GRASSROOTS INNOVATION

PRAISE FOR THE BOOK

'Professor Anil Gupta has proved with his empirical research that human beings are innately innovative and entrepreneurial. I cannot agree more. I invite young people to tell themselves this, "We are not jobseekers, we are job creators" and act this way. I am confident that this book will inspire youngsters to become entrepreneurs and encourage educationists to rethink the message they give their students'—Professor Muhammad Yunus, Nobel Peace Prize laureate and founder, Grameen Bank

'Professor Gupta has made seminal contribution to pushing our country towards becoming an Innovating India. He is almost single-handedly creating a national ecosystem to nurture grassroots innovations, and this book provides glimpses into how he has been devoting his boundless energies towards what he has taken to be his sacred calling'—Dr Vijay Kelkar, chairman, Thirteenth Finance Commission; chairman, National Institute of Public Finance and Policy

'Stating from personal experiences, Anil Gupta weaves the remarkable narrative of a journey that placed traditional knowledge and grassroots innovations on the national agenda. It is also a story of institution-building, the uncertain processes that it involves and the conflicts it creates. Full of insights, the book is an inspiring work from a person who has passionately devoted his life to highlighting the knowledge of those whom society treats as marginals. Gupta's book is a major accomplishment that will interest scholars, social activists and the general public alike'—Kuldeep Mathur, reputed author on public policy and administration; former professor at JNU

'Professor Gupta is globally heralded today as the father of the inclusive innovation movement, which he started more than three decades ago. His firm conviction that "minds on the margin are not marginal minds" lights up every page of this inspiring book. His fascinating journey is filled with great milestones—right from setting up the Honey Bee Network to SRISTI, the National Innovation Foundation to the Festival of Innovation. This is indeed a fascinating story of realizing the dream of democratization of innovation of one of the most iconic innovation leaders of India, told in his own inimitable style. To me, it is a must-read'—Dr R.A. Mashelkar, president, Global Research Alliance; chairman, National Innovation Foundation; former director general, Council of Scientific and Industrial Research

My life turned from being an exploiter in the knowledge market to perhaps a more benign actor, thanks to the thousands of grassroots innovators who taught me how many economically poor people solve community problems and openly share these creative solutions.

May these teachers, grassroots leaders and social innovators reinforce our faith in the future.

CONTENTS

Introduction:
Be a Bee   xi

1. Seeing Beyond What Is Visible   1
2. Evolution of the Honey Bee Network   55
3. Shodhyatra: A Walking Class   103
4. Listening to the Minds on the Margin:
   Sound of a Bird   148
5. Knowing, Feeling and Doing: Expanding the
   Domain of Responsibility   187
6. Fulcrum of Frugality: A Circular Economy   242
7. Mobilizing Social and Ethical Capital for
   Supporting Innovation   301
8. Lessons for Learners   325

Acknowledgements   345
Notes   353

INTRODUCTION

Be a Bee

Sowing the seeds of the grassroots innovation movement twenty-six years ago was a cathartic moment. The search for authentic expression in a world where short-changing knowledge creators and providers is the norm was not easy. But, thanks to thousands of farmers, artisans, pastoralists, students, scholars and many well-meaning policymakers, the movement gained momentum. Slowly but steadily, communities of practitioners, professors and other stakeholders began to recognize the need for reciprocity in a responsible and respectful way towards the knowledge-rich but economically poor people. Commitment towards an uncertain future requires not just faith but also a capacity to cherish fuzziness. I have had a job as an academic and therefore the uncertainties I faced were less consequential for my material survival. But those colleagues who worked with me in taking this initiative forward by showing enormous willingness to pursue a path not traversed so far risked far more. I cannot thank these colleagues enough. Each one of them has given, and many more are still giving, a very precious part of their life to sustain this movement. May their tribe increase.

The contribution of farmers who have walked with me for thousands of kilometres all over the country, despite troublesome terrains and severe conditions, is unparalleled in the history of recent social movements. To some, there seemed no reason to walk through conflict-torn regions as a part of the shodhyatras. But if we listen to those who are angry and upset with the current social arrangements, only then will the legitimacy of these arrangements come into question. Pursuing a non-violent path of change is imperative. But one can persuade others to follow such a path only when we listen to those who don't agree with us. We must try to do that patiently. We often argued that we may not have been able to support the disadvantaged people in their struggles around *jal* (water), *zameen* (land), jungle, but we could certainly tilt the scales in their favour in the struggle around *jaankari* (knowledge). The Honey Bee Network is a manifestation of this solidarity with the *minds on the margin, who are not marginal minds.*

I have shared several personal anecdotes from my life while narrating the story of the grassroots innovation movement. It is only to illustrate that our personal evolution is often intertwined with our professional predicaments and values. It is difficult to separate the two.

It is also possible that the institute that I have been teaching at for the last thirty-five years may not figure as prominently in the narrative as it deserves. There are few institutions which provide more freedom, flexibility and fellowship than what the Indian Institute of Management, Ahmedabad (IIMA) has provided to me. Thank you, IIMA, for making this movement possible.

The story of how Amrutbhai Agrawat, a blacksmith in a village of Gujarat, tried to solve numerous social challenges through his creativity and innovation reverberates in almost every single instance of grassroots innovations. Having lost his father, he was brought up by his mother, a farmworker. None of his struggles ever dampened his spirit. His children are carrying forward the same spirit of social innovation. He was one of the first innovators we came across when we started this journey. His recent stay at the Rashtrapati Bhavan as an innovation scholar, hosted by the office of the President of India, is testimony to the journey the Honey Bee Network has pursued so far. Many times, people ask how many innovations have reached how many million people. A valid question, except that it betrays the case for the long tail of innovation. If we were to ignore these niche-specific solutions, a lot of communities would be neglected, bypassed and alienated. There is nothing more dangerous for democracy than making a lot of the communities distributed around the world feel that their unmet needs are of no concern to those who matter. A distributed, networked, shared economy requires a large number of flowers to bloom and not necessarily of the same species and stock. Diversity is the essence of inclusiveness and creativity.

The evolution of the Society for Research and Initiatives for Technologies and Institutions (SRISTI), the Grassroots Innovation Augmentation Network (GIAN) and the National Innovation Foundation (NIF) provides understanding of the institutional context in which technological, educational, cultural and other individual and collective innovations have been nurtured. Today, there are a large number of groups that are championing the cause of innovations and that is to be appreciated. When this journey began, the National Innovation System (NIS) included only R&D and innovations in the formal sector. The incorporation of the grassroots innovation system in the Indian NIS demonstrates a pioneering contribution made by Indian science, technology and innovation systems to the global repertoire of innovation policy and management.

It might appear that this is a story of a few individuals who believed in the power of creative ideas of local communities to change their own destiny. This formulation would do injustice to the thousands of unsung heroes and heroines of our society who have shared their knowledge, often with no expectation of anything in return. The real genesis of open-source and open-innovation philosophy lies in the culture of local communities. The ease with which people offer hospitality to strangers whom they may never meet again is evident in the millions of villages and slums around the world. A society can be called truly developed only when it is kind to strangers, not just the ones around us, but also the perfect ones—non-human sentient beings and the knowledge-rich, economically poor people. Perfect strangers refer to those who are unknown, and unknowable, i.e., unborn and other small life forms.

This book is also an advocacy for small or large organizations, corporations, educational institutions and public and private supply chain managers to engage with creative communities. It is a reminder of what is being slowly realized that creative and innovative ideas can come from the most unexpected quarters, including workers on the shop floor, farmers, artisans, roadside mechanics, children and young students—practically anyone. If not many such ideas are getting traction, we should realize the need for reforming our mindset, institutions and the polity.

If the reader feels empowered to try new empathetic ideas regardless of fear of failure after reading this book, I would be satisfied. If the reader injects children, colleagues, neighbours and others with the virus of the Honey Bee Network spirit, creative, collaborative and compassionate ideas will get much more visibility, voice and velocity.

I look forward to hearing from you about the ideas that you disagree with, or the ideas that you want to take forward in your own spheres of influence. Every drop counts, every support matters for overcoming our inertia and encouraging inclusive innovations at all levels in society. So, be a bee.

ONE

Seeing Beyond What Is Visible

Many people solve problems not always knowing that their solutions are very innovative, or that they have stumbled upon something that others can learn from. Some, of course, work hard to systematically discover or develop an innovative way of solving a problem. One day, in 1985, a young friend, Nurul Alam, and I were walking together amidst the farms in the Tangail region of Bangladesh. After walking through a few fields, we noticed a lady sitting with a heap of sweet potato vine cuttings and a small wood-based mounted knife, removing multiple roots from various nodes of the vine, leaving only one or two intact. I asked Nurul what she was doing and why. He said he had no idea and with my curiosity peaking, of course neither did I. So Nurul and I sat down beside her[1] to talk. The lesson I learnt from Sharifa Begum is still etched in my memory. She told us that for extremely poor people

1

on highlands, sweet potato was almost like a life-saving crop. They grew it on the homestead as a nursery, and afterwards, if they could get land on lease, they would transplant it. This year, she got a small field on lease for which she was readying the cuttings before planting. When asked as to why was she was removing the roots and rootlets off various nodes, leaving just one or two untouched, she replied, 'If I let all the roots become tuber, these will be thin and long. When I allow only a few to remain, the tuber becomes round. The consumers in the market prefer round tubers.' On further probing, she added that many times when she goes to the market with a bag of tubers—even if the long tubers don't fetch a good price—she still has to sell them because the skin of such tubers is thin and therefore, their shelf life is short. Round tubers have thicker skins and last longer. In the worst-case scenario, she could bring them back the next day to negotiate better prices.

It was an amazing discovery: How an economically poor lady had proved that she was not poor in her mind, even if materially she was a landless woman. The extent to which she was taking consumer preference into account while developing technologies at her homestead was a lesson from which any product or service designer could learn a great deal. For product designers, scientists or technologists, understanding consumer needs before developing solutions to systemic problems is almost a routine step in process, product, service and systems (PPSS) planning now. Many companies engage ethnographers to study the needs of their target markets and potential users, and document the specific characteristics and nuances they find. Yet, the examples where they actually work with grassroots innovators to co-create solutions to the problems of the knowledge-rich, economically poor consumer are very rare. The issue is that not all potential consumers are alike. Some can give feedback on existing or proposed products and services while others can give feed-forward about new possibilities. The grassroots innovators can not only provide new ideas, which companies may have ignored, but can also provide new ways of solving problems. It is this difference between the poor as consumers and the poor as providers that most public and private organizations have failed to appreciate.

In 1980, I was doing a study on communicating with farmers along with a research associate, Mr D.N. Sharma at the Indian Institute of Public Administration (IIPA), New Delhi. A farmer, Ram Nivas of Janjariawas village, Haryana, had shared numerous insights about local agro-ecological indicators through which one could estimate the likely yield of a crop, in this case, pearl millet. The agricultural extension systems in our society have seldom tried to learn from people first before sharing new knowledge or practices. They may not always acknowledge the knowledge provider even if they do make use of some local practices. They may also not prioritize sustainable practices over less sustainable ones.

In 2008, I travelled to various districts of Vidarbha, the drought-prone regions of Maharashtra, such as Wardha, Yavatmal, Chandrapur, etc., as part of another study sponsored by the Department of Science and Technology (DST), Government of India, on reasons for farmers' suicides in Maharashtra. The main purpose of the study was to evolve village knowledge management systems so that farmers could learn about impending disasters induced by climate change in advance and also learn from each other's coping strategies. I wanted to meet the families of farmers who had committed suicide due to crop failure, inability to repay debts or a combination of other distress-induced factors. I had hoped to learn and gain insights from this study that would generate new science and technology applications which in turn could prevent more suicides in the future. What surprised me most when I met the affected families was the complete absence of non-chemical or non-monetary solutions for pest control shared by the agricultural extension department with them and others. It was intriguing because the main reason why thousands of farmers committed suicide was their inability to pay back the loans taken from money lenders to buy pesticides to control cotton pests. Through our research, it became obvious that the cost of various chemical inputs was very high while the effectiveness was too low. I was aware of dozens of examples in our database of dealing with pest control mechanisms in cotton, using local knowledge and innovative practices. Ironically, one of the solutions had come from the Jalgoan district within Maharashtra itself, where the farmers' new innovative measures were to grow bhindi (okra) as a border crop around the cotton field. Bhindi belongs to the same botanical family as cotton. The flowers they yield are also very similar. But since the crop blooms much earlier than cotton, the pests gravitate towards bhindi. One could uproot these plants and bury them in the ground, or spray herbal pesticides and control the pests at much lesser cost and far more quickly. This knowledge could travel from Jalgoan to Ahmedabad, where SRISTI and I were, but it was not shared by the local administration or extension workers with their fellow farmers in Vidarbha. Naturally, in the absence of sustainable practices, the farmers' families would continue to suffer. There could be nothing more tragic than to have somebody ending one's life just because the public extension system and private actors would not share extremely affordable innovations. When an innovation is not only frugal but also sustainable, its lack of diffusion automatically indicates something fundamentally amiss in public policy and the working of public institutions.

Despite the outreach of broadcasting communication systems like television stations and public radios in the country, it is both surprising and frustrating that such knowledge and technical know-how has not become available to farmers, for example, even a simple fact that farmers can easily make herbal pesticides themselves to protect their crops.

But just as two decades ago it was difficult to find a toothpaste made with herbal ingredients, today it is difficult to find one made without them. The consumer preference and buying behaviour has changed so drastically that many of the traditional herbal tooth powders are now ingredients in toothpastes of popular brands. Such a development in another aspect of the consumer goods industry prompts me to think that perhaps in the agriculture sector, a similar transformation can take place even without public policy support. Till then, the database of sustainable innovations will provide a point of reference for those wanting to try low-cost, high-impact methods. The journey described in this book is not only about the discovery of innovations but also about insights learnt from common people. The book also addresses how one can observe creative and innovative ways of solving local problems through patient and respectful attention to small oddities. The grassroots innovators don't hang a board outside their home declaring their innovations. Many times people who have developed innovative solutions don't even know that what they have done *is* really innovative. Given the sociocultural context in which people often laugh at someone who tries to break the existing mould of thinking, it is not surprising that people often deny when asked about any knowledge of local innovation. Our approach has been different and how we have discovered creative people during our different shodhyatras is discussed at length. The book also dwells upon the paradoxes involved in changing public policy or the outlook of institutions involved in supporting innovation. Finally, the book acknowledges my own naivety and not letting it get in the way of learning from the ingenuity of knowledge-rich, economically poor people.

My own journey on this path was triggered by a personal dilemma that had created an almost unbearable moral pain.

I had spent a year (1985–86) in Bangladesh on the invitation of the Bangladeshi government to help reorient agricultural research to make it more people-oriented (but more on this later). Prior to my departure, in 1984, I had begun to research the match or mismatch between farmers' priorities and scientists' goals to address the same. The contrast between what farmers know, both traditionally and also through contemporary experiments, and how scientists deal or do not deal with this knowledge became more pronounced after my stay in Bangladesh. The more I thought about my experiences in Bangladesh and the results from my research of their agriculture systems, the guiltier I felt. The paradox was that conventional on-farm research had neglected the farmers' wisdom and its incorporation in institutional research planning. For overcoming this gap, I pursued an action-research approach to help my scientist colleagues see the merit of learning from people while designing experiments on the farmers' fields. The traditional research was focused more on developing cropping patterns and input-use levels for the same. Given the ecological diversity, climate-induced risks and a very small size of average landholding, the cropping patterns had to be dynamically evolved in the given local socioecological context. The challenge really was to improve productivity by using knowledge more than the material inputs.

While I was being paid in dollars for triggering this transition, the scientists in Bangladesh with whom I worked on the project did not have any such incentive. Yet, even on Fridays, their prayer day, they would be willing to work with me to discuss and design the participative on-farm research strategies. The grassroots communities and individual innovators who shared their knowledge did not get anything directly in return either. It occurred to me that just like moneylenders exploit players in the money market, traders exploit consumers in the commodity market, and the big farmers exploit workers in the labour market, I was also exploiting the poor in the knowledge market. I was learning from them. I was writing about this learning. I was becoming famous. I was being paid for learning and sharing that learning. And yet, none of what I was gaining was going back to those from whom I was learning. This kind of knowledge exchange seemed very asymmetrical. It dawned on me that I was no different from those who took advantage of others in the markets in which they had control.

This realization that I was an exploiter was not very comforting. I looked at my income tax return and I could not establish any clear link between my income earned and the outflowing share that went to the people whose knowledge I had used to further my research and be paid for it. I had tried to argue that I was trying to work for changes in public policy so as to favour the disadvantaged communities, but my motivation no longer seemed completely convincing to me.

When I returned to India in 1986, I began to reflect on the experiences and insights I gained in Bangladesh. I also wrote a review essay on the ethical dilemma and value conflicts in social science research with specific reference to management science. While introspecting in my subsequent research, I realized that the dilemma I was facing was perhaps not unique but the answer I had to find had to be unique.

It is at that stage that the idea of the honeybee came to my mind. I was returning home from the office at lunchtime from the IIMA campus. I don't know if it was because I saw a real honeycomb or the concept just crossed the mind, but it was as if a light bulb had gone off in my head. It occurred to me that the only way out of this pit of guilt was to mimic a honeybee.

Honeybees do what we, intellectuals, seldom do: While they cross-pollinate flowers, we do not facilitate people-to-people learning because we don't often communicate in local, regional languages. When the bees collect the nectar from the flowers, the flowers don't feel short-changed. Flowers, in fact, invite the bees by bearing different, attractive colours. When we collect knowledge from people, generally without reciprocity, we cannot claim that people don't mind. The bees don't keep all the honey themselves. They in turn share some with us. We as researchers or intellectuals need to ensure that we share the interpretations of our research and analysis that we draw back with the people who provided the data to us in the first place. Such action must be taken not only as a mark of ethical responsibility but also for scientific reasons: Ethical responsibility, because we have no right to use the knowledge given by common people for any purpose without their consent; the scientific reason is that only when people come to know why we were asking the questions that we did do they realize the full context of the study or the interface. Then, they offer new information or insights which one cannot get by any other alternative methodology except sharing back the findings at different stages of the interface.

The concept of prior-informed consent takes care of the first ethical inadequacy. The Articles 8(J) and 15.5 of the Convention on Biological Diversity stress upon the need for involvement and consent of the people whose knowledge one tries to take while developing industrial products. The second aspect of ethical responsibility refers to the ability of respondents in any social research to understand the larger context of the study. When we share our understanding of the farmers innovative or traditional practices, they offer more information because they understand how it may help others to use their knowledge better. Sharing back also enriches the knowledge context of the local communities, who can consequently pursue better or different experiments to improve their livelihood.

I was once doing a study titled 'Impoverishment in Drought Prone Regions in the Ahmednagar District, 1981–83', in which I wanted to understand, first-hand, the coping strategies of affected families, so I created a set-up for voluntary researchers to stay with the families. The first stage was to develop a questionnaire but not to give it to the researchers immediately. The idea was for the researchers themselves to realize that even after the first round of study, questions which were pertinent to the family under study were not part of the questionnaire while questions that were not relevant were included. The second stage involved sharing of the questionnaire so that the limitations of the expert power could become evident. No amount of expertise claimed by any professional can help in anticipating all the relevant questions that need to be asked to understand the survival strategies of a specific household. Empowerment of the field researcher required disempowerment of the expert, in this case, myself. The demystification of the expert power of the lead researcher was essential if the process was to become authentic and mutually accountable. The third stage was to learn about the perceptions of other institutions and role players through the eyes of the studied family, and the fourth stage was to finally read the entire case study back to the family to share what one had learnt. It is at this fourth stage that we realized the farmer in question had told us many more things which he or his family could not share earlier. Many times, the questions we ask appear segmented or disconnected to the world view of the communities with whom we want to work. Only when they come to know of the fuller context of the inquiry are they able to appreciate the relevance of our questions. Sharing back the findings or our interpretations of the knowledge collected from the people helps them understand the context. Prior to every shodhyatra—learning walks through the villages organized every summer and winter—we collect examples of local creativity in coping with or transcending problems through contemporary innovations or outstanding traditional knowledge. This compilation is shared during the shodhyatra before we begin our inquiry. The feedback process helps in creating the larger context in which the purpose of our walk becomes clearer. We will also share what we learnt from others and not just that community. This builds trust. It conveys the underlying ethics of knowledge exchange which no amount of arguments or explanations would have conveyed as well. The context does influence the quality of the content.

There was an episode in Parner village where a farmer had gone to work on a 'food for work' site (Employment Guarantee Scheme, EGS) and had still not received the payment. His son did not want to go to school since his fees had not been paid. The researcher had written down the part of the discussion about the son not wanting to go to school, but did not know what had happened between father and son later. When the case was shared amongst us all later, the farmer told us that since the researcher had left for a group meeting in the city the very next day, he did not know what the farmer had actually done. He told the researcher that he had actually borrowed money from a neighbour to pay the school fees because he was unlikely to be paid his wages for some time and attending school was important for his child. The farmer did not know that these actions were of interest to the researcher, so until the final debrief, he did not share the remaining part of the thread on his own. The importance a poor family attaches to education would not have become apparent if the sharing or feedback session had not taken place.

The same way, when we started sharing small details of an agricultural practice or veterinary care learnt from the farmers themselves, their respect for those practices increased. When an outsider appreciates, for instance, growing okra around a cotton field for pest control as mentioned earlier, the practising farmers share more knowledge of such practices. In the absence of such a context, the stock answer generally is, 'No, nobody has done any innovation here.' What is routine for one person becomes disruptive knowledge for another, depending on their respective contexts. This is how the philosophy of the Honey Bee Network was being shaped.

In the Honey Bee Network, when we started sharing not only what was learnt from a particular farmer or grassroots innovator, but also what other farmers had communicated with us on that subject, the farmers began to develop trust in the network process, and more and more information about creative solutions began to be shared. In a sense, the ethics influenced the efficiency of knowledge exchange.

What the Honey Bee Network has taught me as well as thousands of others is difficult to summarize in one book. However, the lessons from this journey can certainly be articulated so that the authentic search undertaken by future managers, scholars, students, activists and policymakers for emancipatory knowledge can become more sharp, responsible, reciprocal and mutually rewarding while dealing with informal sectors of the economy. There are very few people who can claim that they never learnt anything valuable from common people—their workers in farms or factories. And yet, when we look for examples of a reciprocal and dignified exchange of knowledge between formal and informal sectors, we don't have much to choose from. The entire literature on knowledge management seems to have missed the crux of the knowledge economy, i.e., how we reciprocate the generosity of those who share their ideas with us without much expectation of return. Should those who share such ideas remain poor or should they receive the benefits yielded through such communication? It is our belief in the network that a more symmetrical relationship between formal and informal sectors will eventually empower, enrich and inspire both.

The Pursuit of Oddity

Oddity is another name for standing out. Every innovator is, in a way, an oddball. In fact, it is precisely because he or she does not conform to the prevailing order, does he or she get our attention. No matter how programmed we are into the culture of congruence, compliance and conformity, some people stand out. But, the scholarship of innovators is indeed a 'deviant research'.[2] However, not all deviants have equally positive orientation. Every grassroots innovator has their own tale to tell about the struggles they've faced in reaching the point where they are finally at. In this book, I will try and introduce you to many such oddballs. In conversation with them, their tales reverberate with me because I found that some of their struggles were my own. Without a shared platform of similar suffering, authentic learning can be obscure or difficult to pursue.

Before I delve into their stories, let me first share some of my early experiences which provide clues to how my mind and spirit have become obsessed with the problems of the marginalized people. Growing up, I studied in schools where a wooden slate was used to write on; a slate which would also readily be used to beat an errant child. Every day the slate had to be cleaned, polished with *multani mitti* (clay) so that it was ready for overwriting by a pen made up of the canna plant. The black, washable ink was made by mixing dried, black ink flakes in water. There are schools where children still use such slates. Only later did I get access to stone slates.

I continued to study in ordinary schools except for a very short stint in Modern School for infants in Kanpur. Later, after moving to Delhi in 1962, I enrolled in Class V at Ramjas Higher Secondary School, located on what was a desolate hillock in Anand Parbat. After the ninth standard, I stayed in the hostel for two years. The first inventor I chanced to meet then was the father of a dear friend, Inder Mohan Mittal and his sister Rajani. Palla Ram Mittal was a maverick mechanic, designer and fabricator. His house was just behind our hostel. There was a workshop adjoining the house which housed all kinds of tools, junk and, of course, a new kind of washing machine that he had invented. Unfortunately, the business didn't do very well. I recall once Inder Mohan and I had gone to some of the dry cleaning machine shops in Faridabad—where my parents lived at that time—to distribute the brochures for the Cleveland Washing Machines and demonstrate their design and operation. This activity was my first exposure to market research as well as the umbrella of marketing (little did I know then that decades later I would end up in a management school). One of the important things I learnt was that the design of the washing machine was quite advanced. It had more features than many shop owners were willing to pay for. Shri Palla Ram Mittal was a diehard tinkerer and was always busy with executing some new idea. He had also made a working design of an underground train, which experts had come to see, but never did anything about it. These were ideas much ahead of their time. His experience was no different.

Because I also used to work with my friend Inder in his workshop after my classes, the early exposure to the life of an inventor remains etched in my memory. That was the first time I saw a gramophone and I still remember some of the old songs I heard on it. We worked on some small experiments including an effort to make a human-powered generator. We also used to catch and listen to medium-wave radio signals with the help of a crystal; it didn't require any battery, just a set of headphones, and a crystal or a diode. That was perhaps my first attempt at tinkering I did at the hostel. I used to go to old junk markets that used to be held near the Jama Masjid, Delhi, on Sundays; later, the scrap market was moved to a place behind the Red Fort. There were several lessons learnt which have reverberated time and again during the subsequent journey of the Honey Bee Network. Many grassroots innovators have a tendency to embed too many features in their initial design. The result is higher complexity and limited ability of the consumer to appreciate the relative merit of each feature. The simpler designs seem to have greater resonance in the marketplace. But, telling this to an individual innovator is not easy. Most innovators are far too convinced of the infallibility of their assumptions about what customers really value. The difference between the few who succeed and the many who don't sometimes lies in this ability to stick to the essentials in version one of the innovation. The concept of different versions for different pockets or categories of customers is also not so well understood by a large number of grassroots innovators. When an innovation is ahead of its time, unless there is a patient support system, it may often either be aborted by the innovator himself or herself or it languishes for want of support. The relative price difference between an existing model and improved model may genuinely be high, given the number of features. Since customers don't appreciate the value of each feature, they think the price is too high. A highly accomplished innovation fails in the marketplace just because it is too good. The contemporary stress on being 'good enough' shows an increasing reliance on the sufficiency of a solution rather than its overbearing excellence, thereby jeopardizing its affordability and frugality.

Innovators are wired differently. Once, we interviewed the children of some grassroots innovators and tried to visualize the lives of the new broom through their eyes. Many of the children grasped that having innovative parents meant having to deal with a lot of their idiosyncrasies. The struggles of an innovator invariably impinge on the career options available to children. Given the nature of intense struggle that several innovators have to go through, children may choose to follow a less arduous path for their future. It is in this context that an empathetic, agile and responsive

innovation support ecosystem becomes important so that
more and more young people do not eschew the painful
path of developing innovation-based enterprises. Let me
recount stories of some innovators whose children were
interviewed to understand the impact of their parents'
struggle on their motivations. Yagnesh got a consolation
award for his innovation from the National Innovation
Foundation. He was a largely self-taught mechanic. He
had invented an air curtain device that is often used at
airports to prevent the mixture of hot air from outside
with cold air-conditioned air from inside. The devices
imported from outside had many defects, and he worked
on the redesign, incurred huge debts but ultimately
succeeded. But in the process, he had to struggle a lot.
When Yagnesh was under debt, he had to sublet the
room meant for his son to study in. Later, he made a
lot of money and prospered in his life, but those dreary
memories are very much a part of his family legacy.
Often, innovators failed to make much headway and
their children also suffered; their education cut short.
In other cases innovators could afford to educate their
children well, and thus could benefit from their skills in
the growth phase of their innovations. Notwithstanding
all these constraints, there are innovators who have
found a way through.

Despite all the struggles, if the innovation either
does not go to market or the innovator does not get the
required support to expand his activities through scaling
up their workshop, additional tools, increasing working
capital or loans in the form of Micro Venture Innovation
Funds (MVIF)—his innovation is futile. The amphibious

cycle by Shri Saidullahji is one such innovation which got widespread appreciation but did not get market traction. His economic condition has not improved significantly, even though he has received a lifetime achievement award from the National Innovation Foundation (NIF) presented by the President of India. Thus, validation, value addition through science and technology input, design improvement, linkage with entrepreneurs, etc., can, with supportive market conditions, transform the lives of innovators. And, of course, not to mention, also that of users who benefit from these innovations.

Most of these innovations have been discovered through the shodhyatra—a journey to explore creativity at the grassroots level by walking through villages in different parts of the country—or, in other words, scouting expeditions. Other ways through which innovations have been scouted include one innovator helping to find another, chance encounters during cultural and agricultural fairs where innovation stalls are put up, media, etc. The students from rural institutions are also engaged to go from village to village looking for oddballs during their summer vacation. A large number of volunteers scout for innovators through their own journeys into the deep hinterlands of our country. Only a few innovators are able to reach us on their own; if we had waited for innovators to reach us, we would possibly have had only a few thousand innovations and traditional knowledge practices by now. The NIF has received more than 2,00,000 ideas, innovations and traditional knowledge practices from over 550 districts of India, thanks largely to the Honey

Bee Network volunteers. I will come back to the birth of
the shodhyatra later in the book.

Mehtar Hussain and Mustaq Ahmed, two brothers
pursuing farming in the Darrang district of Assam,
developed a bamboo windmill to pump water for
a small paddy field. They fixed the windmill on an
axle balanced on two bamboo stands. This windmill
could not change its direction with the movement of
wind, but with gusts of wind behind it and a generally
favourable direction, it could work well enough. The
Honey Bee Network scouted the windmill and assessed
its potential for application in western India. The
Grassroots Innovation Augmentation Network (GIAN)
tried to adapt the windmill's design for the purposes
of pumping brine water to produce salt. However, the
initial reaction of the salt workers to the project was
full of scepticism, while the GIAN saw the potential of
the project's application for the salt farms of Gujarat.
The brothers were subsequently invited to Gujarat
to study the local situation and compare it with their
native environment, where basic research was done.
The salt workers bear with extremely stressful working
condition. They work in the salt pans barefoot and
absorb a lot of salt in their bones, so much so that their
feet don't burn at the time of cremation. Generally, the
salt workers use a counterpoise to lift the water from the
well and guide it through the channels to the salt pans.
Two people are required in the process. Only a few salt
workers can use diesel engines to pump brine. The salt
workers often have to borrow about Rs 50,000 to buy
the required amount of diesel for a season. Hussain and

Ahmed's windmill was expected to reduce not only the labour requirement of the process, but also the cost of diesel at least by half. When both the brothers came to the Rann of Kutch, Gujarat, they worked with local fabricators to design an iron windmill; given the higher speed of salty winds. Several versions were then designed to suit the local needs.

Here, the innovation was not so much in the concept of windmill, which has existed for ages, but in its unique design features. There were two questions which Mehtar Hussain and his brother, Mustaq, asked, which professionals like us may often not ask. Our disciplinary training equips us with lot of strengths. But, sometimes, it also puts blinkers on our eyes. We fail to see beyond what is visible. We take conventional practice or ways of thinking for granted. The irony is that we are not aware of these filters in our perception. Interaction with the grassroots innovators can help us overcome our myopia. Since the brothers had developed the windmill to irrigate a small paddy field in Assam, the first question was, 'Does it matter whether the paddy field is irrigated in four hours or forty hours?' The second question was, 'Does it matter whether water comes in spurts or flows smoothly?' In their design, they had used a handpump, driven by the force of the windmill, to irrigate the field. The answer in both the cases was no—it didn't matter. In fact, slower irrigation is better than faster irrigation because with lower water pressure fewer nutrients are leached from the soil. In any case, plants need moisture and not water, i.e., much lesser quantity of irrigation is sufficient for plants to uptake the nutrients from the soil. Too much of water harms the productivity, but makes the plant more succulent, which in turn makes the plants more vulnerable to pests. More water also helps in leaching of nutrients. That is why drip irrigation often gives higher productivity with much less use of water. Why use a high-horsepower engine and overconsume high energy, when it will lead to fast flood irrigation of the fields, leaching of nutrients, affecting the soil structure adversely, and losing productivity? Accordingly, they didn't use the gearbox which is the costliest component and difficult to maintain in such conditions. Instead of modulating the irregular speed of the windmill, they used a reciprocal mechanism to directly move the handpump. The movement of the handpump obviously didn't require much torque as is the case of a generator for electricity powered by a windmill. Thus, this innovation proved to be a frugal solution, which was also efficient.

One can learn from an innovation at four levels: artefactual, metaphorical, heuristic and gestalt. The learning at the physical design or artefact level is called artefactual learning. In this case, the bamboo windmill developed by Hussain and his brother could be replicated to make an iron windmill with more or less a similar design—a great example of artefactual learning. Here, the same design is adopted, but with different material and some minor design changes in the more or less same domain of lifting water. The artefactual applications are the easiest form of imitations. The positive side of this mode of learning is that one does not need a great deal of derivative innovations. Small incremental improvements help in adapting the original idea to different contexts within a domain. Thus, a micro-windmill by N.V. Satyanarayana was given a consolation award in 2002 by the NIF because it could generate energy for charging cell phone.[3] The scale was reduced but the functionality remains same.

Metaphorical learning refers to the following: If the concept of slower irrigation is used in various other ways to slow down certain energy-intensive reactions without affecting the efficiency adversely, that will be a metaphorical application. Slower cooking in several dishes adds a special taste and the nutritive value remains the same or goes up. Faster cooking may make the food ready more quickly without necessarily the taste or the nutritive advantage. The Slow Food Movement is an example of this model of learning. Another good example of metaphorical learning is the hydrophobic quality of the leaves of lotus flower. The surface of the leaves does not allow water drops to rest on it. It repels it. When artificial self-cleaning metallic or other surfaces are designed using this as a template, one can call that metaphorical or analogic learning. Likewise, Velcro was designed based on the spine of a cocklebur, a natural pod which sticks to our clothes while walking through weedy growth sometimes.[4] The spines of the cocklebur are curved slightly inward. They interlock with the fibre of the cloth and stick to it. Many of us in our childhood remember the sticking of cocklebur.

The learning at the heuristic level implies identifying the thumb rules underlying an innovation or a phenomenon. For instance, it is often suggested that good heuristic for climbing mountain on a foggy or misty day is to take every step upward and forward. When visibility is low, such a thumb rule may help one reach the top of a mountain. With limited information, a quick assessment has to be made of a complex phenomenon. These thumb rules have a much wider cross-domain applicability. Though a grassroots innovation may look simple at design or artefactual level, but understanding the heuristics underlying it may make handling many complex problems (even in other unrelated domains) easier. When we look at the two heuristics underlying the windmill innovation, we notice the following: (a) A lesser output per unit of time (evident in slower irrigation) could in some cases be better than maximizing output per unit of time; and (b) A smoother flow is not always better than irregular flow. Our training often teaches us to ignore such counter-intuitive heuristics. Wherever applicable, one can apply such heuristics to industrial contexts to great advantage. Sometimes we use a lot of energy to complete a task quickly without sufficiently investigating whether the time saved is eventually leading to a much more costly energy loss.

I don't want to generalize these lessons too much because there are obvious limitations of these heuristics in many cases where maximizing output per unit of time is indeed better, and smoother flow is more efficient than an irregular one.

Learning at the gestalt level implies the relationship among how technology evolves, the normative or value-context institutions provide and the culture of curiosity and questioning triggers in the minds of community members. Let us consider the case of the Assam windmill again, where the culture of using local resources to develop frugal process solutions led to the discovery of the relevant design. Moreover, the technology and the culture would not have worked in the case of salt workers if the selection of households benefiting from the installation of these windmills had not been conducted through a community-wide consultation.

Let me illustrate this concept of gestalt learning further, with an example of the double-decker bridge in Nongriat village, Cherrapunji district, Meghalaya. We came across this bridge made up of prop roots of the rubber tree on both the sides of a seasonal river during a shodhyatra in Meghalaya. The local community wanted to make a bridge over a river. While they had a choice of making a conventional bridge out of rope, wires, concrete, etc., the cultural values of the community triggered an alternative solution—of making something different, greener, sustainable and, of course, affordable. The curiosity to do something different was triggered by the culture. Culture can be a culprit when it sows the seeds of compliance, conformity and too much congruence. It can also be a highly liberating force if it sows the seeds of uneasiness with the status quo. The idea is that once local Khasi culture threw up the right questions, technological repertoire has to be tapped to generate the suitable answers. In the Nongriat village, they discovered that using the roots of the *Ficus elastica* of the rubber tree species, incidentally grown on both sides of the river, was most attractive option.

But, technological options cannot be realized without collective cooperation and consent. No one person could have built it. Institutional development and involvement was inevitable. The group norms, values and a sense of shared responsibility for building a least-entropy (minimum disorder, almost zero waste) design of the bridge required durable cooperation. This is the role of local common property institutions.

The confluence of technology, institutions, and culture are the three pivots of sustainable design. If technology is a word, institutions are like grammar and culture is a thesaurus. We need all three variables for generating sustainable solutions. The materials used in the root bridge in Meghalaya are so frugal, yet because of its renewable constituents this solution meets practically all the conditions of affordability, accessibility, availability and durability of sustainable design. It has circularity (or cradle-to-cradle approach) embedded in the design.

Conventionally, much of industrial development is characterized by what is popularly called Life Cycle Analysis (LCA) that is, the journey of a product from cradle, its birth, to its grave, ultimate waste. That is why a sanitation mission becomes so daunting. Unless the production of waste itself is questioned, how can we address the problem of ever-increasing waste in our society and its obvious adverse health, environmental and social implications? The circular economy, on the other hand, implies cradle-to-cradle, that is, a zero waste concept, which will be discussed in detail in the following chapters.

We have seen how one can learn from innovations at four levels. Just because an innovation may emerge from the grassroots level, it does not mean that it is applicable only at the grassroots. One can learn from the metaphorical/analogical, heuristic and gestalt level as well to apply the lessons learnt across domains, sectors, spaces and social contexts. Lessons can be drawn not only from the physical aspects of innovations, but also from their ethereal dimension.

The spirit behind the innovation matters no less, so let us look at the processes of the inner journey, to explore the deeper values one can learn from grassroots actors.

Learning to Unlearn

In Ladakh, when a child cannot handle a cup or a glass properly, and it falls and breaks, parents don't admonish the child. They don't say: Why did you break it? They often say: It was a breakable thing, so it broke.[5] If the early formatting of the hard disk in the brain didn't generate feelings of guilt, or being held responsible for mistakes we did not really commit, would we not have more open outlook as adults? Many cultural communities don't infuse guilt among children at a young age. They don't put a premium on masking and hiding things. They know that an open society is, of course, a happier society. One such community is the Lepcha community in Sikkim, particularly in the Dzungu region, which also brings up their children with openness and compassion. In many other northeastern mountain-dwelling communities, children seem to enjoy a similar culture of happenstance. Mistakes and small deviations are not treated with reproach and anger. Hence, children do not grow up in an atmosphere of fear, but acceptance. Of course, there are cultural norms generating identity, rituals creating social bonds and rules for managing common properties, conserving nature and other regulated collective expectations of good behaviour. But these are embedded in a more easy -going manner rather than enforcing the same through strict sanctions. It shows up in the outlook of the youth which is perhaps more outgoing, friendly, trusting and respectful of elders.

The values are derived not only from elders, parents or sociocultural communities. There are several other processes through which we shape our world view. While pursuing our journey to make sense of paradoxical blend of complexity of institutional structures and yet simplicity of life in many rural areas, we felt the need to learn from 'four teachers'. Maybe everybody learns from these teachers, maybe to varying extents.

These four teachers that we can learn from and be influenced by are: teachers within, teachers among peers, the teacher in nature, and the teacher among common people. These four teachers influence and help forge an open persona, of an individual who is willing to learn from the community at large.

The Honey Bee Network operates informally to harness the voluntary spirit of scientists, farmers, artisans, technologists, artists, designers, entrepreneurs and even investors. The philosophy of cross-pollination, overcoming anonymity of knowledge-holders, sharing whatever we learn back with the people in their language (incidentally, this book will also be shared in local languages), and if any financial benefit arises through commercialization, royalty, or other means, sharing a fair share back with the knowledge-providers, all resonated with thousands of people who have volunteered with the initiative. Meetings like shodh *sankal* (meetings of experimenting farmers), shodhyatras, village visits/ camps, biodiversity contests, idea competitions among children, recipe contests, women self-help groups, bhajan *mandali*s, etc., have helped unravel the creativity and innovation at the grassroots level. Scientists help in validating the innovations as well as traditional-knowledge practices of common people without charging for their time, patent lawyers help in filing patents/plant variety protection without charging their fees, and some designers have also helped generously, though much less than any other professional group so far. The small-scale entrepreneurs have licensed unpatented technologies by paying knowledge-holders. They could have copied these without any restriction. But showing an outstanding example of business ethics, they preferred to compensate the innovators instead in dozens of cases.

Now let me explain how the shodhyatras began. Eighteen years ago, at one of the Honey Bee Network meetings, some farmers asked us why they couldn't join our collective search for learning opportunities at the grassroots level. Hearing success stories of creative and innovative experiments by common people much like themselves, they were intrigued and wanted to participate in our efforts. This feedback led to our establishing 'exploratory walks', which came to be known as the shodhyatra.

Initially, for the first few walks, the Society for Research and Initiatives for Technologies and Institutions (SRISTI) would meet the cost of food and logistics. Since 2002–03, every shodhyatri has borne their own travel and food expenses—only preparatory costs, logistics of portable exhibitions and other support are borne by SRISTI. Generally, those who can convince the coordinator team at SRISTI of a genuine desire to learn from common people, and of their willingness to comply with group norms of simplicity, frugality and collegial secular respect, are accepted. Those farmers, teachers and others who wish to contribute to this cause join repeatedly. Amrutbhai Agrawat, one of the serial inventors and a lifetime achievement award winner from National Innovation Foundation, as well as a former member of the SRISTI governing board, has attended thirty-four out of thirty-five shodhyatras. He missed one due to sickness of his late mother. There are many like him who have attended several yatras, mostly between five and ten. Nowadays, when people do not spend even two to three days in social functions like marriages, spending eight days in travel and five to six days on walk in, say, the northeast region of India at one's own cost is a significant contribution. In the thirty-sixth shodhyatra in Arunachal Pradesh, more than seventy people have registered to walk together. Further registration had to be curtailed because local arrangements for stay and food for a larger number will become very difficult.

The Shodhyatra: Just the Beginning

In June 1998, we (some farmers and I) decided to walk from the farm of Gaffarbhai Qureshi, in the village of Ramdechi, Talala taluka, in the Junagadh district of Gujarat to Gadhada, in the Bhavnagar district—a total distance of about 250 kilometres to be covered in ten days. The temperature in the daytime would go up to 47–48 degrees Celsius. Being the first walk on the shodhyatra, none of us had the prior experience or skill of walking long hours day after day—sometimes without much water, since handpumps would not be working for tens of kilometres. The longest distance we walked in a day that trip was 40 kilometres, the day we missed the right road turning near Dhari bypass. It was a fortunate detour, as we stumbled on to the village of Amreli, walking through which we discovered many ingenious innovations in soil and water conservation, the design of bullock carts for spreading manure in the field and other farm implements.

During this particular shodhyatra, we also had to spend a night in the Gir forest, the only natural habitat of the Asiatic lion. When we set up base, we lit a small campfire nearby. We spread mats to sleep on for the night but the sound of lions' roars made sleep hard to come by. The roars also seemed closer than they probably were. People were afraid. Those who slept facing the open forest felt that if a lion came to camp in the middle of the night, it will probably eat the first person right next to the forest. So the person closest to the forest got up after a while and changed his place. Then the second person became worried about being closest to the forest and becoming lion prey; he also got up and changed his place. Some of the forest guards spending the night with us told us stories of how lions had behaved in the past, all while the game of changing places was going on. I don't think the yatris have been able to forget that amusing night when some people were genuinely scared, while others were merely amused at the others' fear.

Later, we met Maldharis, the cattle rearers who lived on the fringe area of the Gir forest. They shared their anguish at being asked to abandon their settlement in the forest. At the time, the forestry department was relocating forest-dwelling pastoral communities to places outside the forests. The Maldharis asked us a simple question: 'Map the lions and our habitats. If we are indeed the problem, lions should remain in areas away from us. The fact that they prefer to be in areas where we live shows that we are not a threat to them. In fact, even if they attack and take away our cattle once in a while, we take it in our stride. Never once has any Maldhari poisoned the carcass (something that poachers may do) to kill a lion.' But this was not an easy message to be communicated to the forest bureaucracy. Recently,[6] it has been shown empirically that Maldharis don't pose a threat to the lions, rather their presence makes lion habitats more hospitable.

The palpable insight here is that such socioecological interactions at the grassroots level can only be understood when people trust outsiders to share their agony and also achievements. The pastoralists in this sanctuary had understood the need for lions to remain closer to primary prey (deer) and secondary prey, i.e., cattle. They hunt in scrubby vegetation through line of sight. The conservation of wildlife and the ecosystem is no less dear to them than the forestry department. Yet, their voices are seldom heard and incorporated in the policy discourse. The minimum commitment we make to such communities during our shodhyatras is to ensure that their voice reaches the right quarters. The authenticity of the process of the walk, perhaps, helps in achieving trust even during the short time that we are able to spend with them.

The Shodhyatra as a Pedagogical Expedition

In addition to the two half-yearly shodhyatras in the summers and winters, I also teach a course involving a walk through the Himalayas in the autumn break at IIMA. The course was started about thirteen years ago in quite an interesting way. Chandan Agarwal, Hemant Ahlawat and a few other students met with me one day under the mango tree, situated at the entrance of the main complex of IIMA, and invited me out for a cup of tea at a shack outside the gate of the institute. They regretted that the prearranged, twice-a-year, shodhyatras took place at a time when they did not have a term break and thus could not participate. I wondered out loud whether students were truly interested in learning through very unconventional, rigorous, strenuous and demanding circumstances. I mentioned that the physical strain might be high, but learning from the four teachers' concept, discussed earlier, might be worthwhile if some of them wanted to make breakthroughs in life. The more I tried to frighten them about the physical stamina walking in the Himalayan region required, as well as the importance of building inner character along the way, the more determined they became. We discussed a rough array of the topics we might pursue should this walking course were to come to life. Next, I made an outline and sent it to the course committee for approval. The course was highly unorthodox, did not include any reading; in fact, it prohibited books, and instead stressed upon learning from within, life as we know it, surrounding us, nature and the common man. The committee comprised the chair of different disciplines and groups at IIMA who had got together to discuss the outline. After more than an hour into the meeting, a colleague remarked, 'Look, Anil wants to teach, students want to learn, then what is the problem? We can always review the coursework later.' Finally, the course was approved and over the years, became one of the most sought-after courses. Students have developed a system of bidding for the courses with limited registration. The shodhyatra course has only twenty-five seats. Students have to bid for a fixed seat (twenty places for Indian students and five for foreign exchange students) and have to allocate almost 80 per cent or more points for this course alone. So, out of 200 points, some of them have to allocate more than 160 to get into this course.

The idea is that students might learn that for making breakthroughs in life, there has to be synchronicity between the inner and outer being of the same individual. Without such synchronicity, can we really seek authenticity? Authenticity is a necessary condition for making a breakthrough. When we live in a crucible of social scrutiny, the credibility rests on our ability to share our inadequacies as honestly as possible. Authenticity does not imply being always adequate or correct. On the contrary, it is in our willingness to be vulnerable that we are open to learn and share without reservations. But recently I've learnt (and may I say quite late in my life) that authenticity also may require an ability to force a disconnect between the inner and outer being at times—a mild schizophrenia if you will. Who has made any significant difference without this 'affliction' in small measure, any way! Can an outstanding theatrical performance, rendering of a heart wrenching song, composition of a painful poem, or a delivery of a famous speech like 'I have a dream' by Martin Luther King touch the lives of the millions without earnestness? This could happen only when one can disconnect oneself from other identities, to be able to focus on the intended one. The little disconnect within oneself provides space for absurdity, imagination and a flight of fancy that help one transcend the realm of what *seems* possible.

As the teacher, I have learnt so much from this course too. With the first batch of the shodhyatra course, we went to Bhutan. Subsequent batches went to Lahaul Spiti, Kangra, the Valley of Flowers, the base camp of Kanchenjunga, the Dzungu region of the north district in Sikkim, the Murlen National Park in Mizoram, and different parts of Ladakh.

Once, in a village in Sikkim, in the year 2012, when community members suggested we dance together without any forewarning or preparation, an Italian student, Alessandra Martinengo, observed, 'The spontaneous gestures, the desire to get into the game, the

desire to learn and not worry about appearing incapable
are not elements that characterize my culture.' He cited
a poem by Rudyard Kipling, which reflected the serenity
he had absorbed; which in fact not just he, but I had also
absorbed.

> If you can talk with crowds and keep your virtue,
> Or walk with Kings—nor lose the common touch,
> If neither foes nor loving friends can hurt you,
> If all men count with you, but none too much:
> If you can fill the unforgiving minute
> With sixty seconds' worth of distance run, yours is the
> Earth and everything that's in it,
> And—which is more—you'll be a Man, my son!

On the same shodhyatra in Sikkim, Shwetang Dave
narrated an encounter with an autorickshaw driver
which affected the whole class. One day, while walking
back from his friend's place to his college hostel, he was
very tired. He had just nine rupees with him, but in the
auto, the total travel would have cost him at least thirteen
rupees. So he asked the driver to drop him off as far as
where nine rupees would take him. But the driver, seeing
his fatigued condition, took him directly to his hostel; he
even refused to take the nine rupees Shwetang offered
him. Instead the driver told him to give those nine rupees
to someone who needed it more than him. The driver
may have gone away after leaving Shwetang, but he had
returned to our class. Each one of us could feel him in
us. There were none present who had not been favoured
by someone in this manner, and yet they were occupied

with their own well-being so much. I don't think I could have conveyed the thought of imbibing the basic spirit of generosity better.

In another shodhyatra in Ladakh in 2013, a debate took place regarding the trade-off between what one is good at and what one loved to do. For example, one may not be good at playing a particular musical instrument even though one may love to do so. While one's expertise may lie in coding economical programmes, one may not really enjoy that. A lot of arguments were presented on both sides. It seemed that, without reaching a consensus, loving what one is good at was not an obvious choice. But perhaps there was a way of coding programmes that learnt from musical symphonies and rhythm and brought joy, which without being at an intersection of the two may not be possible.[7] Ideally, one ought to be in a place where loving, learning and living intersect. But what seemed obvious to me had not been so easy to communicate or even assimilate by the students. It is not easy to kill one's 'darling' phrases, concept and notions of a 'good and meaningful life'. Dialectical thinking, with the ability to live with paradoxes, seemed one way to move forward towards a breakthrough.

As can be expected, there have been rough patches and risky moments. Once, we had to cross a spate of rocks holding on to the branches hanging from a tree for support, with nothing to keep our feet on. If our grip loosened, then the gorge below, where a river flowed in full steam, was not a far off end. But the group worked together, and we managed to tide over that moment safely. Several students just sat down holding their head between knees in a very fatigued and resigned mood. I kept quiet and ignored the immediate stressful experience as if nothing had happened and walked on. In the evening, during a post-dinner session I was advised to take an indemnity bond from students to prevent being put in trouble due to some unforeseen hazard. I have trusted them and they have always reciprocated. Bonds cannot insulate one from real rubs with rough edges in life. We go through risky moments to feel closer to life; make ourselves vulnerable. It is in the moments of vulnerability that we are closest to our true self, our defences are down and we are willing to accept the truth a bit more. When we feel too much in command of ourselves, our ability to listen to the inner voice perhaps eludes us. Many grassroots innovators put themselves in situations of very high risk without making them vulnerable inside. They commit to some vain designs and hope to achieve breakthroughs somehow. It is not easy to counsel them always, and only subtle feedback is used to bring them out of their pseudo-comfort zone. If they succeed in recognizing the unviability of some of their trajectories, they accept the need to learn, discredit their fondness for particular designs, and embark upon a fresh journey disempowering themselves a bit; vulnerability then induces humility and hastens the learning process.

During one of the shodhyatras in Ladakh, some athletic students walked fast in front and reached the next point much before us—two girls, an overweight boy and me. All three students had difficulty in walking; one of the girl students had asthma. There was no means of communication and no help could be sought, given that so few people live in the cold desert. It dawned on me that I could not have carried three people on my back if, God forbid, there had been an emergency. It was expected that the whole group would be more or less together such that the first and the last persons in the group were in visible sight range of each other. When we all sat for the evening discussion, there was a lesson waiting for us. Most students realized that I was a bit upset over their behaviour but none of us said anything to the other. Then, a student made a remark I find difficult to forget. He said, 'Sir, today we realized that if you are on top and you have no one to share with— you are not there.' Was that not an important lesson of life, in the pervasive race to be ahead of others? But often, what's left behind is one's own notion of self-importance, the *ahankar*, the ego!

Sharing is so fundamental to realize one's experience:

When we care
to feel or just share
what is left, inside
is a cracked layer,
through which the sprout
of serenity, concern and compassion
overcomes the hesitation
to dare.

Inner Shodhyatra: Towards an Authentic Self

The wisdom of common people is often inaccessible to us, because we don't listen enough; we don't listen to our own inner voice either. Is there a connection between the two? Because we don't listen to our inner voice, are we unable to listen to authentic voices outside us—at grassroots, or even at other levels? What can these voices tell us?

As I often say at the beginning of every shodhyatra, we actually embark upon two journeys—one inner and the other outer. We know when and where the outer journey will end. But with the inner one, we don't know. The inner shodhyatra, once embarked on, does not end even when one has returned from the jungles or mountains.

In 2008, when I was invited to give a talk on Mahatma Gandhi's birthday in Rashtriya Shala, founded by Gandhiji in Rajkot, in 1921, I was faced with a dilemma. Many luminaries had delivered talks in this series in the past. I was not even a patch on the credentials of such speakers. How would I do justice to this responsibility?

While ruminating on the right metaphor, suddenly, I noticed that one of the lady staff, Hetal, was wearing earrings which seemed to sparkle like diamonds. I asked her whether they were actual diamonds. She said they were. Then I asked her why the metal holding those diamonds seemed whitish instead of yellow gold. She replied that a little impurity was used in the gold to encase the diamonds to make the earrings stronger. And I realized, I had found the theme for my talk. The next day, when I addressed the audience, I noticed there were many ladies wearing similarly set jewellery. I told them—if Gandhian thought was like a diamond, I am entitled to a higher share of impurity in my life to be able to hold it. Even with my many infirmities, inadequacies, lacunae in my persona and character, I could still access Gandhian thoughts and values because strength of the vessel to hold such precious thoughts comes from human impurities mixed to make what one may call a tenacious alloy. Our ordinariness should not prevent us from accessing values at their peaks or valleys, which otherwise may seem unassailable.

Deep learning can occur during surprising moments in the ordinary chores of everyday life. What makes a difference is our emptiness and thus willingness to absorb the insight.

While returning from attending a debate in Ranchi, I met a coolie way back in 1971 I cannot forget about at the Kolkata railway station. Due to heavy traffic congestion, I was late and had missed my train to Delhi from Kolkata. I didn't have much money in my pocket and was very nervous, looking like I might break down any minute. Looking at an eighteen-year-old boy who appeared lost and panicky, an elderly coolie, dressed in the usual red shirt, took pity on me. He first asked me why I was so worried. I told him that I had missed my train to Delhi from where I had to go on to Hisar, the place where I was studying. He soothed my nerves saying, 'Don't worry, I will get you a seat on the next train.' I said, 'Thank you kaka, but I don't want to travel without a ticket.' He said, 'I will buy you a ticket.' I was very much relieved that my worries had tided over. It occurred to me that I should ask for his address so that I could send the money back to him once I reached home. On my request for the same, he refused. When I persisted with my request a few more times, he got angry and said, 'If you ask one more time, I am neither going to buy you a ticket nor get you a seat.'

I was bewildered at his kindness. Yet I didn't understand what I had said to offend him. I touched his feet and said, 'All right, don't give me your address, but at least tell me what was wrong in asking for your address.' He replied, 'Look, if I give you my address and you forget to send the money back, I will be unhappy. I might hesitate in helping someone else in future. If I don't give you my address, you can't disappoint me. I don't want to bargain anxiety in return for helping you. You will not get my address.'

That debt has multiplied many times over by now. No matter what I do, there is no way I can ever pay it back to him. I am not even sure that I can pay it forward enough. In a sense I have since been asking myself whether such social debts are indeed the real assets of life. Have not all of us been helped by some stranger or the other in our life? And if so, why do we skimp on lending a helping hand ourselves? Why is it that when we are in a position to help others, we think of our kith and kin first? Why do strangers seem so distant? How would fairness ever be achieved in life if strangers did not command respect of consideration at par with those who are known? But then, these questions were too far-fetched for a young mind to understand fully. It was clear to me I was never going to forget the social debt I had incurred. Perhaps this was one of the defining moments in my life when the compass tilted itself towards a new North Star that would help me in navigating the ship of my life in future.

The inner plane of the shodhyatra has many paradoxical moments—though I am not implying that paradoxes are less frequently encountered in the external walks. I cannot claim that I have always lived with loyalty to this principle of paying forward, a kind of anonymous giving, deliberately making it impossible for some IOUs to be settled. But I have tried. I remember that when I came back to college I had reflected on this rendezvous many times. A kind of sadness would creep into my life when I thought of it and realized how those who had so little could find it in their hearts to give so much. Should all debts be recovered? Are not unsettled IOUs the glue which keep relationships alive? Nowadays, many young people try to settle their accounts almost every other day. 'You paid for my tea yesterday, let me pay today' seems to be a common refrain. The tendency is to say, 'We are square.' But, is it really possible to compare a discussion had over tea yesterday with the insights shared while having tea today? In other words, it is difficult to derive the equivalence of two moments over time and space just in monetary value. It is not the value of the tea that makes moments memorable, it is what we feel with or without articulating it. Thus the debts we have incurred are actually not easy to measure. I remember what my grandfather Shri Revati Prasad Vanprasthi used to say. He was a monk and lived in an ashram in Jwalapur, near Haridwar, for over forty years. He once mentioned that if one treats an obligation of an inch as equivalent to a mile, one would always remain under debt but never be short of happiness. This perhaps is the secret to being grateful for the small mercies that life offers.

The unredeemed IOUs are thus those debts which, even if they seem payable, we don't recover so as to maintain a feeling of mutual indebtedness. The unbalanced books of accounts create a similar feeling of being under social, spiritual and emotional debt.

During my summer vacations at college, I often did not go home and instead, tried to cope with being by myself through painting and reading literature, biographies and poetry, etc. The ability to distance myself from my family seemed so vital for cutting the umbilical cord which many of us carry for far too long in our lives. Some of the books I remember I read were: *Our Inner Conflicts, Divided Self* by R.D. Laing, *Magnificent Obsessions* by Lloyds C. Douglas, *Gunaho Ka Devta* by Dharamvir Bharati. Even in my school days, instead of going out to play in the evening, I would read books borrowed from the library, even though my mother would tell me that reading books at sunset was not good for the eyes. So, it is not surprising that eventually my eyes got weak and I now have to wear spectacles. As always, it is easy to be wise afterwards.

Many times in my class, I have to explain to the students that their professors' experiences should not deter them from questioning their teachers, and if necessary, irreverently. I often quote a statement that one of my students, Arvind, shared with me in 1981, 'Experience is like a rear-view mirror; it shows you the road travelled but doesn't tell you where to go.' How many of us have demanded respect and submission because of our so-called professional or domain experiences?

The journey to discover the vast stretches of our ignorance interspersed with our claims to expertise is a part of inner shodhyatra. The more questions we raise about what we thought we knew, the more kindled our curiosity is likely to be.

Sometimes, this experience can also put one in strange situations. From 1978 to early 1981, I was working at the Indian Institute of Public Administration on an action research project to explore whether a district project planning cell could help in revamping the administration in six drought-prone districts. The selection committee for the interview for a higher position on the same project included eminent economists like Professor P.C. Joshi. I had no background or formal training in management science, though I thought I knew *something* because of a four-year stint in a commercial bank as an agricultural finance officer. Various members of the committee seemed both impressed and disappointed in alternation with my responses, but overall, the chairman, the director a bureaucrat agreed—I was good but they thought I lacked experience. But Professor Joshi could not restrain himself and said, 'Is experience worth one year, multiplied by ten years, good?' He meant that if we could do the same thing repeatedly, for a long period of time, we don't necessarily become wiser at it or in general.

Memory-scapes maybe intertwined with one's memories of place, people and purpose, and yet, not just those. Memory-scapes also carry the seeds of both an experienced and imagined world that may later shape one's view about the surprise in everyday life. The more

I start believing that my existing memory can explain a new happening, or idea, the less likely it is that I will be surprised. And really, can an insight occur without being surprised by it? Don't we raise our expectations about the need to understand a phenomenon much higher when we constantly ask ourselves: Did I know this? Did I know this the way the other person sees it? If not, will I admit that I am learning something new? How else could we train our eye for detail—and spotting grassroots innovators? We would be able to see novelty and wisdom on the ground, where earlier travellers had just passed by thinking there was nothing new to learn. Much of the literature about rural development and technological change, making evident the creative and innovative potential of common people, was almost completely ignored till the 1980s and even later, and thus denied them agency and the political–economic space for asserting their identity. Fortitude thus plays an important role in opening new furrows, instead of just deepening the existing furrows.

Thus, there are times when it is important to take a stand; and taking a stand on certain issues costs a great deal. But there is no easy way of building the capacity to stand on one's own feet. I will share several moments in my life when I had to face difficult situations. Thankfully, a quote I read during 1969, when I was in my second year at college, has mounted me on good ground. I had a broken mirror frame in which I pasted this quote to read every day. The quote was: 'Fortitude is the capacity to say no, when the world wants to hear yes,' said by Eric Fromm. Fromm realized that courage, or what Spinoza has termed fortitude, could not be understood without fearlessness. No society can ever be built on the shoulders of those who crawl when asked to bend, as we saw during the Emergency in 1975. I was in the Moradabad district of UP, serving as an agricultural finance officer in a bank during 1975–77, as I already mentioned. The lending capacity to the landless and poor, of the two branches I was serving, was better than any other bank in the region. Therefore, I didn't pay attention to the recommendations of the local politicians. They were quite annoyed on this waywardness in an otherwise repressive environment. The way things were: Many small sugar-cane farmers didn't receive payment against their supply bills during the end of crushing season; they had to wait for the next year to receive payments from the sugar factories. I developed a scheme in consultation with senior officers to pledge the unpaid bills, after getting an undertaking from the receiver of the mill. Thus, the bank would extend loans to the farmers against the unpaid bills of sugar cane in the summer and receive the payment from the mill with interest during the winter months from October to December. This was the first time when more than 6000 farmers, who had had to discount their bills with local traders, had got their payments in time. However, a scheme like this, which cut at the roots of corruption, threatened the vested interests of other parties. The money was recovered as per the plan, though I received an accusatory phone call—that is, I was to explain my conduct and why I had allegedly exceeded my brief—since no superior officer acknowledged his responsibility in the matter. While the inquiry by the local information officer did not deter me from doing the job well, for many others this was a trying time. Many schoolteachers and other state government staff had to produce copies of the sterilization certificate without which the salaries would not be given. The story of forced sterilization of poor men is well known and doesn't merit repetition. The devotion of the bank staff was exemplary because they worked long hours without overtime payment to serve the farmers.

Every episode can be an event, as it often is, and can also be an experiment in the laboratory of life, as Dr R.A. Mashelkar puts it. If I mention my personal discoveries off and on in this narrative, it is only to stress that we collectively cannot learn, unless I learn and vice versa. The moment I separate the two, the authenticity becomes a casualty. The people I met, things I did or did not and lessons learnt and sometime forgotten are not always my individual, voluntary experience. There were situations in which I was put and had to find a way forward or a way out. Sometimes, my situation was like that of Abhimanyu, who would not know the final way out of the *chakravyuh*, or the web of entanglements, and thus would succumb to the situation. The compromises sometimes are necessary in anybody's life and I would share as many of them as possible. But, more than that I have been forgiven by so many so often for having succumbed and not having struggled enough that the spirit continued to become stronger after each reprieve.

The story of my personal struggles is intertwined with the struggle of the new social movement started more than three decades ago. The oscillations in the sea of experience do not allow a linear discourse. And therefore, a zigzag description is more accurate of any design process in life, or product or service, rather than drawing it as a cycle or a linear flow diagram. As I proceed, I will have to impose a similar state of flux to the state of being that I am in.

Serendipity and Navigating the Path Ahead

When a pot is stirred, not all ripples respect the brim. Some embark upon their independent journey. They cease to merely be ripples. Their future trajectory is no longer in my hand. They could become a tear in somebody's eyes or a smile on somebody's face. Who knows? I am just a trigger. Happenstances are the stuff of which life is made. Instead, taking credit for too many things merely feeds the ego and does not nurture the humility that is so necessary for making small or big breakthroughs.

To illustrate, let me go back to 1977. I was travelling in a bus from Moradabad to Kurukshetra. I bought a newspaper to read on the way. While turning the pages of the newspaper, my eyes fell on a small advertisement box on the last page. The ad was a call for a management specialist in rural development by a central institution: the Indian Institute of Public Administration (IIPA). I knew nothing about management as a discipline, as mentioned earlier, except through the practice in my role as agricultural finance officer. But, something in me said, I should give this a try. At that time, I was working at Syndicate Bank, pursuing a reasonably meaningful career with all kinds of responsibilities and privileges. I believe I always had academic penchants, which got sidetracked for the job because of some family compulsions. But reading this advertisement, I felt the old stirrings rise again. When I reached Kurukshetra and met my wife, Sadhana, who was doing her postgraduation in Sanskrit at Kurukshetra University, I told her about this opportunity. Being a daughter of a Spartan professor, having seen how devotedly he had guided his students without any material possessions or attractions in life, she didn't hesitate for even a minute before she agreed. I sent in an application through an official channel in the bank. The bank forwarded my application. Having forwarded my application, the bank could not refuse me leave for taking up the job for three years. This was the first time that a bank had given leave to anybody for such a purpose. The chief of agricultural finance division, Shri K.V. Beliraya was hopeful of my coming back, and also visited me at IIPA a few times to discuss the changes one could bring about in the banking practices. In the interview, they asked me questions about management—Project Evaluation and Review Technique (PERT) and Critical Path Method (CPM)—and a few other routine concepts. Some I had prepared beforehand and answered well, some I goofed. I converted my practical experiences at the bank into general management lessons and that seemed to make a difference. A computer expert asked me a question I still remember: Whether the flood in Brahmaputra basin was a problem of risk or uncertainty? I replied that over space, it was a problem of risk but over time, it was a problem of uncertainty. We can assign probability with a reasonable degree of certainty as to which regions are likely to be flooded. But we still cannot predict when exactly floods will occur. I got the job. That reply thankfully changed the course of my career.

Once I joined IIPA, New Delhi, in 1978, life got busy: A newly married life coupled with pursuing a PhD at Kurukshetra University (which accepted the stint in IIPA as equivalent to two years of residential requirement in the university), doing my job as a management specialist in the action research project, and at the same time, learning social sciences—in particular, economics which I had never studied before formally except in an undergraduate course. The guards at IIPA were my constant companions when I used to work well into the cold wintry nights. Some of them would bring me tea from the Express Building, a short distance behind IIPA on Ring Road. They used to observe me working, seeming as if I stayed in the office for weeks and months at a time. When I was tired, I would spread a newspaper on a long table and stretch myself out on it. Two of my colleagues, B.D. Singh and R.K. Hazari, literally fed me by bringing food from their home. I learnt a lot and occasionally friends like Jeff Romm would come in the evening and discuss regional planning theories and the limitations of concepts like growth polls with me.

Sprouts of Inquiry into Local Knowledge Systems

During the course of the action research project, I visited six drought-prone districts, namely, Mahendragarh (Haryana), Jodhpur (Rajasthan), Purulia (West Bengal),

Kurnool (Andhra Pradesh), Ramanathapuram (Tamil Nadu) and The Panchmahals (Gujarat), all over the country. I was doing my own doctoral research in the Mahendragarh district. During this time, I, along with Sharma, a colleague of mine, met Ram Nivas, a farmer from Janjariawas village. Ram Nivas used various weeds as indicators of the impending yields from other crops. By looking at the bearing of fruits on the calotrops, he would, for example, estimate the prospects of the pearl millet crop. Similarly, the bounty of fruit borne by the neem tree in spring gave him an indication of the likely rain profile to follow in the months later. I was intrigued how he would make such close observation of nature and find correlations among different events. With this encounter, my interest in local knowledge started growing.

Dr Y.P. Singh, one of my beloved teachers at Haryana Agricultural University (HAU), Hisar, was teaching at the Indian Agricultural Research Institute (IARI), Pusa Road, New Delhi, at that time. When I shared some of my insights from the field, he narrated his own experience of linking formal and informal science and technology systems way back in the mid-1960s. Back then, he was a young professor at HAU and began to guide two masters' students, Verma and Khanna, in the process of learning from farmers and then validating that knowledge in the lab. Both Verma and Khanna were veterinary doctors and they documented extremely useful animal healthcare practices from local animal-keeping farmers. For the defence examination, Dr Singh invited an eminent scientist and the editor of a famous journal *The Allahabad Farmer*. The expert was a bit aghast at Dr Singh's audacity to redefine the disciplinary boundaries of the scientific method as understood then in agricultural extension discipline. In his view, what the extension science dealt with was taking knowledge from lab to land, and not the other way round. Here was an effort to bring knowledge from land to lab, to take it back to land after scrutiny, and if necessary, value addition. With very great effort, the students passed. But, Dr Singh did not guide another thesis on the subject till the late 1970s. A pioneering work, which perhaps was the first effort of forging such a linkage, was thwarted by the academic establishment.

This episode has remained with me and has continued to inspire me about the need to forge such linkages in the scientific purpose of producing meaningful technologies and institutions, regardless of the inherent challenges posed by both internal and external players. I must admit, however, that my interest in the subject was subdued because of my own involvement in the research on rural credit and how to improve the access of economically poor people in high-risk environments. For the next ten years, even after moving to IIMA, I continued to pursue studies on coping strategies of people in high-risk environments. In 1984, I took up a study on matching farmers' concerns with breeders' and technologists' objectives. During this study, I went back to the Mahendragarh district to learn from the farmers and understand the disjunction, if any, between what scientists understood about farmers' needs and what farmers actually preferred. In one of the fields, I observed that farmers had grown coriander as a border crop around a chickpea (gram) field. When I asked the neighbouring farmers the reason for the same, they replied that it had been done to prevent a pest attack. Later, I shared this knowledge with one of my friends in ICRISAT (The International Crops Research Institute for the Semi-Arid Tropics), Michel Pimbert, who was an entomologist. He took up research experiments at the farm and found that what the farmers were doing was right in practice, but their reasons were all wrong. In actuality, the coriander did not repel the pests but attracted the predators to feed on the nectar-rich flowers. The effect was the same—keeping the pests away from the chickpea. So I learnt that the scientific validity of a practice may sometimes be questioned on the basis of wrong reasoning or incorrect attributions of people. But, for the farmers, I learnt that what mattered more was whether things worked. They did not find themselves concerned with causal mechanisms, given their limited repertoire of tools and techniques. It is exactly in such a context that the bridge between formal and informal sector can be so productive.

TWO

Evolution of the Honey Bee Network

The theory of imperfect beginnings will become evident when I describe the birth of the Honey Bee Network and the various institutions and initiatives that it spawned. The articulation of natural, social, ethical and intellectual capital took place on a platform that precipitated the historical iniquity in the knowledge economy. Imperfect beginnings imply working with insufficient advance information. 'Paralysis through Analysis' is almost completely avoided in such an action-research approach to life and learning. One makes improvements in the strategy incrementally, without having to be sure in advance. This also means one accepts being vulnerable as a normal situation of being a learner. It is possible that this vulnerability may also make one hungrier for even small insights, than would have been the case otherwise. In perceiving a potential for change, the hope for finding an innovation becomes more feasible—all because of imperfect beginnings. How do we really know whether we will find any innovation or not in advance of the shodhyatras? But the faith, or rather the hope, that there *will* be some people who will pass a vote of no confidence in the status quo of inertia, keeps us moving.

In 1980, while pursuing research in the drought-prone district of Mahendragarh, I witnessed how the interplay between communication and power influenced the way farmers in the informal sector, and extension workers and scientists in the formal sector, communicated with each other. The matrix of one-way communication, two-way communication and no-way communication on one side, with one-way power, two-way power and no-way power shows the dilemma involved in this interface. As I became aware of how communication and power were enmeshed, the asymmetry of power between the formal and informal sectors of knowledge, technology and institutions also became more apparent to me.

	Power		
	One-Way	Two-Way	No-Way
One-Way	Authoritarian	Fearful Dictator	Street singer or Tom Tom beater
Two-Way	Farmer Training centre	Empowerment	Collegial learning
No-Way	Power Of silence	Impossible	Indifference

(Communication)

2.1 Communication and power: The dynamics of exchange

One-way communication—one-way power is a highly authoritarian model in which those who rule decide what is communicated. The recipient has to receive the said communication passively. Two-way communication and one-way power could be a situation wherein a teacher may listen to the feedback of the students but ultimately exercises his or her authority to decide which feedback to act upon and which to ignore. The possibility of someone having power and not asserting or communicating it is almost zero. If one has power, then it will flow through communication. On the other hand, one-way communication and two-way power is a possible situation in a democratic election in which the leaders may convey their agenda and the voters may show their power through voting rather than verbally communicating it. Next, one-way communication with no power flow either way represents a tom-tom beater (an announcer on a railway station, or any public place) who announces messages to people in a locality without any power to influence the actual content or its interpretation. Another example of this dynamic is people who manage propaganda dissemination without having the power to influence the content. Two-way communication and two-way power is perhaps the most sustainable and democratic arrangement. Mao Tse-tung called this the mass-line concept. The brigade was accountable to the commune and vice versa. The two-way power makes it democratic and two-way communication makes it humanitarian. The Honey Bee Network has tried to evolve into a social movement with such norms of horizontal and vertical accountability.

Gandhiji called a similar approach the gram swaraj in which the village community was expected to resolve a lot of common issues through collective will and mutual respect, without direction or interference from higher levels of authority.

In our context, two-way communication–two-way power will mean that farmers, or industrial innovators at the grassroots level, will have the power to comment upon and correct, if need be, the research agendas designed by scientists, technologists and firms and vice versa—that is scientists and technologists will also have the power to shape the agenda of farmer experimenters. The lab-to-land initiative will become a land-to-lab and back to land movement. Mutual learning will become a crucial indicator of power on both sides, playing a key role in keeping bidirectional communication flowing. In 1986, during the valedictory function at the Bangladesh Agricultural Research Council (BARC), I had asked a question: Will R&D leaders monitor the number of experiments started, stopped or modified in the wake of feedback from small farmers and their families? This question is often not asked and thus two-way power is not allowed to manifest when concrete decisions are to be taken. Many leaders want a participative culture in their organizations but don't wish to share power with the grassroots level and thus, deny themselves the benefit that could come from the ideas of the people at the shop floor or community level.

Later, while conducting a study on matching farmers' concerns with technologists' objectives in 1984, I realized that there was systematic bias in the perceptions of scientists about what they thought were the farmers' needs. For instance, scientists tended to focus on the role played by a specific crop or its variety at a particular time, in isolation of its linkage with other enterprises of the farmers. On the other hand, farmers, like most of us, looked at their portfolio. Similarly, scientists paid less attention in the early years to both quantity and quality of fodder even in dry regions, whereas the farmers knew that their survival depended upon livestock, particularly in drought years. Therefore, it was not surprising that the farmers' traditional varieties were much larger and with higher fodder content and quality than the modern crop varieties, in the case of millets and sorghum. There were many other disjunctions in the respective perceptions and responses to the environmental challenges noted in the economy. Some of the international centres of agricultural research eventually learnt these simple facts after spending millions of dollars and initiating large-scale surveys over the years.

As I mentioned briefly in the previous chapter, I was invited to Bangladesh in 1985, by the Bangladesh Agricultural Research Council and the Bangladesh Agricultural Research Institute (BARI). This summons came through the International Commonwealth Conference on Land Use Planning that was organized at IIMA by Professor Gopinath in 1984. I had presented a paper on the socioecology of land use planning. One of the participants in the conference, Dr Motlabur Rehman, director of BARI, took that paper and shared it with Mr Anisuzzaman, secretary of agriculture of the Government of Bangladesh. The secretary was well travelled within the country but had rarely travelled abroad. He read the paper and felt that I should be invited to reorient the agriculture research process in the country.

In Bangladesh, the interaction with the scientists, farmers, workers, tenants and policymakers taught me a lot about survival under high-risk conditions. With sixty per cent people being landless, the amount of creativity I noticed in their practices was inspiring. For example, the secretary noticed that fresh tomatoes were being sold in the market during off season. Such a thing had never happened before. He sent a message to BARI to find out how the farmers had managed to accomplish this feat. A team was then sent to the villages from where tomatoes were being marketed. What they learnt was an interesting lesson in ingenuity. The farmers had hung the uprooted tomato plants upside down, with unripe tomatoes, on a rope in a dark place. Anyone can do an experiment and see how by putting tomatoes upside down (stem side below), one can slow down their maturity. The flow of ethylene, which induces maturity and brings redness in the skin of tomatoes, is slowed when they are hung upside down.[1] A very low-cost, frugal, scientific method had been developed to lengthen the maturity period of tomatoes and thus give the farmers the advantage of higher prices during off season.

One should not assume that the farmers cannot and do not conduct both market and on-farm research to link 'mind to market',[2] as Dr R.A. Mashelkar puts it so nicely. In the Rángpur area of north Bangladesh, it was observed that in several homesteads, farmers planted one banana plant after every four areca palms. While

Bangladesh receives a lot of rainfall during its monsoons, there is hardly any rain during the winter season. The banana plant, after absorbing a lot of moisture during the monsoon, releases it for the roots of the palms in the winter. In situ, biological moisture conservation made the coping strategies of the farmers stronger in the wake of climate-induced fluctuations.[3]

Another occasion in Bangladesh, I was waiting for the ferry to cross a river to go to Ishwardi, an on-farm research centre. Since there was still time for the ferry to arrive, we sat down at a tea shop and started talking to the local clientele. One of tea drinkers was a small farmer who owned hardly 2 acres of land. I asked him which varieties of paddy (rice) he grew in the small field that he had. He said that given the risk and livelihood constraints, he planted two varieties in the same field— BR10 and BR11. We asked him why he specifically planted these two varieties. He replied that one of them was more adapted to climatic conditions and yielded at moderate levels. The other variety when cooked and consumed stayed in the stomach for a longer period. He explained that more than actual hunger, the pangs of hunger were more painful. A variety of rice which kept the belly full for longer periods helped in avoiding the pangs of hunger. Till then, I hadn't known that quantity could be compensated by quality as such. The feeling of fullness of the belly, i.e., how much the rice grains swelled in the stomach was almost never mentioned in any treatise or major policy study on rice breeding.

Now, I am not so sure whether scientists should breed varieties of rice according to the characteristics of the fullness of the belly. But, if the users demanded, they should be willing to at least share the knowledge of the existence of such varieties so that farmers can make prudent choices suitable to their conditions. Another example of the adaptability of the practices these farmers follow comes to mind. The energy needs of households were often precariously balanced amongst different choices. Some farmers put dung on jute sticks, as if intended for barbeque. When they burn these sticks in the clay stove used for cooking food, they can regulate the extent of heat needed for cooking by repositioning the stick with the dung balls.

Like so, there were many other creative ideas that I came across. And that is how the Honey Bee Network was born—partly, as I shared, out of the immense guilt I suffered from about not giving back to those who taught me so much. The Network celebrates the creativity of common people at their doorstep, i.e., recognizes them in the places where they work. The purpose is to convey a message that when somebody solves a problem ingeniously, it is the responsibility of outsiders—the state/market or civil society—to recognize these ideas first in situ, or where they occur. Volunteers organize idea contests among children, recipe contests among women, biodiversity contests among community members to identify outstanding innovations and traditional knowledge practices, such as food made out of uncultivated plants. Unique ideas and innovations— unaided, self-triggered, self-designed and supported (what I have also characterized as the autopoiesis model of grassroots innovation)—are taken forward by linking formal and informal science and technology knowledge economies and institutions. Much of the knowledge is open-source, shared democratically in local languages to pursue cross-pollination of ideas, forging knowledge bridges among people across language and regional cultures. While sourcing these distributed, scattered and uncelebrated ideas across thousands of villages over the country and the rest of the world, one needs the help of scouts or a voluntary network of people (students, farmers, teachers or almost anybody) who search for innovators by visiting different localities. Today, people call this process crowdsourcing or mass sourcing, but the Honey Bee Network started sourcing ideas from the grassroots level more than twenty-five years ago.

The dynamism in this process of mutual learning cannot take place unless everybody's role is properly acknowledged and celebrated.

These scouts are also recognized. Without these scouts, we could not have reached the innovators and other knowledge-holders. Whatever is learnt from people goes back to them in their local languages, and in this way, anonymity is overcome. If any benefit arises from commercial applications, or any other form of sharing of people's knowledge, a fair share should go back to them. These basic principles have since guided how the network functions in India and abroad.

The Honey Bee Network started growing with a lot of volunteers, including some former students, teachers and friends, realizing the validity of the philosophy of the network. Our mission to search and spread, and honour and harness creativity at the grassroots began to flourish. A lot of hitherto nameless and faceless minds started gaining recognition after coming in contact with the network. In 1993, SRISTI was set up as a voluntary organization to provide backstopping support to the network. The idea was to create a new kind of collective human consciousness or plural identity. People imbued with such a spirit will leverage the collective good over the individual good. It was not an easy feat, of course, but slowly and steadily, lot of people joined the network who genuinely wanted to pursue the Honey Bee Network philosophy of reciprocal, responsible and mutually respectful knowledge exchange. At that time, nobody was talking about the intellectual property rights of the poor people. When we argued that the knowledge rights of the economically poor people must be protected, the idea was met with amazement. Nobody thought that these minds on the margin have rights over their intellectual property. Today, when NIF has filed for more than 730 patents and about two dozen plant variety protection applications on behalf of the grassroots innovators, the world has begun to slowly take note.

SRISTI focused on four areas of creativity: education, technology, institutions and culture. In 1997, the first International Conference on Creativity and Innovation at Grassroots (ICCIG) was organized at IIMA. One of the recommendations was to set up a risk fund to take the innovative ideas forward. Mr S.K. Shelat, then chief secretary, Government of Gujarat, heard at the conference that we were facing a dilemma whether to stop documentation. After all, we had not been able to make much difference in the lives of common people except enrich their repertoire of knowledge through sharing. It is then that the idea of the Grassroots Innovation Augmentation Network (GIAN) was born.

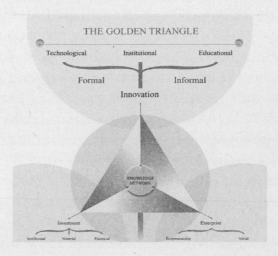

2.2 The golden triangle of the Grassroots Innovation Augmentation Network (GIAN)—reducing the transaction costs of innovators, investors and entrepreneurs to join hands and build a sustainable value chain for livelihood support.

The GIAN was, what we later understood, a kind of incubator. The golden triangle linking innovation, investment and enterprise was a kind of incubator. The ex ante and ex post transaction costs of innovators as well as other stakeholders were brought down. The concept of the Micro Venture Innovation Fund (MVIF) emerged in the form of the proposal for SRISTI Social Venture Fund at the ICCIG. By March 1997, the GIAN was in place.

The institutional context of each initiative was different. SRISTI was set up when the Policy and Perspective Committee of the IIMA felt that a *Honey Bee Newsletter*, with unverified claims of farmers, did not behove an institute like IIMA to publish such a newsletter. They suggested that a separate institution should be set up for the purpose. I was hesitant, but reluctantly agreed. I had applied for leave for doing research on the creativity and knowledge systems in local communities in 1991, but till 1993 I did not get leave. Generally, faculty took leave to go abroad or work within the industry, but I wanted leave to study the roots of Indian creative knowledge systems from the ground up. Once I got leave and set up SRISTI, the process of discovering and documenting grassroots innovations began in right earnest. Subsequently, the GIAN came into being to convert some of these innovations into enterprises. Kirit Patel, who had started with me, just a year or two after the founding of the Honey Bee Network, also helped in setting up the GIAN as its first acting chief innovation manager.

Genesis of the NIF

In mid-1998, I began to meet different secretaries to the government to share with them the progress the Honey Bee Network had made. The hope was that they would be convinced of viability of our approach, and thus help the network in scaling up. But most government branches offered short-term assistance for a so-called pilot project or some kind of feasibility study. I didn't see any point in following this approach of having to prove that Honey Bee Network process worked, because in the previous decade, we had already done the pilot study and achieved the results of documenting more than 5000-6000 grassroots innovations and another few 1000 traditional knowledge practices already. One day, Mr Dharmadhikari introduced me to Mr Gopalkrishnan, the additional secretary in the ministry of agriculture (who later became the chief election commissioner). I talked about the successes and outreach of the Honey Bee Network but also shared my frustrations that despite having met six secretaries in various relevant ministries, not many people understood the essence of the Honey Bee Network philosophy. He suggested that I should meet with Dr E.A.S. Sarma, secretary of expenditure in the ministry of finance. He was a PhD in physics and it was suggested that he might understand the connection between science and technology developments in the informal and formal sectors.

When I went to visit Dr Sarma, I had to wait for a long time. I was about to leave when Dr Sarma emerged from his room, apologizing for keeping me waiting, and took me inside. After hearing me out, he thought that Dr V.L. Kelkar, the finance secretary, should also be invited to join the meeting. He phoned Dr Kelkar requesting him to look at the presentation. Dr Kelkar was, of course, very busy because of the ongoing pressures of the budget-making process. But he agreed, though reluctantly, to join us for five minutes. Our discussion then went on for about an hour. I told them that if they were not convinced, I could come back after five years. With about 8000–10,000 ideas, practices and innovations already collected and documented, I felt that a strong case had been made for the country being innovative at the grassroots level. For harnessing the full potential of the programme, scaling up was necessary. They seemed convinced and asked me for the next steps. I suggested the setting up of an innovation foundation. Later, the discussion was furthered with the then finance minister who also liked the idea. We requested Dr R.A. Mashelkar to chair the National Innovation Foundation. In 1999, the finance minister announced the setting up of the NIF in that year's budget.

It was an important milestone for a new social movement like the Honey Bee Network, to have made an impact on the policy and institutional context of the country. While some sense of satisfaction was there, it was apparent that the change ahead was much bigger. There was no template to copy or learn from. No such foundation existed anywhere else in the world, which made the journey ahead very exciting but also made us more anxious.

I proposed a national fund for connecting innovators all over the country. This fund, with an initial corpus of Rs 20 crore, would build a national register of innovations, mobilize intellectual property protection, set up incubators for converting innovations into viable business opportunities and help in dissemination of information across the country.

Soon after the announcement, that same year the Kargil war took place and the government was excessively stretched for resources. There was a point when the then secretary of science and technology, Professor Ramamurthy, felt constrained in allocating resources to our cause. However, when Finance Minister Yashwant Sinha learnt about this issue, he was categorical that the foundation must be established. The assurance given in Parliament had to be respected. Instead of the request for a corpus of Rs 200 crore, the National Innovation Foundation received Rs 20 crore on the last day of the financial year 1998–99. The foundation had already been registered as a society in anticipation of the impending approval.

A distinguished board, chaired by Dr R.A. Mashelkar, took over the responsibility of guiding and supporting the national urge to be a global leader in sustainable technologies.

But the dealings of the government are seldom straightforward. While sanctioning the corpus, the finance ministry decided that the NIF should have only three senior professionals instead of five, that too on a contractual basis and they should be paid much less than what was requested. Every year, the finance minister would invite senior scientists and other professionals for pre-budget consultations. For several years, I was also extended an invitation. In one such pre-budget meeting in 2001, the finance minister inquired about the progress of the NIF. I couldn't restrain myself and shared, in an anguished tone, that while the NIF had done very well, it had decided not to hire any staff and work through volunteers instead. I said that there must be something seriously wrong with the structure of governance if the finance secretary, who decides matters costing say Rs 20,000 crore or more, also wanted to decide matters of less than Rs 2 crore (incidentally, the interest on the corpus of Rs 20 crore). What was the point in having a board[4] with such illustrious members, including former finance secretary and advisor to the finance minister, former expenditure secretary and several other senior officials, private sector leaders and eminent social change agents, if the board cannot decide the number of people to be hired and the amount to be paid? It is better to work without staff at all, I had declared. It was indeed remarkable that despite relying on volunteers, the NIF had been able to mobilize a large number of innovations from the northeast, breaking the myth that marginal regions had marginal minds. In the first year alone, the NIF had managed its scale of operations through volunteers from SRISTI without any staff. Moreover, the NIF had mobilized more than 1400 innovations and outstanding traditional knowledge practices. I also offered to restructure the ministry of finance without any cost to the government so that such anomalies don't exist and the best use of talent could be made!

Soon after, the NIF received approval for all that it wanted. The reason I have described this incident is to show that at the time, the government respected a reasonable position and, without getting into ego hassles, resolved the issues appropriately. I was happy that the then finance minister didn't take my outburst unkindly and in fact, continued to invite me in the subsequent years for more pre-budget consultations. There are few organizations like the NIF in the country which could have delivered so much output at such a diminutive unit costs. The entire credit for this goes to the hard-working team—the very sincere collaborators of the Honey Bee Network, and its thousands of volunteers in different parts of the country and in different industrial, rural and educational sectors.

Despite steady success, constant innovation is a necessary condition for organizations to remain vibrant, responsive and agile. In the budget speech of 2002, the finance minister announced yet another window of opportunity for grassroots innovators at our behest. This proposal was regarding the setting up of a Micro Venture Innovation Fund in collaboration with the Small Industries Development Bank of India (SIDBI). However, even with this initiative, the beginning was not easy.

The Swiss Development Cooperation (SDC) had given some funds to SIDBI for promoting innovations. SIDBI wanted to use these funds to create the Micro Venture Innovation Fund at the NIF. In the initial discussions, the SDC suggested that they should have a role in monitoring the use of these funds. The NIF refused to accept such surveillance for two reasons: (a) SDC had no special expertise in handling such funds, whereas the NIF had evolved the concept through learning from the Honey Bee Network, which had set up the GIAN in 1997; and (b) SDC had given funds to SIDBI, and the NIF had no obligation towards the organizations which funded SIDBI. The NIF was accountable only to SIDBI.

The matter took more than a year to resolve. Finally, the SIDBI agreed to the NIF's position and no third party monitoring was installed. The takeaway here is that many international organizations try to go beyond the boundaries agreed between the parties and unless one resists such attempts, their influence can exceed their contribution. Lack of tact in this regard may not be good for the developmental autonomy and freedom of institutions in any country.

The annual budget of the NIF was Rs 1.6 crore (8 per cent interest on a corpus of Rs 20 crore through RBI bonds) which was grossly inadequate, given the challenges the NIF was facing at the time. Initially, every year, and later every two years, a presidential award function was held to honour the grassroots innovators. The function itself cost upwards of Rs 45 lakh, including nominal award money. The first award function was chaired by Shri K.C. Pant, then deputy chair, Planning Commission. In fact, he was so moved after meeting with the grassroots innovators at the exhibition organized on the occasion that he invited them to visit the Planning Commission. He also asked many members of Planning Commission to visit the exhibition. A display of grassroots innovations was organized in the lawns of the Indian Agricultural Research Institute in New Delhi where the first function was organized. Each innovator got the opportunity to explain his or her ideas to the chief guest, Shri Pant. This was the first time such an exhibition had been organized in the capital, and at the NIF's expense, the innovators, along with one or more friends or relatives, had been invited to attend. For most of the innovators and their family members and friends, it was a rare occasion when they were being honoured in such a ceremony. Later, Shri Pant organized a presentation on the NIF for the entire Planning Commission, and decided to write to all the chief ministers for the purpose of appointing various nodal officers to coordinate with the NIF.

The next year onwards, Dr A.P.J. Abdul Kalam, then president of India, agreed to give away the awards every year. Since Dr Kalam's involvement, the NIF awards have always been honoured by the President of India. Dr Kalam talked about grassroots innovations in various fora and created tremendous awareness about the work of the Honey Bee Network and the NIF. The next president, Ms Pratibha Devisingh Patil, after visiting the innovation exhibition held at the Indian Agricultural Research Institute in Delhi, announced in her speech her decision to host an innovation exhibition at the Rashtrapati Bhavan. Ever since then, the President's office hosted an exhibition of innovations every year and the awards are given biennially at the same location. India is probably the only country where the head of state hosts an exhibition of innovation. The present president of India, Shri Pranab Mukherjee, took the entire movement and effort to another level. From March 2015 onwards, he decided that his office would host a Festival of Innovation at the Rashtrapati Bhavan. This has heralded a new chapter in the continuing march towards an inclusive society through grassroots innovations in India.

The kind of message that this gesture gives can only be appreciated if one looks into the eyes of those reaching the pedestal of the Rashtrapati Bhavan. A lot of policymakers, distinguished members of the diplomatic community, entrepreneurs and at least half a million other common people who visit the Mughal Garden come to visit the exhibition. New partnerships are forged, new bridges are built and new agendas are set.

Indian society is going through a fundamental metamorphosis. Popular aspirations are rising, patience for institutional inefficiencies is decreasing, and young people are not willing to live with inertia and indifference towards larger social change anymore. In a way, this is a very promising situation. A demanding youth is the biggest guarantee for democratic and demographic divide to converge, for harnessing the potential of an inclusive innovation ecosystem. President Pranab Mukherjee has taken several concrete steps to promote innovations, reinforce the social, ecological and industrial connect of Indian academia and galvanize societal will to serve the underserved, as well as reach the unreached.

Various institutions of excellence also need to become outstanding examples of social and environmental accountability. They can do so by: (a) creating standards of excellence; (b) responding to the unmet needs through high-quality basic and applied research; (c) learning from and sharing with the grassroots innovators the productive ways of blending formal and informal knowledge systems; and (d) recognizing the limits of what they know or do not know about solving social problems.

Institutions of higher learning are expected to produce high-quality research minds who will be productively challenged by not only esoteric theoretical problems, but also by persistent or 'wicked problems'. Shri Pranab Mukherjee has taken several initiatives which can help build bridges between the formal and informal system. I will now move on to describe some of these initiatives in detail:

National Innovation Clubs (NICs)

Every elite academic institution is expected to motivate its young students to search, spread and celebrate innovations and sense the unmet needs of the public. Institutions can encourage students to implement and share the innovations not only with them but also those available in the NIF's database with the communities and school children in nearby localities. They can draw upon the innovation database of the Honey Bee Network (nifindia.org, sristi.org, honeybee.org and techpedia.in/ awards), or their own institutional innovations, and share not only the actual inventions but also the science behind them with local communities. In the process, they might come across some intriguing, interesting and inspiring questions, which will reinforce their spirit for discover and inquiry further. The logic is simple: When we share what we know we invariably also share what we do not know. A resultant acknowledgement of inadequacy and insufficiency may trigger the search for new ideas, as philosophically put, we can reason that there are never any perfect solutions. All over the world, even the large corporations are realizing that internal R&D is not equal to innovation. They are also realizing that all good ideas may not come from within the organization.

The search and sourcing of innovations from the common man, pursued by the Honey Bee Network for the last twenty-five years was a prelude to open innovation framework in the country. All over India, the IITs (Indian Institutes of Technology), NITs (National Institutes of Technology), IISERs (Indian Institutes of Science Education and Research) and numerous other establishments can be a pivot for two-way flow of ideas and knowledge between the formal and informal sectors, looking to source innovative ideas from schoolchildren in the hinterland as well as from villages, slums, workshops, Micro, Small and Medium Enterprises (MSME) clusters, etc.

Unless we systematically map the creativity as well as unmet needs of our society, how can we ever develop a collective determination to meet these needs in the near term? Sensing the gap between availability and needs is thus one of the important goals of the National Innovation Clubs. We are aware that a lot of social anomie and alienation results from the persistence of unmet needs which both markets and the state continue to either ignore or address improperly. And every innovation, in some form, is a response to a gap in the local aspirational ladder and available choices. But there is also a lot of inertia which can be overcome by sensing the gaps, scouting or spotting any solutions that may exist or have been developed by local community member, documenting them, parameterizing and then reducing to its solvable components and converting these ideas into viable products and services.

The celebration of innovation, the fundamental approach of the National Innovation Clubs, includes inviting innovators in various fields to the classroom, honouring them and understanding the ethics and the rationality underlying their frugal solutions. It also includes inviting outstanding innovators on board as adjunct faculty to help our young students learn the art of converting an unmet need into an affordable solution.

Validation and Value Addition

Validation by the formal scientific institution is necessary, not only to enhance the scientific temperament among knowledge-providing communities, but also to understand the scientific principles underlying a functional practice. Validation also helps in increasing the self-confidence of the knowledge providers by enhancing their ability to solve their own problems. Once validation through on-farm research or in-lab testing is complete, further value addition may help in improving efficacy of the solution. Sometimes innovations dependent on natural resources may reduce the raw material (including biomass) and thus reduce pressure on environment and help in conserving biodiversity. The students will also better grasp the basic scientific concepts when they address real-life problems in the lab. Thus, NIC aims to strike a balance between scientific theory and practice as taught in the classroom as well as real-world creativity, coping strategies of communities with climate changes and other socio-economic stresses, developmental politics and social situations.

Exhibition of Innovation/Festival of Innovation

As I've mentioned, the Rashtrapati Bhavan holds an exhibition of innovation every year in March to engage young and old, rural and urban, experts and laymen alike, so as to expose these parties to the innovation and creativity at the grassroots level. If every school and higher education institution also organizes an innovation exhibition or festival of innovation at their individual, local levels, it will sensitize the faculty, staff and students to the creativity of common people. These will also create a new social festival where every year, every region will celebrate local creativity and innovations. Nations like India that need to constantly improve living conditions of people will need new ways of galvanizing social energy and motivations.

The first festival of innovation was organized during 7–13 March 2015. The second festival was organized during 12–18 March 2016. Undoubtedly, the legacy of such initiatives conveys to the nation that the country cares for the creativity of common people—young students, schoolchildren, the economic poor and other members of society. In due course of implementation of such programmes, it is possible that the mood of the nation may change. The impatience with the inertia of development may increase. Diffidence may get diluted and start-up culture, being currently advocated strongly in public policy, may be strengthened. There is perhaps no nation in the world in which the head of state, the President, hosts a festival of innovation in this manner.

Innovation Scholar-in-Residence Programme at the Rashtrapati Bhavan

In 2013, Shri Pranab Mukherjee, apart from inviting an artist and a writer, also invited around ten grassroots innovators, school and college students to stay at the Rashtrapati Bhavan for a period of two to three weeks.

The purpose of creating a temporary community is to build their linkages with policy, technology and other institutions such as industry associations, relevant wings of the government, private corporations, science and technology institutions including the Indian Council of Medical Research (ICMR), the Indian Council of Agricultural Research (ICAR) and the Council of Scientific and Industrial Research (CSIR) etc., the Bureau of Indian Standards (BIS) and other stakeholders. The NIF has supported the residency and has begun to provide post-residency mentoring as well. In 2013, five innovation scholars were selected to join the residency by a committee chaired by the secretary to the President, Ms Omita Paul. These included two grassroots innovators, Dharambir of Yamuna Nagar, Haryana, and Mr Gurmel Singh Dhondsi of Sri Ganganagar, Rajasthan. Two winners of the Gandhian Young Technological Innovation Awards given by SRISTI as a part of techpedia.sristi. org were also selected, namely, Abinash Kumar from the Jawaharlal Nehru Centre for Advanced Research, Bangalore, and Manisha Mohan, a student of SRM University, Chennai. Teneth Adhitya of Virudhunagar, Tamil Nadu, a school student and winner of the NIF's

IGNITE award for innovative children was also selected. It was an extremely unusual opportunity that these five innovators got to expand the horizons of their thinking and strengthen their commitment towards the nation.

The second batch of innovation scholars-in-residence included Priyanka Mathikshara, aged fifteen years, an innovator from Tamil Nadu who invented the Super Stocker 3C Ultra Model Dustbin; Mukul and Diptanshu Malviya, two innovators from Rajasthan who invented the Wrapper Picker; Mansukh Jagani, an innovator from Gujarat who invented Bullet Santi, a multipurpose agriculture machine; Rai Singh Dahiya, from Rajasthan who invented a Biomass Gasifier System; Kamruddin Saifi, from Uttar Pradesh, who invented a chaff-cutter with clutch and brake system; T.S. Anand, from Tamil Nadu, who invented a prosthetic knee for uneven terrains; Shantanu Pathak, from Maharashtra, who invented the Care Mother, a mobile pregnancy care kit; Vikas Karade, also from Maharashtra, who invented a 3D model generation from 2D X-ray images; Mohanlal, from Kerala, who invented a reversible reduction gear for marine diesel engines and Z-drive propellers; and finally, Sarthak Shukla, aged fourteen years, an innovator from Uttar Pradesh who invented a cylindrical-shaped refrigerator with rotatory tray.

The third batch of the programme joined and began their residency on 12 March 2016, along with the other invitees of the second festival of innovation, at Rashtrapati Bhavan.

From the first batch of the scholars-in-residence, both Dharambir and Dhondsi received an NIF national award from the President; Dharambir specifically for his multipurpose food-processing machine. Coming from a very humble background, Dharambir has come a long way. He used to drive a cycle rickshaw in Delhi and ferry passengers to Khari Baoli, a big market of medicinal herbs. In the process, he learnt a lot about various medicinal plants and their uses. One day, his rickshaw met with an accident and was no longer fit for use. He was also injured. He came back to his village and began to think about growing medicinal plants and designing a new machine for processing these plants and other horticultural products. He had no experience and no training in mechanical processes. The only thing he had in abundance was a kind of foolhardiness and a stubborn desire to do what had not been done before. He lost a lot of money, came under debt, was scolded by his father, sometimes even beaten for his persistence but he didn't give up. One day, his family asked him to leave their joint family home to live on his own. The family was tired of what they thought of as excessive expenditure on his experiments. By putting him under financial stress, they had hoped that they will 'cure' him of his 'invention' bug. Thankfully, they could not. Thus, he had to begin threading the parts of his life afresh. His wife was a great support and she joined him in facing the struggle ahead. Eventually, he succeeded. He has made a double-storey, fancy house. Today, he employs thirty women for processing the plants grown on his own small farm. He started with selling herbal products on a cycle in nearby villages, but now has a team of sales agents who do it for him. Through his direct business of selling machines and also herbal products, he has helped in generating 6000–10,000 jobs both directly and indirectly in the supply chain within and outside the country. His daughter has done her MBA, and his son, Prince, owns a car. He continues to constantly travel, train tribals and other community members in using his machines. He even helps them to develop various medicinal products, package them and sell them to market. In addition, he has sold more than 300 machines all over the country. In consistency with the Honey Bee Network philosophy of obeying all the laws of the land and paying tax properly, he was featured by the BBC and other media channels for paying an income tax worth Rs 70,00,000 income during the years 2013–14 and 2014–15. His income tax alone may cross a crore of rupees shortly. During his stay at the Rashtrapati Bhavan, he processed the fruits growing in the campus and made various products which could be sold by the local women cooperative run by the families of the staff. The New Delhi Municipal Corporation offered to buy his machines, while the ministry of food processing and various other institutions including the CSIR offered mentoring and technical support.

In fact, the then director general of the CSIR, Dr Ahuja assured all the innovators that all the CSIR labs will welcome them with open arms and support them without any hesitation. Human Resource Development Minister Smriti Irani also met Dharambir and the rest of the scholars, listened to their ideas and offered all kinds of support to each one of them. Minister of Women and Child Welfare Maneka Gandhi also met with them and encouraged them. Dr Prajapati Trivedi, then secretary of the performance division of the cabinet secretariat, gave them an overview of the innovation processes in the government and explained the Result Framework Document (RFD) system. This framework was supposed to help each ministry/undertaking of the Central government to agree upon key performance targets and indicators for annual review. The NIF had played a role in adding to the dynamism of this process by sharing its own experiences.

The standards play a very important role in promoting innovations and creating their markets. Since manufacturing standards exist for products that are known to exist or can be anticipated, they are generally made compatible with global norms. But grassroots innovations don't have standardization. Most fabricators change the design parameters according to the variability in the agro-ecological conditions in which users work. This problem was manifested most prominently in the case of the motorcycle-based ploughing machine also known as santi. The situation became more complex in this case because most fabricators used second-hand parts.

Agriculture secretary, Shri Siraj Hussain and IT secretary, Ms Kumudini both realized that the problem of more than 10,000 motorcycle santi machines (ploughing, weeding, spraying and other farm operations) in Gujarat inspired by the innovation of santi by Mansukhbhai, were all unapproved because standards had not been finalized. They immediately started a formal process and these farm vehicles are likely to receive formal approval, and thus a legitimate economic activity will also become legally validated through its implementation.

Mobilizing Social Capital

About twenty-four years ago, I met an old IIMA student, Vasimalai on a flight from Chennai to Ahmedabad. We got talking and I told him about our then-recently founded Honey Bee Network. I mentioned to him that I was looking for volunteers, geniuses really, who might like to join hands to scout, spawn and support grassroots innovations and in the process champion the outstanding stores of traditional knowledge we possessed as a nation. Specifically, I told him how useful it would be if some young volunteers organized biodiversity competitions among children. Vasi told me about a young postgraduate in agriculture who had resigned from a very well-paying job in an insurance company and had decided to settle down on a small farm to develop a frugal and sustainable model of agriculture and rural development systems instead. He promised to connect me to him soon after reaching Ahmedabad. This young person, whom I later found out was P. Vivekanandan, became one of the oldest and the strongest partners of the Honey Bee Network. Based in Madurai, he desired to push the limits of simplicity and live an extremely frugal life. When he learnt about the idea of biodiversity competition, he found himself intrigued and reached out to me to discuss the same. This alliance, initially forged over a shared interest in the biodiversity competitions, was the beginning of a lifelong friendship. He has been bringing out Tamil translations of the *Honey Bee Newsletter* ever since. To his other credentials—Vivekanandan has attempted many experiments in local, herbal veterinary knowledge and the conservation of local animal breeds. Many of his efforts in this regard have been recognized internationally and nationally. He also organized a national-level, local animal breed conservation conference in collaboration with the National Bureau of Animal Genetic Resources in Karnal, which included participants from Pakistan as well. There were only a few families left in Pakistan conserving the Sahiwal breed of cattle. Biodiversity conservation inevitably requires cross-border cooperation. Vivekanandan has represented the Honey Bee Network at several international fora and has also served on the board of the NIF. He was recently honoured with the Jamnalal Bajaj Award for science and technology applications in rural development. He is one of my idols in terms of frugal lifestyle. Practicing the values that we discover in the lives of grassroots innovators is not easy. But the network has succeeded in closing the gap in a few cases at least. Vivek is the best example of that.

When different volunteers join the network, they not only bring their spirit but also their social capital to the cause. It is this capital which expands the network to new domains.

Brigadier Ganesham was still in the Indian National Army, when we had organized a workshop on innovations in the army. General J.J. Singh was the chief of army staff and Lieutenant General V.K. Dhir was the director general of EME Corps (the corps of Electrical and Mechanical Engineers is an arms and service branch of the Indian army) at that time. After retiring from the army, Ganesham offered to volunteer with the Honey

Bee Network in Andhra Pradesh. Earlier, Dr Geervani, as vice chancellor of the Women's University in Tirupati had tried very hard to continue with the Telugu translation of the Honey Bee Network newsletter. She had taken the help of language department to further the effort. But, after her retirement, the process somehow withered away, till it was revived again by Ganesham. Since 2006, *Palle Srujana*, a Telugu bimonthly is being published uninterruptedly. (It is the Telugu version of the *Honey Bee Newsletter*, just as Vivekanandan brought out the Tamil version of the *HBN Newsletter*.)

Volunteers like Ganesham have been invaluable to the network. In one case, a technology was developed by Makarand Kale in Maharashtra using pulses and other biological materials to make a bulletproof jacket. While some trials had been done, no systematic trial had taken place in the intended field of use—the defence forces. Using his network, Brigadier Ganesham got those tests done. While the network is completely pacifist, it does encourage safety-oriented innovations for saving lives. But as a matter of principle, we don't get involved in aggressive technological innovations. There are several other such technologies that were scouted and recognized earlier, but which were not getting adequate attention.

For example, Mallesham's asu machine, which got tremendous support after the network was strengthened by Ganesham in undivided Andhra Pradesh. Mallesham belongs to a weaver family hailing from Shirajipet village in the Nalgonda district of Telangana. He used to weave Pochampalli saris, which entails a double ikat pattern, incidentally one of the most complicated weaving technologies. The unique property of Pochampalli saris is that the same design is present on both sides of the cloth. The tie-dye system has to ensure that every pixel— so to say, where warp and weft intersect—must have the same colour. The Pochampalli tradition has been practised by the weavers of two districts of Telangana for the last seven decades. One of the pre-loom activities in making saris in this tradition is the asu process, which is very laborious and is traditionally often performed by women only.

Mallesham's mother had to wind the thread 9000 times on different pegs to facilitate transfer of the design to the thread, then tie-dye the spool before it was wound on spindles, and used as weft in the loom for weaving the actual sari. In a day, his mother could manage to do it about twice, which was 18,000 times moving her hand across four-foot-long asu frame, so much so that it would cause severe hand and shoulder ache. Eventually, she declared that it was too painful and he should find some other source of livelihood instead of putting his wife also through similar drudgery.

But Mallesham wondered what else he could do as he was aware of no other skills he possessed. He was educated only up to Class VI. Yet, he was determined to find a way to lessen his mother's pain. The turning point came as he began his experimental journey to automate the asu process. It was not easy for a school dropout living in a remote village to understand the intricacies of engineering and designing such a technical solution. But he was passionate and determined to achieve his goal at any cost. As can be expected, the debts started mounting by and by. A time came when he had to leave the village and move to Hyderabad and take up a job as a casual labourer in a factory to support his cause. Every day in the evening, he would go out in the market and look for different devices that could help him find solutions to the problem of winding the thread.

He divided the entire asu operations into five frames or mechanical operations. In six years, he managed to develop all links and movements for the first four frames. In the fifth frame he got stuck with a movement, wherein a particular lever would wind the thread around a specific peg a given number of times and then move on to the next peg. Mallesham was not able to solve this step. One day, while he was delivering electric supplies to a small industry, he happened to see a wire-winding machine which was directing the wire to a specific point on the drum. Immediately he knew he had found what he was looking for. The next day, he didn't go for work and tried to implement that design element into his prototype. He incorporated similar levers in his machine and it was a perfect fit, and thus, Mallesham finally completed the asu machine after seven years of relentless pursuit. It was his eureka moment; the machine worked as he had expected. The machine could do in one-and-a-half hours what a woman does in five hours.

He went back to his village with his new design and the word spread quickly. Lots of people started coming to him to evaluate his machine. He had not only addressed a personal problem of his mother's pain, but also removed the capacity constraint of the Pochampalli sari industry, whose capacity had hitherto depended on how the number of women manually performed the asu per day. Mallesham's case is special indeed as it is very rare that a grassroots innovation can remove the capacity constraints of an industry.

Further understanding the need and the criticality of the machine for his community, Mallesham decided to supply these to other local weavers. He set up a small manufacturing unit with some assistance in 2001. When steel prices shot up in 2002, the manufacturing cost of asu machine shot up one-and-a-half times. Knowing well that his fellow weavers in the community could not afford the asu machine at that price, Mallesham learnt electronics, micro-control systems, embedded programming, servos, etc., by reading technical books in Telugu and modified his machine to an electronic version from an earlier, purely mechanical one, bringing back its cost to the original, reduced levels. This is an outstanding feat, possible only when one has *samvedana* (sympathy) for the beneficiaries. It brought down the cost, reduced the weight, improved the quality, lowered the noise pollution and enhanced reliability as well. He then supplied these electronic asu machines from 2003 onwards. In 2008, he came to know that embedded systems facilitate storing the designs, and recalling them on demand. Basically, these systems involve memorizing the designs and operations through software. He wanted to incorporate this facility as a weaver so as to reuse the designs according to demand. Mallesham approached the IT experts and they quoted one lakh rupees for incorporating such a facility into his machine. He returned home quietly, decided once again to take matters into his own hands and bought books on component and modular assembly programming. By the end of 2009, he wrote his own software programme and incorporated a control box in his asu machine. The idea behind such a control box was that the weaver could easily set the number of times he wanted the thread to be wound on each peg. Depending upon the tie-dye design that is intended to be created on these threads, this kind of control system reduced drudgery a great deal and improved accuracy, quality and ease of operation. Mallesham is a vibrant example of the sensitivity of a self-driven innovator to his community.

In this way, Mallesham's empathetic innovation changed the lives of thousands of weavers. Later, I got a chance to talk about him in a radio interview in the US on the show, *NRI Samay*, which generated a very large number of inquiries. This programme has a large non-resident Indian listener network. Through this kind of publicity, the Honey Bee Network could expand the stakeholder base of the innovation and create wider awareness. Returning to another beacon of the Honey Bee Network, I recall how Brigadier Ganesham not only followed up on those inquiries, but also visited the US and mobilized significant contributions through his network for providing this machine to women asu workers. He also developed a fund to buy yarn and give it to the weavers who would be using this machine, so that they could come out of the clutches of the yarn traders and moneylenders. A network of asu family consisting of the weavers benefited by the asu machines, the contributors, local Honey Bee Network members and the innovator was formed and it met periodically. He realized that without breaking the link between exploitative traders and the weavers, the real gains of the innovation would not accrue to the adopters.

Today, with over 700 asu machines spread across the Pochampalli weavers, more than 7000 weaver families benefited from this innovation in terms of permanent removal of drudgery to women, which enabled them to continue with weaving—still the only skill they knew. The asu machine also ensured continuity of the Pochampalli tradition of weaving when the availability of women workers for manual performance of the asu was waning to alarming levels during the late 1990s. For such an outstanding contribution at the grassroots level, Mallesham also received a national biennial grassroots innovations award given by the NIF from the hands of the President of India, besides the Micro Venture Innovation Fund support from the NIF.

Here, the synergy of efforts between the back end and the front end of operations clearly demonstrates that without volunteers like Brigadier Ganesham and Dr Geervani, the network could not have made much difference to the lives of creative people such as Mallesham.

Moreover, the Honey Bee Network has focused far more on scouting and dissemination of innovations in the first decade and a half, than on value addition and commercialization of innovations. For the first ten years, there were only two people (actually one and a half—Kirit Patel, full-time, and me, half-time, besides some research staff in the coordination cell). Slowly, more of our colleagues joined in and strengthened the network over the next ten years. Riya Sinha played an important full-time role in coordinating the network besides handling many other responsibilities. She managed the scouting and documentation function of the NIF and later on took over the entire administration at National Innovation Foundation as chief innovation officer. She edited the newsletter, and mobilized the content, had illustrations made by the artists and got the layout done. In other words, she looked after the entire production responsibility of the newsletter. She also helped in making a database on indigenous common property institutions with an intern, Troels Bjerregaard from Denmark. Ramesh Patel joined SRISTI around twenty years ago and steers its activities even now. Dilip Koradia worked for a while with us and contributed many ideas in terms of scouting and documentation. There are far too many contributors who deserve to be acknowledged than is possible in a book like this. But it is important to stress that in majority of the cases, the people who joined us chose to work with me, and not the other way round. There are very few people whom I may have selected, and Dr Vipin Kumar is one of them. He now coordinates the activities of the NIF full-time as its director and chief innovation officer.

Managing Honey Bee Network did not require only keeping all the volunteers properly recognized and motivated, it also required maintaining the motivation of internal team.

Once, Kirit, Riya and a few other colleagues were very upset with me. I had recruited two staff members to assist me in bringing out the *Honey Bee Newsletter*. These colleagues were not cooperating with me for some time and felt that by directly hiring the staff (so-called professionals), I was marginalizing them, that is trying to find ways of coping with the stress by bypassing them. On the SRISTI board and staff meeting, they questioned my prerogative to recruit staff unilaterally. A decision was taken to take away my recruiting powers. They thought by bringing in staff with short-term tenurial assignments, I was sort of doing injustice to those who had spent long innings with the network. So for the next two years, I didn't recruit anybody. They obviously didn't have any doubt in my ability to recruit since I had recruited them. In a way, they were right. A social movement cannot be built on the shoulders of only professionals whose commitment is short-term and who don't see a long-term future in the network or the organization. Building the institution required people who not only trusted the vision and the culture of our organization, but were also willing to make trade-offs in their personal lives in favour of the institution when required. In fact, when SRISTI was set up in 1993, the dream was to forge a new kind of human consciousness which would give primacy to the collective good over private inclinations.

Building the Honey Bee Network as an institution—which aimed not only to ingrain a feeling of collegiality and utmost transparency but also an ability to fight for values while disregarding one's status in the organization—was a true challenge. I can take some satisfaction in the fact that the people who were appointed on a contractual basis and whose term was extended annually had enough confidence in themselves and their relationship with the institution that they could challenge me repeatedly. After a while, they realized that it was only by challenging that they could earn my respect. Everybody had faith that if they contributed sincerely to the common cause, nobody could question their continuity in the network. The contractual nature of staff appointment did not make their stake and voice in the running of the network any less important or strategic. Else, long-term vision would not develop and also such staff will not be able to motivate outside volunteers to have long-term commitment towards the network. No one person, no matter how charismatic, can build a network alone. Likewise, he/she cannot sustain the differentiated needs for recognition, respect and reciprocity among the members without support of the whole team. Otherwise it is so easy to sow the seeds of discord; so many groups have splintered due to internal and external pressures.

I have always reminded everybody we have recruited in SRISTI, the GIAN or the NIF that their jobs have not been generated by me. It is the creative, common people who have done it. They do what they do and have shared their knowledge generously with us without which the financial resources for recruiting and building our organization could not have been raised. We all need to be grateful and devoted to such knowledge providers whose contributions have paved the way for young people who run these organizations.

Another collaborator is Dr T.N. Prakash who played an important role in bringing out Kannada version of the *Honey Bee Newsletter* for many years.

Dr T.N. Prakash, then a faculty member at the University of Agricultural Sciences in Bangalore, took enormous interest in mobilizing innovations in Karnataka. A large number of these innovators receive awards at national and regional functions. He continues to provide support to local creative communities even today.

SRISTI Normative benefit sharing formula

Sr. No.	Index	%
1	Innovator (Traditional knowledge holder)	30
2	Nature	5
3	Community	5
4	Innovation Fund	20
5	Research and Development	15
6	Over head	15
7	Contigency	5
8	Women fund	5

2.3 Normative Benefit-sharing Formula developed by SRISTI

Shri Sundaram is an innovative farmer from the Sikar district of Rajasthan. He has been collaborating with the network and has helped in discovering other innovators, particularly, farmer breeders. He himself has developed several varieties of chili and chickpea. One of his most famous technologies involves growing a tree in arid regions using one litre of water just once, that is once in the entire life cycle of that sapling. Most people plant trees during the monsoon season; the survival rate is sometimes as low as 30 per cent in dry sandy regions. Sundaram would plough the land during the monsoon season to let water percolate as much as possible. After the monsoon, in the month of October, he would complete the steps of planking and laddering to break the capillaries of the plants. Whatever moisture had percolated remained underground because in such a situation, it would not evaporate easily. After two months, he created small pits as openings, enough to hold a seedling. Conventionally, pits of 1x1x1 foot would be dug up. By opening bigger pits, we lose all subsoil moisture. He would then give a measured one litre of water to the seedlings he so planted. Since there was no moisture in the upper layer of the soil (as opposed to the case during monsoon months), the seedling was forced to send the roots downwards, to seek out the moisture which had been previously contained. The monsoon seedlings, on the other hand, had no incentive to spread their roots deep. When the upper layer of the soil dried up, these seedlings often died. But, the seedlings planted by Sundaram's method survived. Thus, the lifespan of these seedlings increased and they were able to survive till next monsoon, unlike the seedlings that were actually planted during monsoon. The Oil and Natural Gas Corporation (ONGC) then took up a larger-scale plantation in arid lands using Sundaram's technology through the involvement of SRISTI. The results were very promising. If this method is followed, a large part of degraded land can be turned green at an extraordinarily low cost. This requires change in the mindset of the forestry department and also suggests a need for new guidelines. But the incentives for reducing cost and increasing efficiency at the same time leaves little margin for distribution. In due course, India will overcome such perverse incentives that militate against the scaling up of frugal, extremely sustainable innovations. Once ONGC supported the larger-scale dissemination, it became slightly easier for Sundaram to convince other officials about the need for using this approach. But any approach which reduces waste, costs less and generates economy in operations is not easy to institutionalize in public systems, given various perverse incentives.

Sundaram has also developed several new varieties of dry-land crops. In 1998, Sundaram visited the village of Khandela, where he noticed a few uncommon plants of guar in a farmer's field. Those plants were taller, bore more number of pods from top to bottom and were free from insect, pest and disease infestations. He specifically selected those same plants and harvested the seeds separately. The next year he grew the seeds of the selected plants in his farm and observed that some plants had fast-growing habits, including early flowering and fruiting. He adopted such mass-selection methods, that is, pooled the seeds of selected plants and plots every year for six years and harvested better seeds separately. The results were a new variety of crop with uniform height, synchronous maturity and higher yield. In this way, Sundaram came to develop several varieties like Guar SR-23, mothbean SR-1 and Kabuli Chana SR-1.

He finally released these varieties into the market for commercial purposes in 2005.

Sundaram's wife, Bhagwati Devi, is no less innovative. She found that termites, a serious problem in the dry lands, used to affect the growth and yield of the crop a great deal. She also observed that pieces of soft wood in the soil attracted the termites. To attempt to solve this problem, she planted small pieces of eucalyptus in the wheat field at different intervals. What she noticed was that all the termites became concentrated under these pieces of eucalyptus. One could then simply remove these pieces and dispose of the termites. Similar heuristics have also been used independently in Africa, by another farmer using bamboo instead of eucalyptus.[5] Farmers thousands of miles apart facing similar challenge often use local resources and solve problem using similar thumb rule or heuristics without often knowing about each other's solution. This means that rediscovery of wheel becomes imperative time and again. The Honey Bee Network reduces this gap, hastens mutual learning and expands scope and scale of social imagination.

There are other numerous collaborators including scientists, designers, fabricators and policymakers whose contribution to the network has been immense. In fact, in the contemporary context, the network cannot progress without constantly bringing new skills, perspectives and capabilities into the mix. There is much more scope for identifying a lot more innovations in every state and therefore the Honey Bee Network welcomes new partners to join and supplement the effort of existing ones. There are several scientists who have added value and or validated innovators' claims at some point of time, without any financial fee or at a very low cost. Almost all the scientists in over 200 labs who have worked with the NIF did not charge for their own time. The same goes for our patent attorneys. If all the ethical and social capital is converted to financial capital, the Honey Bee Network volunteers are estimated to have contributed tens of crores worth of resources for enriching the opportunities for grassroots innovators and traditional knowledge holders.

Father Hubby Mathew coordinates with the Peermade Development Society in Kerala and has helped us in scouting and disseminating innovations in Kerala.

Dr Balaram Sahu, a veterinary scientist, working with a public sector lab volunteered to work with the network and scout for innovations among children and grown-ups alike. He organized workshops for children to generate ideas and promote lateral learning among them.

Dr Zhang Liyan, faculty at the Tianjin University of Finance and Economics in China, has developed and shared with us a very large database of grassroots innovations in China, which is the strongest network outside of India in any one country.

Knowledge Rights of Creative People

The network has diffused tens of thousands of ideas, innovations and traditional knowledge practices in different languages, creating an open-source knowledge base. Volunteers, innovators, those who add value can learn, if they like, but they can also acknowledge and disseminate the knowledge to others to increase the cross-pollination of knowledge in the country.

At the same time, in about 730 cases, SRISTI, the GIAN and the NIF have helped innovators in filing patents under their names, the costs of which were borne by the network. These rights have been protected not only to promote people-to-people learning, but also to incentivize commercial corporations to license these technologies and share the benefits of their commercial success with the innovators themselves. If they could not recover their investment in developing and diffusing the commercialization of these technologies, they obviously do not license grassroots innovations. So the concept of Technology Commons has been developed to not only allow but also encourage people-to-people copying of innovations. Only people-to-firm transfer of technology should take place through licensing. The NIF has also set up a Grassroots Technological Innovation Acquisition Fund (GTIAF) to acquire the Intellectual Property (IP) rights from the innovators and make those technologies available in the public domain, so that small firms and entrepreneurs can license it at no or low costs. The expansion of the public domain may be the primary purpose, but getting innovators their deserved due cannot also be ignored, if innovative culture and mindsets have to be incentivized overall.

More than seventy technologies have been licensed to small entrepreneurs and almost the entire money generated has gone back to the innovators. A benefit-sharing model was developed by SRISTI, which is used as a normative template in the NIF as well. Innovators are encouraged to share some part of their income with the communities, allocate some for nature conservation, contribute some to women's innovations and add a little to the innovation funds for taking care of innovators themselves.

Most innovators have not yet learnt to share the benefits with other stakeholders. The network considers developing this mindset as a part of institution-building process. It is hoped that in due course, most innovators will realize the value of the platform, and its philosophy, and thus contribute more of their resources for the common good. Compared to 730 patented technologies, there are more than 10,000 which are in the public domain, underlying the fact that sharing is the dominant characteristic of the network.

Almost all the IP organizations support the mission of protecting knowledge rights of the common people. They even offer to provide help pro bono. The average cost for filing for patents comes down to just about 300 dollars. These firms have been influenced by the Honey Bee Network philosophy and thus cooperate and collaborate with the network's institutions. The same applies to our collaboration structures with R&D institutions who aim for value addition. Almost all the scientists in the public and private sector who work with the NIF or SRISTI are willing to forego their fees. If they do charge, it is a nominal amount for meeting the cost of research staff and consumables. If we were to calculate the full value of the time IP law firms, R&D institutions, design institutions, scientific labs and other network members provide us through their engagement, we estimate that millions of dollars' worth of contribution has been made pro bono. Even still, we believe that the network has not been able to fully recognize the collaborative potential of R&D, IP and design firms.

So much of social and ethical capital could not have been mobilized if people didn't trust and respect the transparency and purposefulness in the activities of the network institutions. The network mobilizes ideas, documents the experiences of innovators, spreads innovations or their implications and creates partnerships all across the spectrum of the innovation ecosystem in a subtle yet effective way. Many large firms have also recently approached the NIF and SRISTI to explore collaborative product development and commercialization of innovations. It is too early to predict the outcome of the same but surely the search for frugal innovations has made Honey Bee Network databases the destination of first choice.

THREE

Shodhyatra: A Walking Class

Every summer and winter, since the first year in 1998, I, with fellow volunteers, pursue the shodhyatra in different parts of the country to recognize, respect and reward creative and innovative people and communities at their doorstep. We are aware that when outsiders recognize somebody in our country, the validation prompts desire to respect and view the local achievers differently. In much the same way it seems that when we as outsiders recognize local talent, the peer respect for such creative achievers increases in the respective communities as well.

Take the case of Rehmatbhai, an animal healer popularly known as Gwal Bapa, who was honoured by SRISTI for his lifelong and selfless community service of healing animals. Even while his community had benefited from his expert services, no one had gone out of their way to recognize his skill or reinforce his creative spirit. It is true that local recognition from one's own community matters just as much as external validation. Rehmatbhai was called Gwal Bapa because he was able to understand the pain, disease and internal afflictions of cattle sometimes even better than the people to whom those animals belonged. Passionate about sharing his gift, he also does not charge for his services, but if someone offered to reward him for his kindness, he would accept it graciously.

Once Rehmatbhai was summoned to a village six to 7 kilometres away to treat a cow. To get to the animal, Rehmatbhai travelled with the farmer who came to fetch him on his scooter early in the day. It was night by the time he had finished the treatment. On his return, the patron did not extend him the courtesy of dropping him back to his village; yet Rehmatbhai walked back without grudge or complaint. It is a testament to his character that such instances do not dent his spirit at all. He has accompanied us on many shodhyatras, sharing his insights with fellow villagers openly and often relies on easily available ingredients. He not only cares about the effectiveness of what he advises but also thinks of how the user can formulate the solution for himself. A democratizer of knowledge, he is a walking encyclopedia with an open gracious heart. The Honey Bee Network prides itself not only for honouring such creative local experts but also for absorbing their generous spirit into the fertilization of the spirit of the network.

There are many activities we organize during the shodhyatras, such as biodiversity and idea competitions, recipe competitions among women, paying respect to 100-year-old grandmothers and grandfathers, and appreciating collective endogenous institutions for the conservation of nature, in addition to sharing our database on sustainable technologies. While we learn about local innovations and solutions to add to that database, sharing precedes the scouting of new ideas. We have no right to collect any new information from people unless we share with them what we have collected in the past from others. Else the knowledge exchange becomes exploitative. Aside from the practical excursions conducted twice a year, I also teach a more formal shodhyatra course at IIMA where students are taken to the Himalayas for reflective learning about leadership for social change.

As discussed earlier, while the initial structure of the programme focused on the actual scouting and dissemination of grassroots innovators, the shodhyatra course at IIMA began through the initiative of the students themselves. One day in 2000, two students, Chandan and Hemant came to me and asked me why I didn't provide the shodhyatra experience to the students. I used to return to IIMA bursting with stories I'd gathered and adventures we had experienced during these yatras. They wanted me to offer an elective course for the purpose. Chandan and Hemant took me to a tea shop outside the wall of the campus to discuss the idea. Together, with a few other students, we looked at different dimensions of the course and finally, I drafted an outline and sent it for approval from the Centre for Management in Agriculture to the courses committee of the institute. As is customary, I was also invited to defend the outline.

It was mentioned that the fundamentals of the course would entail learning from 'four teachers': from within, peers, nature and common people. No reading material was prescribed, nor was any book allowed to be brought along for the walk. The purpose was to live as frugally as possible so that the distance between the quality of life of common people and the shodhyatris became as small as possible. The courses committee, comprising various chairpersons heading different academic areas, debated the model thoroughly but found it very unorthodox as there was no session-by-session plan. After considerable discussion, a colleague commented that if there were indeed students who wanted to learn and there was faculty willing to teach, why should the administration interfere? And so, with the right persuasion the course was approved. After its conception, the shodhyatra has been organized and conducted every year as one of the most sought-after courses at IIM Ahmedabad.

The concept of learning from the 'four teachers' humbles the participants, and thus makes them aware of the wisdom of the walk, and the Honey Bee Network philosophy as a new social movement. Generally, after climbing the mountain and relentless walking on the second or the third day, students get extremely fatigued. It is at that stage, when their enthusiasm is waning, that I usually tell them a story about one of the greatest teachers ever to walk the earth.

About 2000 years ago, Lord Buddha was teaching his disciples, mostly the youth that was very keen to learn at his feet. Buddha was also a very devoted teacher but he had his own philosophies, convictions and methodologies.

One day, a student came to him, very eager to join the other students in the class. But, when the Buddha looked at him, he thought that student was not ready to join the monastery. So he asked the student to come back after sometime. Promptly the student returned after fifteen days, but once again, the teacher looked at him and asked him to come back later. Like this, the student was asked to leave and return, for a full month, then three months till a year passed. One day, the student got exasperated. He said to the teacher, 'You have so many students. But whenever I request you to join your class, you ask me to leave and come after sometime. What is my fault?' The teacher replied, 'Alright, let me explain. Go and bring a glass of water.' The student complied with the instructions. The teacher asked him to bring another glass of water. The student did it again. Then the teacher instructed him to pour the second glass in the first one. The student was dumbfounded. He said, 'But, Sir, that way the water in the glass will overflow. There is no space in the first glass.' To this, the teacher responded, 'That is the problem. Every time I see you, you seem so full. Unless you empty yourself, how can I teach you what there is to learn?' The student got his answer.

The students in my course understand the implication of the story at its greatest depths. Sometimes they wonder as to why I don't tell them this story on the very first day of the walk. Only when they understand the importance of emptying oneself do they appreciate why learning is not possible without lowering one's defences. We always seem to know why things happen the way they do. We are afraid of being surprised, but growth in knowledge seldom happens without facing the conditions of surprise. I feel that a fatigued mind is more likely to have its defences down and consequently be more open. That is why I feel that manual work, physical labour and the consequent fatigue help us to think better and imagine more empathetically. Perhaps it even trains us to act more intuitively.

Like most philosophies, there are many ways in which we can learn from the 'four teachers'. For starters, the teacher within is very unpredictable. She will ask all kinds of questions about what should one do or not do. But then she doesn't care whether the answers are factually or morally right or wrong. What it really cares for is whether we try to seek answers to the questions honestly and earnestly because cheating oneself is not very difficult. Many of us do it every day. The dialogue within implies living with a sense of tentativeness. Without being sure of what is next, one has to be sure that it will be worthwhile. Such an attitude is not easy to forge. And yet, it is this equanimity which one has to search for within. It is very difficult to be just and fair in life without this ability. The more confidence we have in our espoused positions, our actual positions get masked. Some would call it a search for authenticity. Gandhiji would often say that nobody should tell him that he was contradicting himself because he often said something one day and something else the next day. His response would be that even in a day's gap he had learnt since then. Living paradoxically implies tremendous humility but also intuitiveness and the enjoyment of being the pivot of a see-saw. The swinging of a see-saw is a fact but which side will be up when and which side will be down is uncertain. Maximizing uncertainty makes new discoveries possible. The mind is trained most of the time to do the opposite. The result is that we often bypass the moments of new learning. We actually practise failing. Let me share a story.

A person was sitting by the side of a river in deep meditation. A saint passing by was very impressed on seeing his concentration. He paused for a while and waited for the devotee to open his eyes. The saint asked the devotee what he wanted. Why was he praying so hard? The devotee said, 'Master, I have most of the things that a normal person needs. But I want a touchstone by which I can convert any metal into gold when needed.' The saint smiled and said, 'Is that all?' The devotee said, 'That's all I need.' The saint showed him a heap of stones lying nearby. He said one of the stones in that heap is the touchstone that the devotee was seeking, but he wouldn't tell him which one. After saying this, the saint walked away. The devotee was very happy and profusely thanked the saint and began his search. He took a piece of metal, picked a stone, touched it and threw it in the river. He did it once, twice, fifty times, 100 times. And then, suddenly, after an hour or so, he notices that the piece of metal had become gold but by the time, the real touchstone had been thrown in the fast-flowing river. It was too late to realize that he had practised hard to fail. Don't many of us do the same?

I tried to teach an informal course on ways of knowing, feeling and doing as well. Not just the shodhyatra students, anybody could attend this class for a week in the evening. The basic idea for the workshop was to discover these four teachers and understand the barriers to our learning they can pose if not properly recognized and accessed. The first argument we have to resolve for ourselves is the relationship among knowing, feeling and doing. In truth, we know so much, we have feelings about much less and we actually take actions on even lesser issues. What determines the degree of dilution of desire while dealing with ourselves? Why should only a small part of what we know and care for actually influence our action? It is true that not everything that we care for can be acted upon. There are after all existential limits of 'ought' and 'is'. There is a lot that should change but I cannot change everything. So should I change nothing? The saga of the starfish narrated earlier tells us that if out of thousands of starfish dying on the seashore, we cannot save everyone, we should save at least the few we can.

I recall certain experiences from my own life where I recognized and learnt from my own teacher within. I was finishing up my postgraduate thesis in genetics in 1972–74. I had already been selected to join a bank on the basis of my undergraduate performance in 1973, but took leave to complete my master's degree at the Department of Genetics at Haryana Agricultural University in Hisar. I used to carry a bottle of milk to the laboratory to make tea from morning till evening. And likewise, I would buy another bottle of milk to make tea from evening to morning to keep awake while doing my research experiments. My weight had come down to

46 kilograms. My friends used to make fun that soon I would have to be seen on the slide under a microscope. Given the keen interest that the faculty and students took in seminars, I had several heads of departments and doctoral students present in a seminar I took during the first term of my second year. It was a one-credit course. I got the feeling that the faculty in charge of the seminar somehow didn't like me. By mistake, I once changed the setting of the temperature in the fridge in which his drosophila insects were being reared, upon which the insects died. He got very angry and despite my explanations and apologies, would not accept that it was a genuine mistake. The teacher gave me a B-grade in the seminar which was way below my expectations. I went to the head of the department, Dr J.B. Choudhary and requested him to get me an F-grade so that I could repeat the seminar instead. Next term, I repeated the seminar course but the professor gave me a 'B' again. I requested for an 'F'. On the third try of repeating the seminar, the professor tried to give me yet another 'B'. The teacher's argument was that he had not given an 'A' to anyone, which of course was no consolation to me. I was convinced his issue with me was personal. In fact, during a seminar discussion one day, he doubted one of my arguments upon which I promptly took his permission, went to the library and produced the journal which confirmed my very statement. The professor was embarrassed. But this time, the dean had to intervene because the story had become quite the talk around campus. The mind is not easy to segment. The mind can connect two things, which may be totally unrelated. And

these connections make life beautiful when new insights occur precisely because of such unexpected associations. But, sometimes, these connections are very painful. The teacher's assumption that I had deliberately caused the damage was not right. The fact that damage had been done was true. The connection between intention and action was mediated by an assumption or belief. I wish he had questioned his assumptions. Even by not doing so, he taught me a useful lesson. When I make similar mistakes, which I indeed do sometimes, I should not stand on false prestige when I discover my error. There is no easy way to acquire this humility except by practice.

Retrospectively, I don't know whether taking an 'F' twice instead of accepting the 'B' was worth it. But there was a voice inside me which told me that I deserved better. In the given situation, the only way I could prove myself was by trying again. Perhaps it was something from within that gave me the courage to stand my ground. Why should the voice within torment one so much? It is not always very difficult to silence the voice from within that is protesting against a choice. We invent a reason and convince ourselves of what we do. That is what often leads to self-righteousness. But sometimes, when we invent an excuse and move on with life, we don't realize that something precious was left behind—a moment of truth, of intimacy with oneself or a moment well lived. The closeness between one's inner voice and the external articulation is what I call as inner intimacy. We all embody hypocrisy to varying extents. The challenge is to reduce it. Maybe in some roles, you can reduce it more than others. But learning from the teacher within helps in reducing it more effectively than would be possible by any other approach.

Is it a satisfaction worth craving for that one has proved to be a good student of the teacher within, even if not of the teacher without? I am not implying that persistence always pays. Persistence after an ineffective design, a faulty belief or assumption can prove very costly. But the teacher within sows the seeds of doubt, or better yet, we can call it questioning. It doesn't always dictate whether the right way to go is to weed the sapling or to nurture it. Ultimately, one has to figure out the right course of action on one's own, perhaps falteringly. Too much assertion, too high a persistence of one's point of view may stifle the scepticism that is so necessary for learning and making new discoveries. But the golden mean between too little or too much has to be arrived at on one's own. Here it is enough to say that middle ground is only viable when extremes are wide apart.

When I was in Class VIII, I used to write very badly in English. My teacher would often strike out my entire homework because I didn't follow his advice. During those days, there were answer keys or help books, which contained important questions and answers, besides essays and other helpful tips. Our teacher expected the class to copy certain essays given in a particular guidebook as a part of the curriculum. I didn't want to do that. I wanted to write the essays on my own. In the process, I committed many mistakes. The teacher would strike out my writing every day and the class would laugh, but I would come back to my seat even more determined not to copy. He seemed to have the last laugh when I got extremely poor marks in my Class XI board exam in English. I got about seventy-eight marks out of 150, whereas I had much better marks in science and maths. If I had followed his advice, and mugged up the answers in the guidebook, maybe I would have got higher marks. But then perhaps I would not have learnt to write originally. I paid a price which frustrated my father. He went with me to Pantnagar but when I could not get admission there, he decided he didn't want anything to do with me any further in this regard. At the age of fifteen, I had to fend for myself and finally got admitted into Hisar, thanks to the guidance provided by one of my father's friends. One good thing that happened was that the umbilical cord got cut rather fast. Sometimes, one carries a kind of dependency relationship far too long in life. It was a strange way of gifting me both my autonomy and also my agency. That is, I had to be responsible towards my newly acquired freedom, and I had to decide for myself how I would use this freedom. I completed my undergraduate and postgraduate degrees in agriculture from the Agriculture University, Hisar. Was my English teacher right? Was the teacher within me right? I somehow believe that the teacher within made my life difficult but certainly more interesting and, in the end, satisfying.

When I was writing my thesis,[1] I took my draft chapters to my mentor, Dr S.N. Kakar. He was the dean of the College of Basic Sciences. He was also a very renowned geneticist. He had worked on microbial genetics with the former president of the American Society of Genetics. He was still very young, having become a full-time professor and the dean at the young age of thirty-five. As advisee he only took on one MSc and one PhD student at a time. The advantages of being his student were having ready access to his lab, and at the same time, very rigorous mentoring sessions. He would also not answer questions directly, redirecting you to find the answers on your own. One evening I showed him the results from my experiments using electrophoresis gel and instead of calibrating them, he asked me if I had read a particular paper on the topic. Since I hadn't, I was asked to read that paper and figure out the connection between the paper and the results from my own experiment. It was not easy. But, finding it out was fun. One meets several kinds of teachers in life—some who encourage you to ignore your inner voice, become worldly-wise and live on. For such teachers, pragmatism prevails. The rest doesn't matter. Then there are teachers who make you reflect on your own actions and draw meanings from your own acts of commission and omission. Buddha awakened the inner consciousness of the student by reflecting on a small act of throwing a few drops of water on the ground. Such teachers don't teach, but they make the students learn. The third kind of teacher is the one who forces you to observe, analyse, assimilate and apply the lessons from within. One has to therefore pay attention to the teacher within even when he teases too much.

Setting one's own standards to gauge the progress of one's inner journey is a tough challenge. It is so easy to fall prey to the idea of setting lower hurdles as a means of getting the joy of achievement with lesser effort. I have seen a very large number of people who set the bar too low and then don't even realize that they are setting themselves up for a downward spiral. The adventurous spirit in humankind, which propels one to take challenges far beyond what anybody may have tried so far, has led to so many inspiring expeditions. This spirit is present in all of us. It requires tremendous effort not to subdue this spirit so that we feel challenged.

The grassroots innovators are less privileged, have weaker support systems and yet stronger connects with the teacher within them. Many of them feel isolated from the rest of society because they think ahead of their time. Some of them get stuck in their search for solutions and are not able to pursue the experimentation without support from the teacher within. The persistence in the wake of not only adversity from outside but also a little bit of doubt within requires handling the see-saw of the dilemma with great resilience. Like a reed, the bend when the storm is too strong. And rise, when the wind favours. But they don't break. Mansukhbhai Patel (from Viramgam, Gujarat), who developed a machine to strip dryland cotton so as to separate shell from the seed cotton, failed many times in his experimental journey. Thanks to the teacher within, today he is one of the most successful and extremely rich innovators managing crores of rupees worth of business through the several companies that he set up.

Next, we have the concept of 'learning from peers', which is a game of choosing one's own pond. One can be a prince frog in a small pond or an ordinary frog in a big pond. When we try to excel only within a small peer group, the pressure is not too high, life is not very tough. To make the journey of pursuing innovation through excellence tougher, one can choose peers globally. One can try to excel in a small peer group such as a college, a local community, maybe the best athlete locally or the best potter locally in the village. Or one can try to be better than the best potter or athlete worldwide. One is free to decide with whom to compare or what the benchmark is. In other cases, one does not know what the global standard is. One just tries to exceed one's own best. There is really no one amongst us who has not faced this challenge in some shape or form. But, sometimes ordinary communities create extraordinary standards or benchmarks for younger generations to redefine and recalibrate them.

In December 2007, we were walking in the Purulia and Bankura districts of West Bengal as a part of the twentieth shodhyatra. In one of the villages, we came across beautiful terracotta horses kept under a tree on a small platform. Apparently, these horses were offered as a part of some worship. We asked the local community of potters why they had kept such beautiful horses in the open, under a tree. Somebody could take them or break them. The community members corrected us. By that time they knew I was a professor. They told me, 'Professor, you have made a mistake.' 'What mistake have we made?' I asked. They said, 'We have not kept just the beautiful ones. We have kept the best ones.' Intrigued by this response, we asked them why. And the response came, 'We have kept the best ones so that when our children walk by this path, they can see the current standard of the best. They know they have to do better.' Creating open-source standards of excellence to spur the younger generation to excel is not an ordinary lesson found in a management book. And yet, here was a community which had implemented this principle out of sheer instincts and ingenuous tradition.

What could have prompted this community of potters to create such standards and set the bar high not only for themselves but also for others?

During the same shodhyatra, we met Rebati Mahato sitting on a small parapet outside her hut in the Loahardih village of West Bengal. We had a meeting in this village to share the posters of different innovations and seek creative ideas locally. While returning from the meeting place, when we passed by the wall of her house, beautifully engraved by her with a kind of embossed design, we just couldn't move on further from there. She was a very small farmer and didn't seem to have many valuables in her home. But, the artwork on her wall showed the richness of her artistic skill. It was an amazing work of art by a lady to perhaps challenge the onlookers about their own limitations. Why would she devote so much labour in creating an artistic standard for public consumption? It may appear to be a silly question. After all, why did early human settlers make cave paintings almost 20,000–40,000 years ago? Even before the oral language was perhaps discovered, human beings knew the language of art. This is one of the most primordial instincts in humankind. The question, therefore, should be, 'How do majority of the people succeed in suppressing this primordial instinct which Rebati Mahato could not?' Rebati was invited to the Exhibition on Innovation hosted by the office of the

President of India. She made a panel of clay artwork to show to the President. This was a small tribute to her spirit of excellence motivated by intrinsic desire to excel and be different. During the rest of the shodhyatra, we did not come across any other wall of that kind. Even in the subsequent shodhyatras, we have not come across such a distinctive, humble, grassroots expression of aesthetic sensibility. A culture that does not generate arrogance even if the creativity is so special is worth treasuring a lot. If such artists could be encouraged to teach young children in nearby schools as a part of the National Rural Employment Guarantee Scheme, it will contribute to conserve the culture and at the same time generate interest among the younger generation.

When we compare the self-triggered desire of grassroots achievers like Rebati with rampant mediocrity all around, one has to ask questions about the source of such an attitude. Maybe, raising expectations from oneself is quite painful. One would then no longer find happiness in ordinary achievements. One cannot say my creation is good, when one should say, no, it is just fair. One should not say it is excellent, when one should say, no, it is just good. Many parents fall victim to this weakness. Similarly, many of our friends may lull us into mediocrity by reinforcing feedback of this kind. Being stingy in giving compliments seems to be a character of a very large number of people. But, being overgenerous in doling them out is equally bad and something society is also guilty of. Moderation, or the middle path, as Buddha preaches, is perhaps the answer for most proclivities. Even in many corporate settings, this bug of reinforcing mediocrity bites the community, for whom businesses claim to develop solutions, by not letting the emperor know that he is not wearing any clothes. Or by getting satisfied too soon with too little.

In another instance, while we were walking in Champaran, Bihar, in December 2008, during the twenty-second shodhyatra, we came across grain bins of clay made by people and erected outside their huts for personal storage of their grains. Most of the bins were plain, and a few had ordinary designs on, but there was one by Ram Tamari Devi which was an extraordinary work of art. Beautiful designs similar to prehistoric ancient tribal paintings were made on the bin. And we asked her, why she had taken the pains to decorate so beautifully such a banal object for everyday use. She replied, 'What else could I have done?'

The excellence was imperative for her. She was helpless before her own drive. She could not be satisfied with doing an ordinary thing. What a spirit of making excellence, a condition of helplessness! She had learnt this from her mother who was living in a nearby village at the time. We could not meet her mother. But by seeing her humility and art, we could imagine the values she imbibed from her mother. Despite very little economic assets, the creative and imaginative potential was bountiful.

Back in the 1940s, Abraham Maslow proposed a hierarchical model of human needs, which he later formalized in his book *Motivation and Personality* in 1954. Essentially, Maslow's theory implies that human beings tend to first seek out to satisfy their basic physiological needs followed by their needs for safety and security, love and belonging, self-esteem and pride and, finally, self-actualization, in that particular order. But I have often asked whether the hierarchy of needs illustrated by Maslow has not done a great damage to the human spirit. Especially as to how we view our fellow humans' worth. While we have a plethora of cultural wealth thanks to the ancient greats, like the poets Kabir and Rahim, but as a nation we also have significant contributions from the likes of Rebati Mahato and Ram Tamari Devi, who have created outstanding nuggets of wisdom, art and culture despite being extremely poor economically. Kabir or Rahim did not care whether they had next-day meals assured but that did not deter them from composing some of the timeless nuggets of wisdom.[2] In my opinion, this goes to show that one can attain enlightenment or self-actualize without even ensuring one's basic needs. Maslow has made many useful contributions but the concept of hierarchy of needs is not one of them, in my opinion. Every person, regardless of one's economic or social status, can aspire to produce the most outstanding creative work or find an innovative solution to the local problems. This realization is at the heart of the philosophy of the Honey Bee Network.

My other objection to this Maslow's theory of the 'Hierarchy of Needs' is that it provides no agency and autonomy to those poor people who are not yet capable of adequately meeting their basic food, clothing, shelter— or physiological—needs. Even if people were not sure of their next-day meal, they could still compose poetry or make art. Many innovators have neglected their family, the education of their children and other basic needs to pursue the solution of a problem that sometimes wasn't their own problem to begin with. Many scholars agree that most of these needs can be pursued simultaneously without following Maslow's order. The self-actualization can indeed be achieved without waiting to ensure the satisfaction of other needs.

Let me recall a visit to a slum in South Africa. I had gone to attend a meeting on Building Bridges between Formal and Informal Science at the University of South Africa, Johannesburg, famous for the education of Nelson Mandela. On one of the afternoons, I took the help of a very enthusiastic participant, Ms Lilly Rose Mlisa, and we took off to a slum near new Pretoria, 60 kilometres away, to search for creativity first-hand.

The 'Woodland plastic city' is a slum located behind Woodland Mall, housing some migrants from Zimbabwe but many others from rural areas of South Africa. At the entrance, there were some entrepreneurs who were charging five rands for cell phones (roughly Rs 30) and shaving heads for fifteen rands. As we moved in, our questions about local creativity seemed intriguing to the local community members, but we walked along. One of the first things that struck us was no matter how poor the person, almost every hut had a small green strip having a few plants of vegetables like onion or gourds showing that while people can be moved away from the farm, farm could not always be moved out of people. After about twenty minutes, the word had gone around that there were two people looking for creative individuals in the slum, and soon people started inviting us to see what they had done. Whether it was a carpenter or a potter who had used broken mirror pieces to decorate the flower pot, everybody wanted to show something creative.

Jonas Jacob Mabina came looking for us and showed what he had done by way of making various kinds of structures using stones and other local material on his mobile phone. He took us to his home to show us a whole variety of things that he had done. What was most remarkable was a stone artwork, which he had made partly to estimate the time it takes to make it and also to make the place around his hut more pleasant. He had a small garden, and his daughter made braids for the local girls at a small cost. He had aspirations to make such structures in metropolitan towns if given a chance. Almost everybody we met was trying to do something to improve his or her life. Nobody begged, nor did anybody ask for freebies. It was a very self-respecting culture, which obviously had not heard about Maslow's hierarchy of needs, else they would have never tried this.

Despite all his sensitivity, Maslow did not realize that in the absence of assurance about the next day's bread, poor people do not just keep a long face. They try things out. Some of them try extraordinary things out. The issue is that if we do not accept the potential for people to make breakthroughs in different fields despite being poor, we will reinforce a kind of a dependency syndrome. Somebody from outside will be expected to get such people out of their pitiable condition. However, when we assume agency on the part of economically poor people, we expect at least some of them will try to excel in their chosen fields, no matter what. If we had not made this assumption, would we have discovered so many knowledge-rich, economically poor people? The entire developmental paradigm needs to go through a basic transformation. Even in factories, several innovations take place on the shop floor. Just as rural grassroots innovators find solutions to local problems alone through social connections[3] even if they do not stand to gain privately. There are slum dwellers and roadside mechanics who find new ways of solving problems and share them openly. The contention is that the urge to excel and achieve enlightenment does not have to be preceded by economic self-sufficiency.

In Indian culture, one of the greatest motivations driving the pursuit of excellence is *swantah sukhaya* (for one's own inner happiness) as exemplified by Tulsidas when he wrote the *Ramcharitmanas*. He says he did it to soothe his soul, for his own inner happiness.[4] This personal driver of selfhood is not impeded or abstracted by uncertainty, insecurity and lack of social recognition. Despite the fact that many of these needs can influence our proclivities, we don't necessarily pursue our choices in a linear order. While pursuing our livelihood, we can compose songs, cut jokes and make light of our struggles. If one visits on a winter night a shelter where rickshaw drivers take rest in the night, one would not find tired and fatigued people only ruminating about their misery. Some of them would burn some logs and sing songs around the fire, often composed by the similar people. I also believe that cultures that consider community interest as sometimes overriding the individual interests[5]

may also not follow the
hierarchy of needs as
suggested by Maslow. In the
cartoon below, carried on
the cover page of the *Honey
Bee Newsletter* (Vol.17 [1–2]
January–June 2006), the
poor don't have only have
legs, hands and mouth—i.e.,
their physical bodies, they
also have a head (including
a heart, representing their
capacity for thought and
emotion). The richness of
knowledge need not be a
luxury for those on the edge

3.1 The poor don't just
have legs, a mouth and
hands, but also a head
(*Honey Bee Newsletter*,
2006)

of survival. In fact, being poor in material resources,
such people have no choice but to maximize knowledge
and skill for overcoming hardships in life.

More recently, while walking through the villages
of the Jalandhar district in, Punjab, we came across a
large number of houses, all of which had shared the
distinctive design of an overhead tank. Somebody had
the tank in the shape of an aeroplane, while others had
an eagle, a tractor, a flower and so on. Not in many
places visited so far, had we seen such diversity in the
design of overhead tanks.

The aesthetic expressions of private and public
spaces and architectures through different forms and
shapes is an essential part of understanding any culture.
In many parts of south India, people make beautiful

ornamental designs after cleaning the public roads or ground in front of their houses by using rice powder. Popularly called *kolams*, these are a manifestation of private responsibility for cleaning public passages. The streets get cleaned very well, particularly in the villages, because every household does it. It is expected to take care of the area opposite their house. Such examples illustrate how our society manages civic sense. And in the process, creates, the standards of excellence quietly.

I remember, many years ago, a student told me in class while we were discussing the role of indigenous institutions in conserving natural resources, about a very healthy practice among certain communities living on the riverbank in Tamil Nadu. Every person who goes to take bath in the river has to take out three handfuls of silt from the river bed and put it on the bank in exchange. If everybody does that as expected, the river would not change its course easily (because siltation near the banks would be avoided). Thus, communities evolve unusual norms for dealing with problematic situations.

The cultural institutions for conservation or augmentation of our vision play an important role in deepening creative processes at the grassroots. Communities evolve unusual norms for dealing with paradoxical situations. On the border of the Panchmahal district of Gujarat and the Jhabua district of Madhya Pradesh, we stumbled upon an interesting practice. In one of the villages, we observed a beautiful painting on the wall of a private house narrating the whole story through different forms and figures. The major inhabitants of the area, the Rathwa tribal community is famous for such *pithora* wall painting traditions. When we asked the villagers about the origins of the practice, we were told that whenever somebody in the tribe fell sick, people took vows and prayed to the local goddess, promising to offer her art in the form of a wall painting in the event of the sick person's recovery. What a way of celebrating recovery from sickness! While the local artist gets employment and income, the people who pray feel satisfied, having achieved, at some level, a version of self-actualization. The narrative embedded in the artwork also carries the local interpretation of social mores of the time. In a sense, a memory-scape blends with the art-scape and the landscape. The traditions of devotion, artistic expression, preservation of cultural integrity and celebration of recovery from sickness are all intertwined. Where personal space ends and community space begins, it is difficult to say.

After getting down from the Jangalmahal sanctuary, during the twenty-third shodhyatra,[6] the shodhyatris asked for a little water to drink from the residents of a hut nearby, as there was no well or other source of drinking water. But after drinking the water, the shodhyatris asked for the nearest water source so that they could make the trip and replenish the stock of water for the family. The poor, tribal householder was shocked at the suggestion. He said that he was poor indeed, but not so poor that he couldn't offer even water to his guests. We were embarrassed. But we pressed on because we were also aware that later, the ladies of the house would have to go a few kilometres to fetch more water (I am not so sure they would have such courtesy extended to them by

our brethren if they came to our cities!) Still, they didn't
let us bring the water.

The norms of hospitality vary from place to place.
Do we ever reflect on such asymmetries in the protocols
of what constitutes a valid civic behaviour? What could
explain such contrast in the norms of hospitality between
the city and villages, the rich and poor? The generosity
of common people, evident in such encounters provides
the context of understanding how common people solve
local problems by developing grassroots innovations,
and why they are often so willing to share them these
ideas openly with us. It is said that those who have less
often give more. Thus the act of giving or sharing is not
a function of what one has, but how one perceives the
other's need. This feeling of being responsible towards
those who need something that we have more than them,
at that moment, comes from several facets of our nature.
The more interconnected we see our life as, the more
responsible we become for the people and things around
us as well. Our educational system gives us knowledge,
but often fails to inculcate values followed by people
who keep the creation of public or common good at a
higher level than their own individual needs.

The social norms whether offering water to travellers
passing by, offering shade and shelter to even strangers
are the benign aspect of rural society. But the same
society has norms which militate against gender balance
or bridging other social asymmetries. During a particular
shodhyatra in Alwar, Rajasthan, before it got too cold,
we set up a projector to show the innovations from our
Honey Bee Network database to the local community

members. It was around 7.30 p.m., dark enough to use the LCD projector. Most of those present were men and children. We noticed that there were hardly any women. In villages, sunset is usually the time when people start returning home and women start cooking the supper. We started the projection and slowly and slowly, the curiosity of the crowd peaked. But after a few minutes of the display, we stopped the show. The men didn't understand why we had stopped and urged us to continue. We insisted that unless women joined the audience, we would not resume the show, to which people started responding with excuses as to why the women would not be able to join. They were busy with the cooking and household chores, they said. We were not convinced and remained unmoved. Unless women came, the projection wouldn't continue. Once they realized that we would really not start the projection unless the women joined, a few people got up to call their wives and mothers, and soon most of the women had assembled. Once the women joined, projection continued and there was a good discussion about which of the innovations would be applicable to work there and which wouldn't. After the projection session, we had dinner and then shared our reflections on the dynamics we had just seen with each other. We asked ourselves in a self-critical tone about why it took us so long to insist on women's presence at these gatherings? After all, for a long time, we had accepted their absence and continued to make presentations in other villages even in their absence. Despite our proclaimed gender sensitivity, we had not shown the same impatience on noticing their lack of participation in earlier shodhyatras.

We had knowledge and also feelings but the relevant action took long to take place.

We later made some amends in our response to neglect of innovations by and for women. After heavy reflection and recognizing the trend that the technologies in everyday use by women often go through a very slow change, the NIF has announced three Gandhian Inclusive Innovation Challenge Awards in 2015 to overcome the persistent inertia in this vein.[7] These challenges were first announced in 2012 but somehow no satisfactory solution was received. The announcement was made again in 2015. In 2016, we are planning to organize summer school of grassroots innovators and technology students to redefine the problem, parameterize different components and attempt fresh solutions. We hope that a joint effort between grassroots innovators and technology students will generate a better solution. Considering the typical problems of many women village workers, it may be worth reflection as to why we do not feel the pain of tea workers who have the labour-intensive task of handpicking tea buds for collection for extended hours of the day. And for that matter, the pain of women transplanting paddy has been ignored for thousands of years, though as a nation we all consume rice often knowing the back-breaking, bending conditions of these women. They must keep their feet submerged under water to complete their labour. Similarly, we have hardly considered the plight of women and the children they simultaneously tend in their laps due to smoke pollution, which occurs without proper affordable cooking stoves that work on multi-biomass fuel.

The role of women in grassroots innovations has thus remained rather obscure. The number of innovations by women has also been rather small in the Honey Bee database compared to their real-life societal contributions. There could be many reasons including lack of women volunteers and fieldworkers. But still, no reason can justify this inadequacy.

Yet, the number of girl students who have got awards is significantly higher than the number of women recognized by the network so far. In the IGNITE competition, children in and out of school can participate by contributing their ideas. The NIF screens these and awards the selected ones. Among these awardees, far more girls get recognition for their innovative ideas than has been possible among the adults. There could be many reasons for this anomaly. Till school level, a girl child coming to school does not face much problem in at least using her imagination. Once the family and social responsibilities burden the women, their ability to assert their creativity gets compromised. It is not that they don't have ideas any more, but there are not enough avenues for them to share their ideas.

It is worthwhile to recall the contribution made by Autumn Stanley,[8] who had spent thirteen years in reviewing 200 years history of the US Patent Office to find out the share of women inventors.

Stanley, in her much neglected masterpiece, *Mothers and Daughters of Invention*, lamented at the share of women patent-holders in the US, which was less than 1 per cent during 1809–1985 in the USA. She shows instead how many times men were given credit for the inventions actually developed by their wives.[9] This number has increased to about 4–8 per cent in recent times (by different estimates). Her main contention is that women actively invent. There is no question of that, but they are not recognized as inventors. Stanley's work is an extraordinary study of women's creativity and inventiveness. And yet, despite the fact that the author spent thirteen years to write this book, and provided unassailable evidence of how women have invented new technologies during the last 200 years in the USA, the work has remained obscure. Grace Hopper's contribution to COBOL programming language was ignored completely; another example is Madam Jacquard who developed the much improved loom also called jacquard loom but it was credited to her husband. During my lectures at Harvard as well as MIT, I asked as to how many students knew about Stanley's work, but not a single hand went up. In the literature on inventions and innovations, her work is seldom cited. Thus, it is not only just that women's creativity is ignored, even evidence about this is ignored. Moreover, women writing about women's inventions seem to be ignored as well. The self-effacing nature of women comes out in several interactions with local populations during the shodhyatras. When asked some specific questions about farming, some of them will invariably defer to their husbands for answers, claiming that the men only know everything.

Gangaben had written a book titled *Hunnar Mahasagar*—an encyclopedia of 2080 self-employment practices in 1898. It is said that 1000 copies were sold in one day. SRISTI has republished this out-of-print book in Gujarati and Hindi. It shows that there were women writers who pooled the popular knowledge for self-reliant development more than 100 years ago. By neglecting such literature in the contemporary history of science, technology and innovation, we do a great disservice to pioneering women innovators and chroniclers. Many of these practices she had collected from women, though as per the prevailing norm at that time, these were not acknowledged in her text. Gangaben had become a widow at the age of fourteen and later became a schoolteacher. There is no department of everyday life for which she has not a solution, be it removing stains, finding adulteration in different edible things, making one's one ink or dyes, etc. The work of Gangaben is no less ignored than that of Autumn Stanley.

The inertia in converting feelings into action takes place not only while recognizing the gaps in women technological use but also in many other areas. Many times, we continue with our inertia even in matters where we are convinced about the need for change. There are several forces at work, which may perhaps make the inertia acceptable. Sometimes, I don't even observe the problem. How does a country, which keeps the insides of the house so clean, keep public places so dirty? And it has nothing to do with education or convenience. It is more just a force of the habit. And habits are not formed by chance. We work hard at them, but sometimes we fail. For instance, we should drink six to eight glasses of water a day. Despite knowing the benefits, it is very difficult to practise this ritual and convert it into a habit.

While writing this chapter, I got upset and had a glass of water, which ideally I should have taken at least two hours earlier. I am convinced of its utility, but by not keeping track, I forget. Some people follow the practice of self-flagellation, i.e., self-punishment, whenever they realize a deep contradiction between what they do and what they think they ought to have done. Inertia also comes in when I am not aware of the consequence of my inaction on others. Or, even if I am aware, I am not too perturbed by the consequences. Inertia becomes inevitable when one's expectation from oneself go down. Still, a balance is necessary since sometimes inertia is necessary to let the right moment emerge for change to take place. Not everything can change all the time. We will have no peace in life if everything is changing all the time. In fact, no social relationship is possible without something remaining constant. Therefore, we have to choose aspects of life where we must accept inertia and where we must not, we must challenge it.

Our willingness to live with the absence of women in most of the meetings during the shodhyatras was one such case where inertia should have given way long time ago.

Inertia, Initiative and Innovation

Let me highlight another few other cases where inertia in our work and lives is still very much prevalent. When we look at the number of ideas and innovations scouted and the number disseminated across the country, the former is found to be much higher than the latter. Part of the reason is that we cannot share all the information we learn without proper validation. And validation takes a long time, because multi-location trials are required in the case of agricultural technology and repeated for at least two to three years to confirm the claims. Still, despite the bottleneck, our share of dissemination must be much higher than what it currently is. Let me share some more examples of inertia in our work and life.

The ability to adapt, adjust and accommodate the constraints becomes the first step in the ladder of inertia. We tend to explain and justify the inevitability of a situation and, in the process, also legitimize our inability to change the process. As is often said, there are many reasons for not doing a thing but there is only one for doing it—wanting to do it. However, the roots of inertia are deeper and sometimes run deeper than the seeds of initiative that take longer to germinate. By making our willingness to take initiative contingent on others becomes an alibi for inertia. Being bothered by social consequences of 'what will others say?' is another reason why many people continue to be conformist and compliant. There are many who believe, 'I am alone and can't change the world by myself.' This is a mindset of those who believe that change only comes from a group action. They don't realize that many changes can also originate from non-descript individuals. 'My learning is not enough, others must also learn.'[10] By making our willingness to take initiative contingent on others becomes an alibi for inertia. As if this is not enough, sometimes we are not even convinced that we are capable of initiating a change. Sometimes, we internalize the inefficiency of an external system as a sign of our own inadequacy to expect more. And worse, the absence of discomfort also staggers our growth. We don't change, and we are not disturbed by the fact that we don't change. The sum total of such belief systems perpetuates inertia. Moreover, habits get reflected and articulated in the language we use. Reification is an inevitable consequence. We start using more and more phrases which pass on the responsibility of our inertia to the reality of things outside us. For instance, in the simplest example, imagine the difference between my saying, 'The car doesn't start,' instead of saying, 'I can't start the car.' A car is essentially a passive phenomenon. It cannot start on its own; it needs a driver. But, if I were to choose instead to say that I am unable to start it, the responsibility of its not working comes on to my shoulders for either not maintaining it properly or doing something else wrong to it. Most importantly, the accountability to fix it also becomes mine.

However, despite such a widespread feeling of inertia in society, some people still channel their drive and take initiative, and thereby convert developing the same into innovation in various fields. Many of the change agents are impatient, sometimes impulsive and often dissatisfied with the status quo. They are motivated intrinsically, though rarely do their efforts translate into institutionalization. Those innovators who overcome their inertia and generate some innovative solutions are not always successful in finding sufficient support in the ecosystem for making a major impact. Diffusion of grassroots innovations require the overcoming of inertia on the part of potential adopters. Large corporations through massive media campaign can sometime create market for ideas which may not even be so necessary for the users. But creating demand for useful simple technologies is not easy because sometimes complexity becomes a sign of credibility.

The fact that this book itself took so long to come out was a sure case of inertia. There were stories people wanted to hear; there were ideas which I wanted to share. But I was writing a lot of papers and teaching six to seven courses a year. I could have cut back on my teaching and other work to prioritize writing this book, but I didn't do that. Why didn't I do that, you ask? Perhaps the task of narrating a cogent story requires going through a laborious pain, which I was avoiding. Sometimes, we invent pressures of work, which legitimize inertia when actually we should be feeling uncomfortable about it.

Even in many villages, we come across the need for change but for which internal mobilization does not take place. Recently, during the 32nd shodhyatra in Punjab, we came across an elderly farmer spraying pesticide in the field. There was a young fellow standing on the roadside with a bucket of water and pesticide in his hands. We asked him, 'Who is the person spraying in the field?' The young man replied, 'Sir, he is my uncle.' We further asked him, 'Do you really love your uncle?' 'Of course,' he replied. We were still curious and asked, 'Then why was your uncle not wearing any mask, gloves or any other safety gear?' He replied, 'I never thought about it.'

Neither did the company manufacturing the pesticide think about it while relaying the same information to its customers. The public policymakers also did not think about it, and therefore did not take any steps to create awareness on the safety hazards, or sanction the behaviour of the companies, which didn't do anything to educate the people. One is hardly likely to find any billboard or advertisements in the chemical-intensive agricultural regions creating awareness about the safe ways of using pesticide in farming practices. However, in relatively inaccessible fine small print, the precautions are included in the pamphlet of the chemical pesticide bottle. Thus, here, the inertia is evident at several levels and among several actors. Despite well-known consequences of exposure to pesticide, we have not taken any concrete steps to educate farm workers and provide them with the right kind of skills to maximize productivity while ensuring their own safety. While legal requirements are met, the operational impact is not achieved because sufficient social awareness is not created. The purpose of public policy is defeated because the relevant indicators are not monitored for ensuring compliance among the industrial actors.

The case of manual paddy transplantation, briefly mentioned earlier, is one of the most unfortunate examples of policymaking and institutional inertia. Millions of women transplant paddy with a back-bending posture. Most of us while consuming rice don't even think for a minute moment about the pain of the women workers transplanting the paddy, literally straining their backs. The women develop ulcers on their feet due to the long periods for which they must keep their feet underwater. The machines exist for mat nursery, i.e., the nursery grown on fibre mats. These are cut into pieces and put on the auto feed transplanters. There is no fully successful device for the normal nursery of paddy yet. Two grassroots innovators, Photo Singh in the Baghpat area of western Uttar Pradesh, and Ranjit Mirig[11] from Sambalpur, Orissa, have tried developing a manual paddy transplanter, but the final prototype is still a long way off. How is it that policy planners and scientists cannot observe this problem and begin a systematic attempt to solve it? Neither the industry nor academia has taken any worthwhile step so far. And even the informal sector has failed to produce a solution in this case. Is it because the technology that involves women faces much more societal inertia than the ones used by men?

The case of plucking tea leaves is a similar example of persistent inertia. Millions of people consume tea but none can visualize the pain of the tea garden workers who have to pluck and collect the buds carefully and then put in the baskets they carry on their backs, constantly moving and lifting their hands against gravity. We would experience pain if we just were to move our hands in that manner even just for eight to ten times. Neither the consumers of tea nor the owners of tea gardens have thought about finding a solution to this problem. This is also a case where the informal sector has failed so far to generate any solution. But when I posed these problems to the students in the Centre for Environmental Planning and Technology University (CEPT), some of the students came up with an interesting proof of concept solutions. One group added a small tape recorder motor in a bowl into which the plucked leaves are kept. And then with the press of a button, the leaves are sucked and delivered in the basket behind. In another variation, the bowl is connected to a pipe resting on the shoulder. When the bowl is moved up through the hole and the pipe, the tea leaves are delivered into the basket still behind them. In theory, this discussion proves that it is not impossible to overcome the inertia that often prevents progress and development.

Most of us have got our shoes or chappals repaired by a roadside cobbler. Let us take the case of three cobblers from China, Mongolia and India. In the case of China and Mongolia, the cobbler has a seat, a table and a very dignified way of offering his services. There is a folding chair to help for the customer to sit in while his shoes are being repaired. But in India, the cobbler is seen using primitive tools, and sitting undignified on the ground with often no comfort facility for the customer. The iron stand for shoe repair was designed when shoes were made of leather and the nails had to be fixed on them. Now the shoes need adhesives or stitching. And yet, there are no tools for the purpose developed by the cobbler or by the engineers in public or private sector.

All these three examples show the deep-seated inertia at multiple levels in society within which policymakers, the youthful technologists and the community themselves have decided not to change the situation in spite of being privy to the problems the said situations entail.

Inertia in Personal Life

The problem of inertia, being deep-seated institutionally, suggests that inertia is deep-seated individually as well. There are also several other areas of our personal lives where we live with inertia. Let us now look at those.

Most of us have steel almirahs at home. Almost everyone in India has struggled with shutting the door of a steel almirah after it becomes old with years of use. It's common to curse the maker or designer of the almirah while continuing to push and nudge the door hard because it doesn't shut smoothly any more. Some put the blame on the hinges and some on the handle, but essentially this complaining goes on for years. The inertia just persists. Any society which learns to live with unsolved problems indefinitely is condemned to live with inefficiency and inertia. The simple solution for this problem, if the initiative has been taken to find it, is to put half an inch of pegging under the front legs of the almirah to raise the front portion slightly. Because the ground level in most Indian houses is not perfectly even, the movement of the door is not smooth. The new balance allows the door to slide open and close more smoothly. Ideally, one needs to act on the simple and obvious solution. In this case, the inertia I highlight doesn't arise because the problem is complex or resources are scarce or that people are ignorant. It arises from lack of proper definition of the problem and a habit of doing without questioning.

Moving on, who doesn't have unsorted papers at home or in their office? I definitely do. And I have deferred the task of organizing them indefinitely into the future to a day when I will have time. Honestly, I don't know when I will ever get the time. But hoping someday to be able to refer to use my old notes, I continue to keep them rather than throwing them away. Some students interested in studying how my mind worked might want to look into these notes later. In this case, the inertia does not result out of laziness alone. It could also be borne out of a hope that somebody, someday will sort out the mess for me.

On an even more relatable scale, there are friends whom we have not met for a long time despite greatly wanting to. The pragmatic concerns of time and schedules sometimes overrule the philosophical concerns. Recently, I remembered a student of design who had worked with us ten years ago. He had made some of the most beautiful posters we ever got made for the Honey Bee Network. I tried to find him but didn't succeed for a long time. Then, one day I succeeded. I told him that I was unhappy with the way he was treated by my colleagues ten years ago. He had forgotten what had happened but I hadn't. I expressed my regrets and requested him to rejoin the effort. The inertia to reconnect was partly circumstantial and partly born out of an ability to live with the dissatisfaction for such a long time. The human mind learns to live with less when it can get more out of life.

Inertia also occurs when we are not ready to face the uncertainty of a situation because of the likely adverse consequences of failure. When I joined IIMA in 1981, the then dean gave me two choices of a course to teach.

One was titled, 'Indian Social and Political Environment (ISPE)', which had not been doing well. The other was called Economic Environment and Policy (EEP II), which had previously been taught by established economists. After giving me these choices, he also made it clear that even if I did well in the ISPE, it might not mean much because it is seen as a soft course. But, if I did well in EEP II, I would have probably essentially made it as a professor. There would be less to worry about. My own degree background was in biochemical genetics and undergraduate degree in agriculture. Having worked in a bank and in action-research projects, I had some understanding about how markets worked and had learnt the economics the hard way. I chose the harder path with greater uncertainty about my success. If I failed, I would have had to quit. Risk was higher, but the challenge was also higher. The rest is history.

I am sure there are people who deal with bigger uncertainties and are able to come out relatively unscathed or mildly scathed. The grassroots innovators with whom we work have often dealt with huge uncertainties in the design, implementation and delivery of their innovations. Yet, they deal with their inertia courageously and have thus succeeded many times in making a difference. My feeling is that as a scholar or activist, I cannot appreciate the ability of innovators to deal with uncertainty if I don't have the same attitude. A risk-averse professional is unlikely to spot or sustain the risk-taking attitude among the common people or youth which is so vital for progress, research and development. That probably is the reason why when risk-averse leaders (who do not take chances and consequently do not set themselves up for making honest mistakes) in so many organizations reach the top, they are not able to tolerate others who do have a more creative outlook on decision-making. Yet, the same leaders complain that they do not have enough juniors employees pursuing innovations or entrepreneurial endeavours within the organization. My point here is that risk taking in personal life is closely intertwined with not only risk taking in professional life but also encouraging others to do so. We need to overcome timidity in ourselves to be able to do justice and encourage the risk-taking behaviour of other innovators.

Nattubhai Vadher, who lives in the Ervada village in the Surendranagar district of Gujarat, has been working on a cotton-stripping machine for the last fifteen years. Here was a relentless struggle of a pioneering innovator who was trying to do something that had not been done before in dryland cotton and at this scale. For hybrid cotton, numerous cotton-picking machines existed, but none existed for cotton-ball picking. Nattubhai's risk-taking ability was being reinforced by risk-taking people in the ecosystem. Recently, he organized a demonstration of the sixth version of his design for farmers from the neighbouring regions in his field. In rain-fed cotton, varieties 797, the balls do not open. The labour requirement is high for picking the cotton balls. Later, with the help of a cotton-stripping machine the balls are broken down and the cotton with seed cotton is taken out. It is then processed in the ginning factory to separate the seed from the cotton. The separated cotton goes to textile mills for further processing as yarn and then finally as textile. Deciding to attend the demonstration, I had taken three other innovators along with me to give feedback to Nattubhai. The ideal time for the demonstration would have been the afternoon, when the plants are drier and thus processing efficiency is higher, but unfortunately we couldn't make it till much later due to some logistical problems. During the field test, the machine picked the cotton balls very well and delivered these into a bag on the back of the tractor. But, some of the cotton lint remained stuck to the plants. The results were not as good as the innovator expected. Yet the farmers who had gathered on the occasion gave positive feedback and conveyed very clearly that they would be willing to buy the machine even with 50 per cent efficiency because that would still considerably reduce the amount of labour involved. They would require that because of much reduced labour involved. It seemed then that labour supply was a real constraint. For a period of fifteen days to one month, when the crop was ready for picking, enough labour could not be mobilized. The other innovators who had accompanied me also offered to help Nattubhai in improving specific features and functions of the machine. Even when the results were not assured as favourable as expected, Nattubhai, a grassroots innovator didn't mind discussing his work, without fear of being criticized or rejected completely. Maybe he had faith in his design and also the peer group from whom he was seeking consultation. Maybe he truly wanted the feedback to improve his design further. He also trusted himself enough to know that there was no one else who could do it better than he could. Given such a confluence of personal confidence, situational constraints and the community support, the ability to take risk perhaps increases. The Honey Bee Network was evidently underwriting some of the risks by not only investing in the prototyping through the NIF and the GIAN, but also by mobilizing the feedback of other innovators through SRISTI. Here was a relentless struggle of a pioneering innovator who was trying to do something that had not been done in dryland cotton yet at this scale. For hybrid cotton, numerous cotton-picking machines existed. But none existed for picking dryland cotton balls.

I can recall many examples where innovators have spent decades in solving a problem and did not get any support from the community or clients or investing companies. Shib Sagar Mandal from, Guwahati, Assam, worked for almost two decades to improve the efficiency of an engine. He used three approaches to improve the energy efficiency: (a) Use a one-way valve to ensure re-combustion of the unburnt oil which goes into exhaust; (b) mix hot air with the fuel to improve combustion efficiency; and (c) allow cold air to be sucked in the engine to improve the piston efficiency. Once when I was a jury member for the Tata Innovation Awards in 2009, I was requested to organize a workshop for the participating Tata Group companies. Shib Sagar was one of the innovators invited to showcase his innovation prototype. It is a different matter that even after bringing a horse to the water, the horse may refuse to drink water. No real connection was forged between him as a creative community member and the corporation. The inertia at the institutional level is undoubtedly much higher; else the rate at which these innovations would have progressed could be very high. The whole country and the world could benefit if such specific and ingenious innovations get incorporated into the design of industrial products, and thus make the economy more energy- and time-efficient. The question still remains: Why does Shib Sagar Mandal bear with so much uncertainty for such a long time? Why does he not give up earlier?

While tracing the stories of unusual lessons learnt during the shodhyatras, I discussed how inertia prevents us from taking action that we see the need for. It is not enough to have a lot of knowledge about a situation, it is also necessary to have the feeling, or the empathy towards affected communities and then convert that pain into action. We can see how many grassroots innovators also overcome their inertia, though the related formal sector is often unable to do so enough. But the bridges will be built, knowledge will be exchanged, the blending of two systems of knowledge will take place. Given the economic squeeze worldwide, the search for frugal innovation is bringing many large corporations at the door of the Honey Bee Network and the NIF and SRISTI. Sooner rather than later, Indian industry will also realize the need for similar handshaking.

FOUR

Listening to the Minds on the Margin:
Sound of a Bird

We only really listen when we have the ability to reflect. Very often, lots of sounds pass us by because we are not tuned into them. A sound becomes noise when we cannot decipher its meaning. Then how do we listen to 'noise' to understand them as sounds, without knowing their meaning? Let me share a story which perhaps some of you have come across before.

Two friends were walking down a crowded street when one of them asked the other, 'Hey, did you hear the sound of the mynah bird?' The friend replied, 'Don't be silly, how can one hear the sound of a bird with traffic making so much noise on the street?' To which, the first friend commented, 'Of course, what a foolish thing to ask!' After walking for another fifteen minutes, the first friend accidentally dropped a five-rupee coin on the road. The second one immediately said, 'Did you hear a coin drop?' The first friend wondered how his friend had heard the sound of the coin, but not that of a bird in the same crowded, noisy environment. Perhaps, our ears are tuned and trained to hear the sound of a particular thing, say a coin. Therefore it is not surprising that many of us don't hear the sound of the birds—the few that are left.

Similarly, listening to the voices on the margin requires effort. Just as an expert music teacher can notice when a student makes a mistake in a single note of the music, the same way, we can train our ears and eyes to hear and see, and consequently make sense of, the less visible and obvious sounds around us. But to kindle our curiosity towards such feeble creative voices, such training of our perception is needed, but it is not easy. Most of us are not even convinced that we need this skill at all. About 200 years ago, when African people were sold as slaves in Europe and the USA, not many of their owners paid attention to the unique skills and creative thinking abilities of these oppressed workers. But those who did have left a rich account of how some of the slaves solved problems and developed innovative solutions.[1]

While the slaves were bought and sold much like commodities in the oppressive conditions of slavery, Roderick Macdonald notices that many slave-owners in England highlighted specific skill sets while posting sale advertisements. In one of the rare studies of the 'forgotten labourer', what Macdonald describes is both fascinating and distressing about how even in such harsh times, the creativity of people who were essentially oppressed was also noticed. Yet, in the so-called democratic societies, we have failed to listen to the creative voices of workers, labourers and other marginal communities. A quick web search for innovations by labourers or low-rank workers will yield convincing results about this inference.

As a part of the research for her PhD thesis, Riya Sinha, former chief innovation officer of the National Innovation Foundation and a senior colleague in SRISTI and SRISTI Innovations (a not-for-profit company set up by SRISTI), we met a labourer named Walla in Jamnagar, Gujarat. He looked after the part of the farming chores of Alibhai, the developer of a particular improved *rasham patto* variety of chilli. Walla explained to us that while planting the chilli seedlings, he used his left hand, not the right one, because the pressure put by the left hand was lesser. He also mentioned that when seedlings were young, one needed to water them through slow irrigation, where water is allowed to spread in a larger plot or subplot, instead of the usual fast irrigation, where water is concentrated in a smaller plot. Like Walla, there are many employed workers who have unique knowledge of their concerned enterprise.

It is for this reason that during the presidency of Dr A.P.J. Abdul Kalam, a proposal was mooted to reorient the National Rural Employment Guarantee Scheme so that one did not focus only on menial work but also required mental work. Kalam wrote a letter to the prime minister on the subject but nothing really changed.

During the severe drought of 1971–72 in Maharashtra, an employment guarantee scheme[2] was developed to provide employment to poor people. It was a variant of the 'food for work' programme that colonial rulers had evolved to avoid extreme distress in economic situations. The workers were generally asked to dig the earth, break stones and perform other such menial tasks since they were considered unskilled in nature. Imagine the plight of 250 million people whose prior skills are completely neglected under this scheme in the pre- and post-colonial period all this while.

About 250 million people are systematically deskilled through this programme by providing wage employment not for tasks which they are good at but for simple labour instead.[3] This means that people with unique skills, say a sculptor, leather worker, folk singer or songwriter or an outstanding mason, will have to perform day-to-day labour jobs, like dig the earth and break stones, to earn their wages. They cannot improve their innate talents and skills and be paid for using those skills for public purposes. If a wall of every village or urban school is painted by local artists, will it not make the learning environment more joyful for the children? Does this act of painting not constitute work? Why not then pay local artists for such work under rural employment guarantee schemes and urban poverty alleviation programmes. Likewise, all public offices can perk up their working environments if one wall in each public office is painted by local artists every year. If wood and stone sculptors are invited one day a week to schools to teach their skills to children, some respect for manual work and these arts will emerge. In addition, some children might like to pursue these talents as a vocation. Folk singers can be invited to perform and share their art; healers can be invited to share their insights about the local biodiversity-based knowledge system with highly effective, somewhat effective and occasionally effective range of solutions. Apart from respect for local knowledge traditions, students will also develop a sceptical attitude, which invites questioning rather than rote acceptance. Why should we not invite a local grandmother to school to teach students how to cook traditional nutritious dishes and also how seasons, species, spices and spaces are linked? Why certain ingredients are good for health in certain regions and seasons may be explained. This can be considered common knowledge, but it too has to be learnt. This is work too, though its contribution to the GDP of any country is most often neglected.

This is an example where a public policy systematically marginalizes the people who otherwise may have specialized skills, knowledge and perspectives. The dream of making India a knowledge society obviously cannot be fulfilled by pursuing such misdirected policies. It is a tragedy that at the time, many of the intellectuals and social activists supported the government spurring a massive deskilling programme. By devaluing a particular skill, one ignores the potential of all the diversified skills through the NREGA, an act which ensures 100 days of employment to a rural household. There was no incentive for one to specialize. There was no market created for these skills. It did not matter how well one sang, or rendered a story or epic or described local biodiversity. There is no platform where this content could be uploaded so that the diaspora as well other resident Indians could access links with their cultural roots and donate a small amount to the account of the narrator. The process of uploading cultural content is not considered work, so it is not surprising that much of this rich heritage of knowledge is getting eroded.

Listening to the marginal voices would thus require questioning the frameworks in which the voices are deliberately muted. Imagine a portal through which tens of thousands of stories, folk songs and traditional knowledge practices could be recorded and shared in local dialects to not only enrich those languages or sub-languages but also help society to understand how different ideas fertilize popular imagination in different communities over time and space. And while making and collecting such recordings the artists could be paid dignified wages. Some of these artists could even become popular and could even be invited for live performances. A society which respects cultural diversity also becomes entitled to a more refined way of dealing with diversity, differences and the divergence of meaning. Consequently, social imagination and creativity can then be fertilized even more.

The fact that such a portal has not come into existence so far should not make us cynical or despondent. Some day the country is sure to rise to the occasion and begin to recognize culturally well-endowed individuals and communities.

In a knowledge economy and society, one cannot only focus on codified, formalized or institutional knowledge. Even while taking note of the informal sector knowledge produced at the grassroots, one should not stress on the knowledge of farmers, and other propertied classes. The land-less and the asset-less but the skill-rich, knowledge-rich, and/or culturally rich communities also need to have a place of their own to assert their identity. In the process, we should ensure that mediating institutions will emphasize less on method, more on ethics and still more on authenticity in engagement.

Historical studies have shown that through experience or repeated practice of certain tasks, cognitive skills of workers improved and they began to perform more complex or varied tasks better. The labourers could specialize, could be above average in some skills while still remaining average in others like the rest of us.[4] But they were still not paid much differently than us, the professional class, for similar disparities or divergence in our skills. Perhaps the innovations by labourers have remained obscure because we do not expect them to innovate in the first place, though the experience of farmers who work on many more farms is different from farmers who often remain tied to his their farm only. In some of the socialist and post-socialist countries, workers' cooperatives are developing new models of designing machines for customers which are unique and not based on the standard format.[5] They ascertain the needs of the customers, then advise why specifications should be changed and then design the machines in Macedonia.

I recall a visit to Pipavav, near Amreli in Gujarat, two years ago, where the GIAN (West) had installed metallic windmills based on the design of bamboo windmills by Mehtar Hussain and Mustaq Ahmed from Assam, discussed in a previous chapter, with the support of the Alstom Foundation, Paris. While looking at the wells still using counterpoise-based water-lifting arrangements, I came across a brine-water well in which a bird's nest was floating in a basket tied to a thread at one end. When asked why they had done it, the workers explained that this bird had nested almost at the bottom of the well, and whenever they were to pump water, the nest would have been damaged. So they decided to save the nest by placing it in a basket and letting it float. Now the bird continues to live there and comes back every evening after flying around for food. When the water level goes down and the bird flies out, that indicates that it is not safe to descend into the well to clean it up.

We gained a similar insight in another salt-making context. In the Little Rann of Kutch, where Ganatar, an educational NGO had been educating the children of salt workers, we had a mini shodhyatra in 2009. A salt worker explained why they rear and train pigeons and other birds: When they descend into the well, the birds sense the presence of toxic gasses and fly out immediately. This provides the signal for the workers to also come out quickly lest they get affected by those gases as well.

Seeing as how valuable such information can truly be, how can one go about tapping such distributed knowledge from workers and peasants?

Crowdsourcing has become a popular mechanism of seeking ideas from anywhere and anyone who has access to online platforms. I had suggested an idea to the National Innovation Council of engaging with 20 million people who travel by train every day. One could disseminate positive ideas about preventive health, legal entitlements, continuing education, etc., and at the same time seek solutions to the wicked or persistent problems. Of course, inertia took over and nothing happened. The railway ministry then did not respond to these ideas. However, recently the discussion has been re-initiated and let us see if any sort of action gains momentum now. In many public systems and sometimes in private systems too, inertia takes deep root. The habits formed over a long period of time do not give way for new ideas easily. A self-reference system does not become an autopoiesis system without self-correcting, self-design and self-governing attributes. Inertia gives way when new criteria emerge to assess system performance. If the prime minister were to assess the learning potential and openness of different ministries to learn from the grassroots level, he will monitor the processes used by line departments and ministries to seek ideas from outside and act on them. The suggestion schemes in most organizations become dormant and operate more as a formality because no action on these suggestions was taken, and if taken, was not shared widely. I agree with the statement and have always argued that 'a change not monitored is not a change not desired' (Gupta, 1984). If one relies only on a line-feedback system, it is obvious that millions of people who lack access to the Internet will be disenfranchised and their votes in the policymaking process will be not registered.

Thus, feedback received from passengers travelling in ordinary class, deluxe or high-speed, air-conditioned, superfast trains will come from different classes of commuters and thus reflect obvious biases. Learning from the working class will require paying attention to these structural factors.

For instance, some day, while booking a ticket for long-distance journeys, one would also be able to book material for different courses that one would like to study during the journey.[6] If millions of people continue their education in a large number of domains through such channels, the ability of the average Indian to process information and articulate new ideas will increase manifold. If they are exposed to creative and innovative solutions developed by the working class as well as roadside mechanics, farmers, artisans, etc., deeply entrenched inertia, indifference and perceived insularity of the middle class towards neglect of creativity as well as the constraints of economically poor people might give way. The crucial point is that we have to use mass contact platforms to *expose*, provide opportunities for face-to-face *encounters* to hopefully trigger *engagement* with the mission the Honey Bee Network shares.

In the summer of 1999, we were walking in Kutch as a part of the half-yearly shodhyatra. It was around noon, when all the walkers were perspiring and there was not much water in sight, we saw a shepherd walking merrily ahead of us with his herd of 200-odd sheep. He stopped when we waved our hands at him, requesting a small discussion. I asked him (which, incidentally, I thought was a smart question), 'If one of your sheep gets mixed with somebody else's herd, how will you find out?' The shepherd gave a mischievous little smile. He saw a paper in my hand which actually had the route plan for the shodhyatra. He took the folded paper from my hand, opened it and said, 'To me all the letters look alike.'

In just one line, the shepherd had taught me a humbling lesson that I would never forget in all my life. Before I could ask him his name and locality, he ran away to be with the herd. The other shodhyatris and I were left dumbfounded. I realized that the question I had asked was actually quite foolish and naïve. Just as I was illiterate in the language of sheep or the taxonomy of sheep, he was illiterate in my language of letters and words. I was trying to, in a way, mock him or unwittingly belittle his ability to distinguish one sheep from another (I did not genuinely realize that he would be able to recognize each sheep distinctly). He taught me how ignorant I was. I have shared this lesson with my students at IIMA and friends elsewhere every now and then. Every time I recall this moment, my ego takes a sound beating. My pretensions evaporate. Why do we then close our minds to the possibility of learning from all around us? Knowledge is not gained only in classrooms or in structured situations. We can learn from anyone, anywhere, any time.

In the summer of 1998, we walked towards the Gir lion sanctuary in Gujarat on the very first day of the first shodhyatra. The villagers told us during the first night halt that we should not forget to stop by the place of Ismailbhai, who lived a short distance from the forest with his family. We all had many questions in our mind about the behaviour of lions and the way they interact with their habitat. The previous night, hardly any of us slept out of fear from hearing the lions roar nearby. When we reached Ismailbhai's house, the first thing we did was drink a lot of water. After we settled down under a tree, the questions started pouring out, 'Ismailbhai, how often do lions come by here? Do they visit your place to drink water in the trough that you fill every day?' Ismailbhai replied, 'Professor sahib, this is the land of lions. The lion lives here. It is people like you who come and go.' And suddenly we realized that our frame of reference had been inverted. This land of the Gir sanctuary belongs to the lions. It was us who had drawn boundaries and encroached upon their territory. If the lion visits places outside what we think is his territory, the problem lies with us, who have defined a territory too narrowly. One of the traits that innovators have is their ability to invert the frame of reference.

The ability to see a situation completely differently from how others may see it makes the life of an innovator so much more intriguing.

Context Changes the Content

Akbar and Birbal used to enjoy an ongoing game of one-upmanship. Birbal, one of the nine wise jewels on the advisory board of the medieval king, Akbar, was a very clever person. Birbal had taken the role of the court jester and resident rebel upon himself. He always tried to argue that Akbar was king, simply because of the rule of ascension, because his father was king. Other than that, he held no merit. Akbar, tiring of his barbs, asked Birbal one day to consent to his wisdom through the test of the people in his kingdom. If he was wise, so would the people in his kingdom be (*yatha raja, tatha praja*). Birbal designed a riddle and asked Akbar to have it announced to the kingdom. If the citizens could solve it, Birbal would accept the claim of Akbar's wisdom. The riddle was as follows: A line was drawn on a paper and people were asked to shorten the line without rubbing it. Many people tried. Finally, a young boy came forward and drew a bigger line right next to the original line. The original line thus became shorter.

My story begins from here, beyond what the boy did. In this tale, what got changed in the process? The answer is: the context. And consequently, the change in context modified the content. Similarly, in a process of innovation, the innovator often changes the context of the problem so that it becomes partly or wholly solvable. When Mehtar Hussain and Mustaq Ahmed designed a bamboo windmill to lift water, through a handpump powered by the windmill, they changed the context in which the two unconnected devices worked. The windmill had been used to pump water for a long time and, separately, so had the handpump. But till then, nobody had used the windmill to run the handpump.

Likewise, when Mansukhbhai converted a clay cooking pan into a non-stick pan, he transformed the very meaning of not only affordability and frugality but also sustainability. After using a normal non-stick pan for a while, the bottom of the surface gets worn out.

The metallic surface shows up and the Teflon coating disappears. But where does the Teflon go? It goes into our stomachs along with our food, even though it's not meant for that purpose. What Mansukhbhai did was to develop a process so that edible-grade coating material fills into the pores of the clay pan. One cannot scrape it off. Thus, the pan is not only safer and healthier but also extremely accessible to the needy ones. Those who cannot afford a pan that costs five to ten dollars can certainly buy a cheaper one worth one or two dollars. In this way, Mansukhbhai changed the context of both the conventional non-stick pan and the clay pan.

This story of Mansukhbhai's Mitti Cool, though somewhat famous, I feel the need to share some less appreciated parts of the story. During the 2001 earthquake in Gujarat, Mansukhbhai suffered a severe loss due to the breakdown of almost his entire production line. His family had already incurred debt. He used to hide behind a tea-vending cart in which he worked for some time to eke out his living, because he didn't want his relatives to see him pursuing this profession. One day, when the idea of Mitti Cool came to him, he realized that making it would need several moulds and furnaces, which he would have to purchase. So as he pursued the invention his debts mounted further. He made seven different machines to make and bake different pots and plates. Mitti Cool uses evaporative cooling to keep vegetables and milk fresh. So he tried to attach a solar fan also to improve its cooling efficiency. An engineer from the National Chemical Laboratory (NCL)[7] had once explored the possibility of painting the inner surface of the clay fridge with a paint mixed with nanoparticles of titanium dioxide to extend the shelf life of the items by using an antibiotic surface. However, the idea of that scientist did not progress. To call such a thoughtful design of a clay refrigerator requiring not only great skill and workmanship but also several complex design principles just a jugaad is a great injustice to an innovator's creativity.[8]

Another time, while walking through the jungles in Narayanpur, part of the Bastar region of Chhattisgarh, we came across a very innovative institutional approach to dealing with the dead. While entering a particular village, we saw many graves. We thought that it was strange as there were no Christian or Muslim houses in sight. The local tribal community, when asked, gave a very interesting explanation for the scenario. They said that whenever a healthy person died, they buried him. When a sick person died, they cremated him. The point was that a sick body could not be consigned to a grave. How could an unhealthy body be offered to the revered earth, they asked? What a transformative change in the cultural context! The theologians do not think of inverting their frame of reference, yet here were grassroots practitioners, doing this very thing in their practice of religion. Perhaps, the way to respect the sacredness of earth *is* not to put any diseased body in it.[9] It was not surprising, therefore, that the region was also very clean and even a dry leaf was not found in the courtyards despite so many trees around. The context of death and the way the sacredness of earth was interpreted was completely different here.

The root bridge in Cherrapunji, Meghalaya, described earlier, similarly changed the context of bridge making, or for that matter, using living materials for construction. Choosing to stay away from existing designs of bridge across the local river, community members in Nongriat village in Meghalaya decided to change the *context* of sustainability. They raised the bar so high by choosing tree roots—living material—to accomplish the design. The entropy or the waste produced from the project was practically zero.

The nature within and the nature without are not completely delinked. Many times what we see outside is linked to what we are either capable of seeing or want to see. So how do we generate the capacity to see and hear more clearly? How is it that so many organizations are working at the community level all over the country and around the world, and yet are not able to find enough creative people whose ideas they may like to adopt? Perhaps the earnestness with which one looks for creativity outside may be linked to one's humility inside. Or maybe it is a matter of redefining the frame of reference.

Once, during a walk from the Panchmahals in Gujarat towards Koba in Rajasthan, we stopped for a discussion at a village school as planned. The schoolteacher received us kindly and had invited many children to speak to us. During the discussion, we talked about our work about learning ideas from common people in uncommon ways. At this point, the teacher gave us an example of a problem he had faced many years ago. He pointed towards some mango trees growing nearby. He said that before he planted those trees successfully, he had failed many times; each time he planted the saplings, either termites or some other insects would devastate the seedlings. One day, as he waited at a bus stand, he met a person with whom he started a casual discussion about growing mango trees. By the time the teacher returned home that day, he had forgotten about the practical tips the stranger had shared with him. After a few years and repeated failures of not being able to grow the mango seedlings, he suddenly remembered that discussion. He went to that person's village and asked him to narrate again the process through which the seedlings could be grown successfully. He learnt that before planting mango seedlings, he should be spreading the ash of teak leaves (*sagwan*) and also put some dry leaves around the roots of the seedling. He did as advised and the trees survived and had been bearing fruit ever since.

Pleased to hear of his personal experience, we asked the teacher whether he had told this story to his students. His answer stumped us, those in the field, but also provided a unique insight into the scope for cross-pollinating communication. He replied, 'I didn't tell this story to my students because the context for telling such a story never arose.' The story had travelled to us, coming from such a great distance, but it could not travel a distance of just a few feet in the classroom. This incident reminds me of the famous dialogue in Sherlock Holmes's story in which the guard is asked by the judge about a theft that took place the previous night. The guard explains that he was very watchful, so much so that even the dog didn't bark. It is then the judge asks, 'Why didn't the dog bark?' Apparently, the guard had been sleeping and the thieves had fed a piece of meat to the dog to keep it quiet while they proceeded with the burglary. The context of a situation makes a big difference and focusing on the content of an idea or innovation may mask the real motivations underlying it. After all, asking the obvious question would not have led to the truth about the guard not doing his duty well. The frame of reference was changed by the question: Why did the dog not bark? The dog barking would be normal, expected behaviour.

Many times, knowledge can travel hundreds of kilometres, as it did in this case since we had come from such a far-off place. But in other cases, it cannot transcend even the most routine face-to-face interactions. Why had the educational system not created a context for such discussions to be held and such stories to be told? How is it that successful examples and even examples of failures in various experiments never get discussed as a pedagogic tool for sharpening curiosity of children? It is not difficult to understand and appreciate that such examples would not only enrich the class discussion but also encourage children to conduct their own experiments. Perhaps the policymakers are afraid that if children in government schools learnt to experiment and innovate—i.e., think and question—their own children, studying in the elite schools, will have no comparative advantage. Maybe the administrators and the ministers are afraid that they will lose support of affluent and elite in society, who will no longer have a mass pool of cheap labour to hire as housemaids and servants at a low cost. Surely, there is a method in their madness.

We have met a large number of schoolteachers who have been great experimenters and innovators despite being in government schools, and no matter how hard educational administrators might have tried to stifle teachers' spirits by engaging them in numerous non-teaching-related tasks, or by being oblivious to their initiatives. One can pick up any textbook from any class in India and one would probably never find an example of experiments undertaken by the teachers, the students or other common people to inspire children to create and pursue higher goals. Only once did we come across a primary school in the last eighteen years of the shodhyatras—in Nashik, Maharashtra—where a schoolteacher had painted the names of those students who had achieved some status in life on the classroom wall—names of half a dozen officials who had studied in that government school and distinguished themselves in life. Just imagine, if every government school had such an honours list of real-life, accessible examples, wouldn't it motivate children to strive for achieving better results in life, despite their economic hardships? The teacher who conceived of this idea had remained unrecognized. Apparently, it is not easy to facilitate autonomous diffusion of such good ideas. Despite tens of thousands of such ideas, spurred by schoolteachers in government schools, available at teachersastransformers. org (compiled by Professor Vijaya Sherry Chand, IIMA, with help from several institutions and volunteers including those from the Honey Bee Network and

SRISTI), not many have been replicated either for improving educational practice or for acting as a point of reference for further experimentation. There seems to be a particular reluctance to learn from examples of even outstanding performance at the grassroots level. This inertia, or unwillingness to bring about change, is not a special attribute of policymakers alone. Majority of us prefer to stay tuned to existing ways of dealing with life and its challenges. That is why bringing about social change needs so much persistent effort.

But without that possibility of overcoming our own inertia, a book like this will serve no special purpose. How can the readers overcome their own inertia? I will like to reflect on the processes that may provide clues to the persistence required to overcome inertia and also its dissolution through both intrinsic motivation in some cases and extrinsic triggers in others.

Knowing, Feeling and Doing

Many of us *know* a great deal but feel emotionally affected by only a few out of the things we know. From among those few things that we *feel* about, we act on even fewer things. Take for example how, while walking on a road, we observe a whole lot of things. It is true that not all of these observations affect us equally. But some of those which do affect us do not leave a lasting imprint. They do not make us impatient enough to conceive of an initiative for changing a particular situation we've noticed. From among the things that affect us, how do we prioritize those experiences or feelings which enable us to take some action to alleviate self-imposed or socially defined pain? Is it necessary that we should suffer equally from all the exposures that do not agree with our internal notions of right and wrong? Some experiences get buried in the layers of the memory-scape and thus are awakened through one or the other trigger. This happens at an individual level and also at a communal or societal or national level. Our country adopted a constitution which gave primacy to achieving free and compulsory education within ten years of its adoption.[10] Some states like Tripura and Mizoram made tremendous progress not only in the field of education but also in the elimination of child labour. The rest of the country still struggles with the problem, except Kerala. It is not that policymakers in other states (some far more economically developed) are not aware of the role education plays in unleashing the potential of all human beings. They are aware. But then their feelings on the subject do not translate into similar urgency as is shown for many other hard infrastructural projects.

At an organizational level, similar inertia may persist. Despite the national policy requiring that all public institutions be enabled to cater to the disabled, many elite institutions are not completely so. At an individual level, our past inertia may make us less sensitive to contemporary problems which we still recognize as valid. Or we may manufacture reasons which reduce our sense of autonomy as well as agency. Autonomy defines the *freedom* to take decisions, and agency points to our *willingness* to take decisions. Thus, there is an inverted triangle of a lot of knowledge, lesser feelings and even fewer actions. Sometimes, too much exposure to knowledge immunizes people towards the problems that the rest of society faces. One either stops or experiences reduced feelings of empathy; soon this feeling converts into a sense of learnt helplessness. There are, however, people who don't fall into a state of helplessness vis à vis society and its problems. They take initiatives, they experiment, they don't feel ashamed when they fail and they can laugh about their foolishness or naivety. It is not difficult to overcome inertia, if one is willing to fail and not feel embarrassed in sharing such failures, or is willing to raise the bar of what quality of life one should be entitled to. Our quality of life cannot be very good if we are accepting of inertia. We will always find or give excuses for not doing something about something . . . anything. We may also develop a habit of externalizing reasons for our failure on to others.

However, there are some who believe that in this paradigm, feelings come first, knowledge next and action later. One could argue that whenever we act, we evaluate the impact of the action on us and others and then, in that process, some kind of knowledge precipitates. Action, feedback, reflection and further observation, feeling and action are iterative processes. In fact, the connections between knowledge and feelings can be tested easily. Once, while looking for various meanings of the word, *samskara*, I came across several definitions and the one which appealed to me most was: The reactions produced in the mind almost instantaneously when we act or are reflective of our 'samskara'. These are a kind of embedded values or sensors about what *is* and what *ought* to be. The feedback is immediate and often very truthful. We may not accept it, we may not reflect on it and we may not feel too much about it. That is possible. Feelings are not always immediate. There are times when actions of the long past trigger contemporary feelings. And there are times when we fail to feel the seriousness of what we are going through in the very moment in which the feeling is realized. How feelings are evoked has much to do with our emotional apparatus. We can feel guilty for things we haven't done, but we can also feel grateful that despite not doing what we should have done, we have been forgiven and welcomed into the sentient community. Our peers accept us as 'normal' persons who, like them, are quite insular to many inadequacies in their proximal environment. All of us make such trade-offs. Which of these trade-offs make us guilty or disappointed with ourselves and which of these helps us raise our self-respect is up to us to decide.

The neglect of a large number of social problems, which should have been addressed long time ago, does not produce enough or perhaps any guilt among the planners, thinkers and the executors. We have such a huge distance between the haves and the have-nots because of precisely such neglect. Many innovators don't know how to sleep with an indefinitely unsolved problem on their minds. They overcome societal inertia by converting a persistent problem into a personal challenge. That's how many grassroots innovators solve societal problems, which did not necessarily start out as personal problems, but eventually became just as meaningful to them.

Both drivers—guilt and gratitude—can evoke deeper feelings to generate the search for more knowledge. This search can also become a prelude for inertia. I have seen many students and professionals who substitute reflection with reading. I am all for reading widely, but I also realize that the quest for knowledge should not become an alibi for inaction, or in other words, acting with imperfect and inadequate knowledge. So how do we tell the difference between knowing when we should act and knowing when one is not sure that one knows enough? There is always uncertainty about the sufficiency of knowledge, and it is also not definite whether action based on the available knowledge will always be right. This kind of uncertainty, often leading to inertia, is dealt with the arousal of impatience, uneasiness and a feeling of dissatisfaction with the status quo.

One of the most important drivers used by the innovators is that of the samvedana, a Sanskrit word that signifies the immense potential for converting knowledge into feeling and feeling into action. Samvedana is composed of two root words: *Sam* meaning equal, *vedana* meaning pain. When a person feels somebody else's pain as his or her own, it no longer remains a third party's pain. It becomes personal pain. Such an internalization of pain triggers *srijansheelta* (creativity) from samvedana. The closest English word for empathy is samvedana, but the difference is this: one has empathy for others but samvedana is inside oneself.

Many women in the Gadha village of Gujarat complained to Khemjibhai, a serial inventor, to develop a solution for their problem. These women used to carry a lot of weight in water pots on their head, like so many other rural Indian women. Naturally, they felt a stabbing pain in their necks. On hearing their plight, Khemjibhai felt their pain as his own. First, he commented jokingly, 'The head is not meant to carry load, it is supposed to think.' Then he developed an empathetic, frugal, affordable and simple solution in the form of *panihari*. He designed a ring on two shoulder rests. The pot was meant to be kept on the ring and after walking a few steps, the person was to pull the stands on to the shoulders, lifting the ring just a few centimetres. The load of the pot would then be transferred from head to the shoulders. Khemjibhai is a terrific example of how samvedana gives rise to a beautiful *srijansheel* solution.

The example of Ram Tamari Devi which I discussed earlier illustrates the case when excellence becomes imperative, action becomes a way of dealing with helplessness. She had made beautiful artwork on clay grain bins outside the huts. No one else had done that over the next 125 kilometres on the walk.

One doesn't manufacture a choice. If we keep looking for choices, we may miss the opportunity for learning early, and eventually we may never end up with a perfect choice. Those who yearn for the perfect choice actually celebrate inertia every day. Life passes them by and they don't even realize it. I have met quite a few outstanding Indians (out of a very large number that live and work there) during my travels abroad, many of whom have carried dreams in their eyes for many years, yet they are still waiting for the right moment to engage with their communities and society to make a difference, to make *their* difference. And that day often never comes. Compare this trend with Bhutan, a small country, which had till recently almost 95 per cent return rate of students who went abroad for higher studies. In China's case, the diaspora makes a much higher contribution to research and publications and other developmental partnerships. It is understandable, therefore, that different cultures create different criteria for deciding what socially admissible levels of inertia are. It is my belief that Indian society is moving and changing for better. Hopefully, not in the very distant future, we will lower the acceptable social levels of accepting inertia and indifference considerably. My hope stems from the evidence of: a) a large number of highly qualified Indian professionals coming back every year to establish themselves in India or sending remittances;[11] b) the country is majorly focusing on encouraging entrepreneurship through a start-up revolution; c) an increasing number of self-regulatory experiments, be it in traffic regulations aiming at reduction in pollution, sanitation, voluntarily relinquishing LPG gas connection for the poor, etc.; and d) the younger generation is far less patient with inertia as compared with our generation, which is evident from the IGNITE awards.

Inverted Model of Innovations

The inverted model of innovations can be another pivot for generating frugal innovations. Simply put, it implies that children invent, engineers fabricate and companies commercialize. Children are not seen as receptacles or a sink of knowledge but as extremely creative and original sources of often extremely frugal solutions. Before the NIF started formally organizing its annual IGNITE competitions for discovering creative ideas from children, the Honey Bee Network and SRISTI had experimented with the idea many years ago during earlier shodhyatras and also otherwise.

Vivekanandan had another friend, N. Muthu Velayutham, from the Covenant Centre for Development (CCD), who jointly organized the biodiversity competitions in a village at the foothills of a small forest in Madurai district of Tamil Nadu, south India. The student who won the competition knew about 112 plants along with their uses. The adults in the same village knew about 225 plants and their uses. This child had covered half the intellectual journey of the community maxima of biodiversity knowledge by the age of twelve. But, he still had to spend the rest of his life learning 'A is for apple', 'B is for ball', and other such subjects which may not build upon what he has learnt outside the school, based on his lived experience. He was expected to unlearn his 'real-life' knowledge such that he had to focus on classroom discussions to become successful in life. Not that one does not need classroom education, but it can easily build upon the prior knowledge children have of nature and other resources. Paradoxically, the people who have never lived with biodiversity often get entrusted with the responsibility of conserving it as forest officers (though many pick up the science and technology of forest management, and associated conservation principles very proficiently). Those who know a lot at the early age become unskilled labourers or sometime even school dropouts because their innate talents and abilities are not encouraged or recognized. The irony of the education system is evident in such cases. The Honey Bee Network decided that we need to recognize such children who have talent in conserving nature and/ or learning from it. In another biodiversity competition organized in Viramgam village of north Gujarat, apart from the children, a middle-aged potter also brought a gunnysack full of plants to share his knowledge and expertise on the topic. His name was Karimbhai, and he became very regionally popular afterwards, when SRISTI widely shared his knowledge about his herbal healing skills.

In these competitions, there were other remarkable insights, despite the outstanding cachet of the winners. For example, there was a physically challenged girl who came to the competition with just a bounty of just one leaf stitched on to the cover of an old notebook. It was clear that with one leaf, she had no chance of receiving any recognition or winning. But that did not matter to her; what she probably cared most about was the sense of participation. We have become so victory conscious that many times we do not participate in competitions in which we believe we have no chance of winning. It was inspiring to see that this child didn't care about winning. Another interesting insight was that girls outperformed boys in the early years, up to the sixth grade. After this age, the girl students seemed to be tasked with looking after their younger siblings, and they started losing out on opportunities to grow their knowledge base.

During the eighth shodhyatra in 2001, from Bhikampura to Nilkanth Gadh in Rajasthan,[12] we had organized yet another biodiversity contest among the local school children in the premises of a temple. A student named Giriraj Prasad Mina was given the third prize for having named about seventy-five plants. I referred to the example of a boy in another village who had named 271 plants and their uses. Giriraj piped up and said that they weren't given enough time or else he could have named 500. He asked for a day's time and promised to find us himself with his list of 500 plants and their uses. We proceeded with the yatra. Sure enough, the next afternoon Giriraj was there, having crossed five villages to locate us to show off his knowledge. We were, to say the least, overwhelmed. Why couldn't we challenge more and more young kids with seemingly impossible goals and turn the tide of inertia into that of innovation?[13]

Later, with the help of Shailesh and Vijay (currently a senior faculty member at IIMA), many more competitions have been organized. Slowly, these competitions have expanded and evolved into idea competitions in general and we started focusing on the collection of ideas from children during our shodhyatras and other activities in rural areas. These have evolved into countrywide contests for scouting ideas from children. In the last round in 2015, the NIF received more than 28,000 ideas from all states and Union territories. There were thirty-one awardee teams from eighteen states, honoured by the President of India, Shri Pranab Mukherjee at IIMA on 30 November 2015. So far, beginning with 2007–08, more than 90,000 ideas have been received from children alone.

Can Children Help Us in Overcoming Inertia?

Over the years, I have realized that children have far lesser patience with inefficiency and inadequacy than we adults do. It is not just the children in so-called English-medium, better-endowed schools but also the children in government or municipal schools, and even dropouts that share the impatience with inertia and insufficiency. As they grow up, they acquire our habits of explaining away the inefficiency rather than gathering the strength to overcome it.

Let me begin this section with one of the more recent examples. Dr Kalam was to lay the foundation stone for the NIF campus on 19 February 2014 at Amrapur, in the Gandhinagar district of Gujarat. The collector, Mr P. Swaroop, whom incidentally I had taught at the Lal Bahadur Shastri National Academy of Administration, Mussoorie, was very keen that some outstanding children from the district of Gandhinagar have the opportunity to interact with Dr Kalam so as to be inspired by him to aim for higher goals. Ramesh Patel, secretary of SRISTI and a believer in the Spartan-Gandhian lifestyle, decided to take the plunge and reach out to the 600-plus schools in the district. With the help of volunteers from the NIF and other segments of the Honey Bee Network, three posters were put up in every school and idea competitions were organized. More than 5000 ideas were collected from the children within a month. Five were shortlisted for recognition on 19 February 2014. One idea which touched my heart the most was given by a young girl named Chhaya Thakore from Class VII. She was short in stature and faced difficulty in drinking water during recess every day because the tap was located much higher than she could easily reach. Knowing that many other children faced the same difficulty, she came up with an idea for a water pipe made with taps at an inclined angle, with one end high and the other low, so that children of different heights could easily drink water from the fountain.

While as adults, we probably never cared to think about the untold difficulties that have been faced by little kids or do anything about them, this little girl couldn't live with the problem anymore. The new kind of tap is being fitted into the school with a small plaque underneath it crediting Chhaya for the invention. We've further encouraged other children that if they notice anything inadequate in their personal lives, society or environment, they can submit their ideas to SRISTI/ NIF and action will follow, if found feasible. Imagine, if millions of children in India and elsewhere start thinking and acting on the unsolved problems of society, perhaps India would not remain trapped in quagmire of mediocrity for too long.

There are many problems from which we adults suffer and yet do not learn to improve our living style. But children sensing our discomfort come out with somewhat coercive solutions directed in our own interest.

How many of us have either suffered ourselves from pain in the lower back due to bad posture or have known someone who has suffered likewise? I myself have had an episode of back pain every third year for over the last decade. The answer might be almost everyone. But what have we done to address this very serious and common need? How many of us have thought about modifying the design of the chair, or adding support options for the back or invented something else that could possibly alert us whenever our posture is wrong? The answer would be: very few of us. We know the problem; we live with it and do nothing about it except suffering voluntarily. But three young students—Sunvi Agarwal, Class X, Chandigarh; Kulsoom Rizavi, Class V, Lucknow; and Tarun Anand, Class X, Ghaziabad—have suggested modifications in computer screens or desk chairs which can make us correct our posture when needed. The first idea was to fix a sensor in the computer screen or a television, which will notice the slip in our posture and immediately switch off the screen. A message would appear, 'Please correct your posture, sit properly, else no view or no work.' The second idea was to fix four or five pressure sensors on to the backrest of the chair. If all the points are not pressed at a particular point of time, the chair will start reminding you by making noise or singing a song till you regain good posture and sit properly. When a working model of such a chair was kept at the innovation exhibition hosted by the President of India's office at the Rashtrapati Bhavan during 7–13 March 2014, it was appreciated by most of the visitors. People wanted to purchase such a chair right away. The response validated the children's feelings about the seriousness of the problem. Yet, neither the general manufacturers of chairs nor the occupational health specialists have considered this idea. Is it too small a problem to garner attention or is it that as a society we wait for someone else to solve our problems?

In another instance, many of us have seen women, old people and others tripping while getting on or down from buses because drivers always seem to be in a hurry. It is unfortunate that drivers have not been able to develop enough patience to let passengers get down or board the bus properly. Sometimes, passengers also try to board the bus even when there is not much space. For whatever reasons, the fact is that no sustainable solution for safe boarding and de-boarding has been found yet. But, four students of Class X and XI, from a government school in Thiruvarur in Tamil Nadu decided they would not live with this problem anymore. R. Santhosh, J. Rajesekhar, A. Nivashini and K. Rathna together suggested the installation of a sensor on the steps such that the bus would not start as long as there was someone standing on the boarding/de-boarding area. If the bus bodybuilders' association can ensure that all their members install such sensors, the drivers of public and private buses will have no choice but to let passengers get down and climb on safely. If the Bureau of Indian Standards creates standards that make it obligatory for buses to have such sensors, without which they will not get clearance from the Regional Transport authorities for plying on the road, the problem will get solved. This scenario is one case where institutional failure requires technological innovation to solve social problems, and also reinforces the value of inverting the innovation model every now and then to expand the space for ideas from children.

We often hear about someone's grandma or grandpa and their deteriorating health. Many of us have also faced the dilemma when mostly old people, who suffer from motor issues, fall down or hurt themselves and there is no one to take care of them. In case of such an incident, how do the old people convey their distress? Even if there are near and dear ones living together or close by, they may be in a different room or out of earshot. Somaya Ranjan Behera, Class VII, from Jagatsinghpur, Odisha, conceptualized a wearable device which can inform close family members in the event of an accident. The students from BITS Pilani, Rajasthan, have already designed a belt of this kind which communicates an SMS to the pre-assigned numbers in the event of an accident. It will provide relief to so many families around the world who face this problem.

Shalini, Class VIII, from Patna, Bihar, observed her grandfather facing a problem in climbing the stairs using a walker. She suggested an adaptation in the walker so as to fix it with flexible front legs. The NIF got a prototype made in which the front legs could be adjusted to become shorter while climbing up and longer while stepping down. Again, we see how small innovations can add value to the quality of life of so many people afflicted with day-to-day problems. This has been licensed to a company which paid two lakh rupees as licence fee besides paying royalty on each walker. She has thus become one of the youngest entrepreneurs.

Many young people, particularly boys, don't wear helmets while driving two-wheelers, even though there is a law requiring the same, but many young boys are careless. Sometimes when accidents take place, one pays with one's life for this folly. Three girls from Thiruvarur, Tamil Nadu, Laila Banu, S.M. Arthi and Vinotha, suggested a mechanism where the motorcycle should not start if the rider is not wearing a helmet, using a Bluetooth signal. A fabricator from Odisha designed a wireless blue tooth mechanism and the idea soon became a reality. If an innovation of this kind can save lives, wouldn't we call them empathetic innovations? In the case of majority of grassroots innovators and their children, innovative ideas are triggered not by one's own problems but by being *samvedanasheel* (empathetic) towards somebody else's problem.

Five different groups of children, including a few selling eggs on the street, were aware that many times the adults do not carry drivers' licences with them when they are behind the wheel. They suggested a system that unless the licence was inserted in a socket, the vehicle would not run. Children don't like adults breaking the rules. Varsha Kumari and Durgesh Kumar from Bihar; Jyoti from Haryana; Raviranjan and Shiv Kumar also from Bihar; and Krishna Kumar from Tamil Nadu independently thought of this idea for which a prototype was developed.

Mohammed Usman Hanif Patel, Class II, from Jalgaon, Maharashtra, thought of using a windmill to run ceiling fans in localities where there was no electricity.

Chris Anant, Class I, Tamil Nadu, conceived of shoes which could become vacuum cleaner because of the pumping action involved in children's shoes that whistled to produce sound. Chris saw his father vacuum cleaning. He asked him why his shoes made that sound. His father replied that the shoes had a whistle in them, upon which Chris surmised that air must be going out and also coming in through the nozzle. This led Chris to conceive of shoes which could become vacuum cleaners by sucking the dust while drawing air inside. Earlier, his mother complained whenever he spoiled the carpet or ground. Now she would purposefully ask him to walk over the dirt. The whole context turned on its head. Such flights of imagination are not uncommon for children. And yet, which theory of innovation has really considered dialogue with children as a way of generating new ideas?

Arnab Chakraborty, a student of Class XII from West Bengal thought of the plight of cycle-rickshaw drivers while climbing upward-sloping roads. Sometimes they get off to push the rickshaw manually while the passengers keep sitting. He suggested a design for a rickshaw that enabled passenger to also do co-pedalling with the cycle-rickshaw driver. Today we call this concept of collaborative problem-solving as co-creation.

Many people forget to take medicine on time. Mohit Singh, Class X from Sidhi, Madhya Pradesh, conceptualized an idea for a medicine box with an alarm on it to remind users of the time for taking medicine. Such boxes are since available in local markets, but Mohit was a pioneer in thinking about it. Chhavi Dutta, Class IX from Jalandhar, Punjab, was not very fond of playing outside, for which she would often get scolded by her parents. She thought about an idea for shoes which will record the time one spent playing outside. The idea was meant to be a compromise between parents and child— one could only see television for the time equivalent to what was spent playing outside. The less time recorded outside, the less access to the television. After the clocked time of play, the signal from the shoes was supposed to switch off the TV automatically.

Farhin Banu, Class XII, from Ahmedabad, Gujarat, and Amlan, Class X from Bhubaneswar, Odisha, devised a jacket that could sense one's body temperature and also rate of heartbeat so that if health parameters went beyond range, doctors will automatically be informed.

In the wake of so many assaults on women, the NIF got many entries aimed at improving women's safety. Manu Chopra, Class XI, Delhi, developed a bracelet which, if pressed hard, would give a shock to the assaulter. A working prototype was made.

All these examples show not only the impatience of children in solving unaddressed social problems, but also the social sensitivity in their perceptions. In all such ideas, the NIF gets the prototypes made based on children's ideas. When they come to receive their awards, they are given a pleasant surprise. Yet, it is not enough to just give prizes to such students. It is also not enough to recognize their social sensitivity. Identifying unmet social needs and responding to them should become a regular part of their education curricula. When children learn to overcome their inertia at a young age, the probability of their taking on an indifferent attitude once they grow up is reduced. It is predominantly this reason of an expansion in outlook which should justify a special window of opportunity for such children. While academic scores matter for admission to higher-level programmes, and rightly so, such sensitivity to social changes and mores should also matter. Brilliance without social conscience makes the world less responsible. Social conscience without extraordinary brilliance may still contribute to make the world more beautiful and trustworthy.

At present, the academic system doesn't build on flexibility to accommodate such students, with maverick mindsets and early developed social consciences. So I have brainstormed many steps that we can take to encourage the creativity of our children at the local institutional level. We can organize idea competitions every week or fortnight as an exercise to stimulate innovative thinking about unmet needs, whether in aspirational, experiential or emotional domains. For instance, when Rudra Prasad Goswami from Ranchi, Jharkhand, thought about a pencil or pen having a pressure sensor to alert him to the loss of his concentration, he was recognizing his own need to self-regulate his concentration while studying. He realized that when his concentration was week, the grip of the pencil or pen became loose. This invention would be useful for teachers as well, who can figure out how many students sitting in the class are paying attention or not. A small light on the top of the pen or pencil will blink the moment the student's concentration goes down. This is an example of an experiential unmet need. When Mayank Walia thought of combining a scanner with text-to-speech software, so that blind people can read any book, he was articulating a social aspiration of the blind internalized by him as his own need. This became an empathetic innovation. The medicine reminder contraption was an emotional need of a child whose grandfather was lax about taking care of his own health. There could be many other such internal and external triggers for thinking about unmet needs. There are many other examples where children have been able to think of solutions that have eluded adults. Naturally, as we gain more experience, we seem to become more aware of practical limitations why things cannot be done. The naivety of the children is perhaps their strength. They are not afraid of being proven wrong or becoming irrelevant. Exercises for idea generation could make children not only socially and personally more sensitive, but they could also become more responsible vis à vis their own reflections. So what happens when they grow up? Many of us have needs which we don't reflect on; therefore, we do not *feel* them and don't even articulate or express them to ourselves or others. There are hardly any lessons based on the hundreds of innovative ideas generated by children or other marginal minds that have been recognized so far by the textbooks of any class. Students must be exposed to such real-world case studies from an early age to avoid the inertia which tends to slowly creep in their life as they grow older. Exercises can also be included in which children are exposed to unmet social needs through social work and philanthropy projects and are then challenged to solve those problems.

FIVE

Knowing, Feeling and Doing: Expanding the Domain of Responsibility

Given our constant exposure to the media, our stock of information and knowledge, whether relevant or not, expands every moment of the day. As our reserve stock of knowledge grows, we become increasingly aware of the possibilities; both outside our life and inside our spirit. In our tradition, we call such awareness *para* and *aapara* gyan. Para gyan refers to the knowledge about our material life, and apara gyan is our ethereal knowledge. These two types of gyan are very much connected; sometimes, one even feeds into the other. But if we focus too much on our consumptive nature, we tend to mask and mute the ethereal or spiritual reflections flowering inside us. If we introspect purposefully and reflect on both aspects of knowledge—essentially the antecedent and the subsequent impact of our actions—we can reduce our focus on material needs. We become frugal and can even hope to reconcile ourselves with the philosophy of *aparigraha*. The concept of aparigraha was first defined by the Jain religion 2500 years ago and it states that one must not accumulate more than what one needs. This sentiment was echoed by Gandhi when he said, 'There is enough in this world for everybody's need; but not everybody's greed.' It is my belief that the interaction between material and ethereal knowledge can also trigger the search for empathetic innovations.

Languages, Intuition and Empathy

Evolution of intuition may help us to understand why some of us have more of it than others. Before understanding the evolution of intuition, let us explore the evolution of human brain itself over millions of years. A very large part of the brain evolved to deal with sensory signals, especially from the hands, or through touch.[1] After all, till stone, wood or metallic tools were invented, our ancestors used their bare hands as a major means of tools. Even when tools started progressing, for a long time, these tools were predominantly operated by hand. Once the thumb separated from the four other fingers, hominids separated from chimpanzees or apes, they were walking straight and were able to hold tools in a way, which never happened before. Similarly, the desire to reflect while acting was also developed in human mind long ago. Human intelligence and agency as distinct from autonomy were evolving through *hands-on* learning.[2] Autonomy refers to the freedom to act while agency indicates willingness to use that freedom, and thus actually act.

It is natural that some of early ancestors might have developed expertise in handling tools more than others by practice or individuals tendencies or even by chance sometimes.[3] When tools had to be shaped cooperatively, the exchange of ideas, instruction, experience and sometimes scolding for not listening carefully must have become imperative. Gestures, sounds and, slowly, words began to be formed. Sharing one's learning with others was done not just through oral or textual language but also artistically. Feelings became art. When feelings had to be understood even without explicit articulation, one needed to develop intuition.

In central India, we have cave paintings which are as old as about 25,000 years. Elsewhere in the world, cave paintings as old as 40,000 years have been discovered. While civilization history comprising formation of languages, communities, norms and rules of conduct, institutional structure of governance may hardly be less than 10,000 years ago. The point I wish to make here is that the reflective ability to contemplate on *things* and produce *thoughts* has been with us for a very long time. The urge to share these reflections, therefore, must have preceded the formation of communities. Unless there is need to exchange ideas and reflections, and get feedback through repeated exchanges, why would one need a stable community? Transient communities existed when different people may have used the same caves and tried to overwrite to create new artwork as history has shown. Or they migrated over long distances and made paintings or sculptures wherever they made short-term halts. When reflections could not yet be articulated in languages or written scripts as we understand them, these contemplations had to be coded in pictorial symbols. Metaphors have low entropy, that is, their meanings last long and don't disintegrate easily. That's why some of the cave paintings still evoke the same feelings in our hearts as hominids might have tried thousands of years ago. These feelings showed concern towards animals just as they showed tendency to tame or hunt these animals. Group behaviour and concern for each other also starts appearing in these images. Images show that people are moving in lines or clusters to hunt animals or simply move altogether. Without concern for each other, cooperation is unlikely to ever emerge. Knowledge was accumulating in communities and not just individual minds and hearts. But even before sharing them in this form, human feelings indeed existed which promoted attempts to share the emerging knowledge. Empathy (*samvedana*) towards others who might have struggled with similar feelings might have been an early precursor of a shared community.

The evolution of community was not a gender-neutral process. The role differentiation began to evolve among women and men due to several evolutionary processes such as the intensification versus extensification of agriculture—the former reduced the role of women in managing resources outside home while the latter did the opposite.[4] Even today, in many communities that are dependent on food gathering and limited hunting, the gender roles are less differentiated and less status-linked.

But with intensification, power, accumulation and differentiation set in.

These role differences became more conspicuous historically when domestication of agriculture started and irrigation required channelling water over long distances to begin with, or drainage of water in paddy fields. In a recent study published in *Science*, Dyble et al.[5] observe, 'Gender inequality reappeared in humans with the transition to agriculture and pastoralism. Once heritable resources, such as land and livestock, became important determinants of reproductive success, sex-biased inheritance and lineal systems started to arise, leading to wealth and sex inequalities.' Mark Dyble, who led the study further adds, 'There is still this wider perception that hunter-gatherers are more macho or male-dominated. We'd argue it was only with the emergence of agriculture, when people could start to accumulate resources that inequality emerged.' Hannah Devlin,[6] drawing upon Dyble's work adds, 'The latest findings suggest that equality between the sexes may have been a survival advantage and played an important role in shaping human society and evolution.' 'Sexual equality is one of a important suite of changes to social organization, including things like pair-bonding, our big, social brains, and language, that distinguishes humans,' Dyble says.

Coming closer to recent history, interestingly, the dresses of women did not have pockets till 100 years ago maybe, while men seem to have had them for a long time. Ever since men wanted to keep things handy, which they might need while hunting and travelling. Women did not keep their hands in pocket unlike men. Even at leisure, they kept their hands busy. They would break seeds, knit sweaters, do embroidery, stitch, peel nuts or do something or the other. They were acting even at the time of reflections. Men predominantly separated the time of action and reflection. The neural networks in women's brain developed differently. They developed intuition which men often lack. Though, by learning to use our hands while thinking, we can perhaps develop similar abilities.

A recent study by Ragini Verma and her colleagues is worth quoting at length:

> In one of the largest studies looking at the 'connectomes' of the sexes, Ragini Verma, PhD, an associate professor in the Department of Radiology at the Perelman School of Medicine at the University of Pennsylvania, and colleagues found greater neural connectivity from front to back and within one hemisphere in males, suggesting their brains are structured to facilitate connectivity between perception and coordinated action. In contrast, in females, the wiring goes between the left and right hemispheres, suggesting that they facilitate communication between the analytical and intuition.[7]

Those thinkers and creative people, who simultaneously reflected while doing work with their hands, tended to produce remarkable intuitive insights, be it Kabir or Rahim, or many contemporary grassroots thinkers, innovators (and even formal sector scholars who tend to pursue some physical labour while reflecting occasionally or regularly). Men can develop intuitive faculties by learning from women's unique strengths and bring greater intuitive and empathetic concerns in their problem-solving pursuits. That's why I stress on the concept of voluntary suffering and students learning how to combine their head, heart and hand in practical ways, while reflecting on deeper questions about passion, purpose, process, etc., during the shodhyatras. Thus the connection between material occupation, physical activity and reflections reinforces a profound sense of empathy or, in other words, the connection between intuition, concern for others, empathy, compassion and creativity of course becomes apparent because of less reliance on the analytical faculties alone. When action and reflection happen hand in hand as often it happens with women, one's intuitive sense becomes more pronounced.

Moreover, all the knowledge we possess does not necessarily convert into feelings. When we travel on the road, we are bombarded with information: signs, people, animals, sounds, etc., yet often we just keep on driving. But sometimes we pause, even stop. The interruption could come from an old woman struggling to cross the road, or a wounded dog squirming in the dust, or an injured person who just fell down from a public bus because the driver was in a great rush. The sad truth is that while majority of us may notice these incidents and pause, very few would actually stop and take action. It is not that we do not have the knowledge of what has happened, but that knowledge does not always activate the feelings button. So why do only certain types of knowledge incite powerful feelings? Perhaps only certain feelings like those of guilt, gratitude or some specific memory associations directly connected to recently acquired knowledge are able to empower us to action. When guilt triggers the feelings button, you feel responsible for whatever has happened even if you are not involved in the accident or event in any way. It is ambitious to expect one to develop feelings for all situations that one faces. Sometimes, emotional attachment to an issue prompts the search for knowledge. And in some cases, the knowledge may reinforce prior feelings or even alter them. Yet this search for knowledge seldom leads to complete contradiction or negation of the initial feelings. Attachment to the knowledge one seeks makes objective evaluation of that knowledge difficult, however, this need not impede one's quest as biases are not bad if they lead to useful action.[8] But in such a case it is only when some of the issues on which feelings become very intense does one resort to doing. The ratio of knowing, feeling and doing is like an inverted triangle. As explained earlier, our awareness about new knowledge is expanding exponentially. But are we developing feelings about some of these unsolved problems that we are coming to know about? The proportion of these problems which we actually act upon is even lesser.

A lot of people have known about the problems that creative people face in thousands of our villages. The buzz about start-up support systems often remains restricted to metropolitan or bigger cities. Even smaller towns are not touched, much less villages, except through the limited resources of various rural entrepreneurship institutions including the NIF. In such a case, either we can claim lack of knowledge of innovation-based entrepreneurial potential at the grassroots level in urban and rural areas, or maybe we acknowledge that our feelings are not as intense as to bring about policy and institutional reforms.

As mentioned earlier, I had thought about creating a portal like Techpedia back in 2002 and talked about it in an IT conference organized by the ministry of information technology. I had the know-how to create the portal to pool engineering projects from different colleges to promote originality in social and technological innovations. I felt strongly about this project because it was obvious to me that the tremendously talented youth were being overwhelmingly underutilized. But neither this knowledge nor my emotions succeeded in overcoming my inertia at the time. The project did not take off till a young boy named Hiranmay Mahanta offered to execute the idea in 2009. He has undertaken many more initiatives with other technological universities and institutions as a part of the SRISTI team. The idea has since evolved a lot more through the collective contribution of many other colleagues within and outside SRISTI and the *Honey Bee Network*. I still have many other ideas which I have not yet been able to implement, for instance, adopting a 'granny on the net'. The idea is that tales told by grandmothers and grandfathers should be recorded and uploaded on to the portal in order to preserve the wisdom of an entire generation that's increasingly lost on the youth. Children who want to partake in such storytelling, and whose parents have no time, or perhaps no skill and repertoire, to indulge them will be the intended audience. When they have already heard the existing stock of stories by a particular grandmother, whose tenor and tone they like, they will have the opportunity to request more stories. Their parents should then have the incentive to write to the portal, and pay for getting additional stories recorded (assuming that the same grandmother is still alive!). This is a sustainable system of storytelling, recording living traditions for the future generation to learn from and evolve with. Nothing of this kind exists at present, unfortunately. While we could accomplish a book on centenarians (*Shatayu: A Life Well Lived* released by the President of India, Shri Pranab Mukherjee, on 26 November 2015) in collaboration with Helpage Foundation, we have not been able create the portal as yet. Perhaps it is because we are missing a maverick who will passionately pursue this goal. Or maybe, the lack of this repertoire has not induced enough guilt. Maybe both.

Sometimes people do manage to modify the ratio of knowledge, feeling and doing and thus the steepness of the aforementioned triangle. The way feelings create restlessness and the consequent impatience for action also depends on the nature of gratification one seeks. When egoistic gratification (yearning for personal name, fame, wealth, recognition, etc.) is overpowered by social, result-oriented gratification (satisfaction from getting things done, by overcoming inertia for the larger social welfare), our actions may be influenced by altruistic motivations. This kind of behaviour is the opposite of what Ayn Rand recommends. She asks people to pursue self-interest and not be responsible towards others. One has one life to live (I agree with this part) and thus cannot be in pursuit of any goal other than the maximization of one's own happiness (I don't agree with this part), through self-esteem, reason and not faith (but without faith, can one ever take up seemingly impossible missions?). Instead, I argue that when reasons reach their limits, how does one get that extra ounce of energy which propels one to move over the hump? It comes from faith, in randomness, spontaneity and paradoxical ways of thinking.

When Mohammed Rozadeen, from Champaran, Bihar, inventor of a modification process that converts a pressure cooker into a coffee maker, was offered a small working capital support, he refused. He said that people who want a coffee maker generally bring their own cooker and copper wire into his workshop and then he modifies it for them. Whatever little he earns from that is enough. He didn't want more. We suggested that he could keep a few ready-made coffee makers on hand to sell. His reply was that his cost of production might go up, and the street vendors and tea shack owners who bought his device might not be able to afford it. Moreover, what motivated him to invent such a device in the first place? Surely, he shared the knowledge most of us have that a cooker produces steam. We also know that when ground coffee is processed with steam it becomes drinkable, like a cappuccino. Then, why was it only Rozadeen who made the connection between the pressure cooker and making coffee? It was his drive of providing additional means of livelihood to vendors, combined with his creativity, which converted the equation from knowledge to feeling to action.

Many innovators don't want to become entrepreneurs or earn too much money for themselves; some only wish that their knowledge is shared widely with those who can benefit from their work. Of course, a few are genuinely desirous of profiting and that's fine too. Greed of a few and need of many (as Gandhi said) have to be matched, through multiple pathways.

Earlier a number has been written as 200,000, using the international million/billion system. It has been marked. Here the Indian system of lakh/crore is used.

The story of Dharambir Kamboj, that I shared in chapters one and two, shows how he balanced the pursuit of personal profit with the creation of common goods. His enterprising spirit was reinforced by his *need* to convert his knowledge into feelings and then into action. His own past, in which his family had mistreated him for having wasted a lot of resources on experimentation, had made him more sensitive towards the struggles of people who were not appreciated by community members. He visits various communities in Meghalaya, Manipur, Sikkim etc., trains community members and shows them how to use machines to make products like juice, jams, jellies and sweets, and to extract essential oil from the seeds or peels. He has spent days at a stretch in the tribal regions of Rajasthan, like parts of Udaipur, where one discovers the most transformative story through the installation of his machine in the area and its linkage with markets. The local district forest officer, Mr Sharma, installed this machine along with Paresh Panchal's machine for making incense sticks and consequently increased the daily income of the tribals manifold. There are many forest offices but only a few care about really helping tribal communities in this manner. May their tribe increase. May they increase the connections among knowledge, feelings and actions.

Thus, there are many other people who may have knowledge as well as feelings, but are still not able to convert them into action because of missing triggers, a certain kind of personality, lack of spirit or just lack of impatience with the status quo. Sometimes, lack of resources may also come in the way. But those who believe in the dictum of imperfect beginnings don't complain about lack of resources. They just start somehow.

For example, when Abhishek Bhagat was a schoolboy, he was very keen to build a machine that could cook food that tasted exactly like his mother's when he would be away at a hostel after a year or two. He didn't know how to ensure that different ingredients as per a particular food recipe are dropped into the cooking vessel in a specific sequence in a given proportion at specific intervals. To solve the problem, he used a mechanical alarm clock in which the hands of the clock triggered the action of adding ingredients at the designated times. Many of us miss the taste of the food cooked by our mothers' hands, and yet, none of us have thought to invent the machine that Abhishek did. His feeling for reproducing the taste of his mother's dishes as closely as possible led him to experiment with the design of the machine. Abhishek later went on to receive the IGNITE award in 2009 and also the National Award from the president in 2012. We engaged a design company to make the machine better but a great deal of improvement is still pending. In any case, conceptual inertia was overcome.

Feelings can arise at any stage in life and be triggered by various causes. All of us feel good or bad, sad or happy, at different times in a day. Most of these feelings are ephemeral. They disappear. Sometimes they evaporate. Sometimes they are substituted by other feelings. But the same feeling or feelings of a similar intensity can produce very different reactions. We can reinforce or strengthen our inertia (or inaction) by dissipating these feelings. Some people convert these feelings to overcome their inertia and thus evolve them into art, and some take them as a motivating force for turning the gears of the engine of invention and innovation.

There is a very interesting passage in the book, *The Human Situation*[9] by W. M. Dixon published way back in 1937. The book is based on the Griffith Memorial Lecture delivered at the University of Glasgow during 1935–37. Once upon a time, the angels descended from the sky and met a beautiful little girl playing in a garden. 'You are a lovely girl. God will like to play with you. Will you come to heaven?' they asked her. The girl replied after a pause, 'Yes, I can come, provided I have the devil to play with.'

We know that whatever concept of God one may have, He is expected to play by the rules. But where is the fun in that? The devil will be mischievous because he is expected to challenge or change the rules of the game.

In the story, the little girl also thought that playing with the devil would be a more fun-filled experience. Many times, in our life, we restrain ourselves from taking action because we are afraid. This little girl was making a trade-off that favoured uncertainty of rules as well as outcome. With such dauntless spirit, she might actually become an entrepreneur! Here I don't want to be misunderstood. I am not recalling this passage (which I read in 1975 in a small lodge in Kadapa, Andhra Pradesh) to pass moral judgement about the need to follow rules. Obviously, nobody can make a lasting impact by not following the rules. But it is also clear that nobody has made it to the top by not breaking some rules. However, what rules we break and for what purpose determines the direction of our moral compass, an idea we will discuss in detail later. At this point, I must stress on the importance of courting uncertainty as a means of exploring new ideas.

Breaking Rules

One of the major factors that dampens initiative, despite having strong feelings about making a change, is the fear of an unexpected outcome and failure. Interestingly, even when the real probability of failure may be lower than the estimated probability,[10] we seem to avoid risk. But there are times we overestimate our ability and cause catastrophic failures. However, my view is that when extreme events are difficult to anticipate anyway, why should we reinforce inertia? When the cost of failure is low, we *must* try. When the cost of failure is high, we *should* still try if our heart says that we will lose our sanity if we don't. As I relayed before, there are 1000 reasons for not doing something, but there is only reason for doing it and that is wanting to do it. We need to now dig deep to understand the bedrock of these different feelings.

Feelings emerge both when our beliefs or memories are reinforced by circumstances and they also evolve when we face contradictions or paradoxes that challenge our belief systems. It is not always easy to be aware of the source of our feelings. Suppressed desires can create strange spectacles of feelings inside our hearts such that when somebody opens a door we might not accept what we see behind the door. It is our lack of control over our feelings after all that makes us human. If we control the moment, we will miss the opportunity to surprise ourselves.[11] Nevertheless, too little control makes us impulsive while too much makes us extremely introverted, and sometimes we may appear stony. A river cannot flow without being restrained by its banks. How much restraint we exercise is an appropriate measure of our moral strength.

In the famous novel *The Mandarins*, Simone de Beauvoir narrates an interesting dilemma faced by Jean-Paul Sartre, Beauvoir's lifelong companion, as the editor of the famous French paper, *Le Monde*. Sartre, rather Henri as fictional character in the novel, had sent a correspondent to the USSR to ascertain the veracity of the rumours about concentration camps in the country. The correspondent came back with evidence of the presence of such camps in which several famous dissenters had been sent for forced labour. Henri was in a difficult position: Should he publish the story in *L'Espoir* or not? If he were to publish it, he would harm the interests of socialism. If he were not to publish it, he would disregard the ethics of journalism. Eventually, Henri chose to run the article. Beauvoir had written critically about such ambiguity in feelings.[12] Many of us are confronted with a choice to bend, crawl or stand upright. The whistle-blowers face this dilemma most intensely.

The famous case of the biggest class-action suit against the cigarette industry in the USA brings out another interesting dilemma faced by an executive. Despite persistent denial by the cigarette industry, Jeffery Wigand knew that companies added certain chemicals to the composition of the cigarette, which caused addiction. He decided to establish evidence against the industry regardless of numerous threats and the breakdown of his own family. He lost almost everything in his life, but the evidence, which he was finally able to procure and present, helped save millions of lives. As one of the first whistle-blowers, he must have found it very difficult to control his feelings for sharing the truth. When silence envelops problems affecting millions in society through a kind of hidden conspiracy—a common mindset which legitimizes neglect of that problem for a long time—one needs whistle-blowers to battle this kind of inertia. In fact, innovators are actually like whistle-blowers, since in a sense they are questioning a kind of silence. That is how the concept of deviant research (*New Scientist*, 2007) makes sense.

Another case of whistle-blowing is narrated by Sucheta Dalal, then a young journalist. She was once invited to lecture in my class at IIMA. She described the story of a series of events, and provided the evidence that blew the curtain off the Harshad Mehta scam. It was a scam in which bankers through fictitious receipts had lent a lot of money to brokers and speculators who in turn manipulated the stock market. They had inflated the prices of shares of certain companies almost 100 to 1000 times over a short period. When Sucheta exposed this scam in 1992, the market crashed, one bank chairman committed suicide, and thousands of investors lost all their life savings. There was a whistle-blower who used to meet her in a nondescript Irani restaurant in Mumbai and provide her with insider tips for each article that she wrote. Nobody knows much about the source except her. But the country wouldn't have been able to get to the truth without his help. To understand the whistle-blower's point of view we must ask: Why do some people develop these intense feelings for doing with determination what they think they must? They take the necessary risks involved even while knowing the consequences of failure, should the powers that be become vindictive. This fortuitous capacity can emerge in our heart with a little effort to be more ourselves. Once the feeling of intense discomfort with a given situation takes hold of us, we tend not to worry about other consequences. Has anybody ever achieved anything meaningful without somehow being possessed by the feeling of doing something risky, uncomfortable? Basically, it may appear irrational to many as to why a person wants to pursue one's passion so uncontrollably that it makes no sense to most people around. But if approval from people around became a condition for taking initiative, how many innovators would actually exist in the world?

Whenever we take recourse to an alibi, an excuse or a subterfuge, we short-change ourselves. We deliberately discount our beliefs. We tend to treat our feelings with less respect than they deserve. And every time we do that, doing it again the next time becomes easier.

While knowledge keeps on expanding, the breadth and depth of feelings don't necessarily follow suit. Feelings can get constricted. That is why those who have less often give more. The ability to feel more, connect more and give more are linked to the ability to go through samvedana, as mentioned earlier.

Philosophically speaking, it is difficult to argue that we ever give anything. We only share. There is a very meaningful concept in the Vedic mantras vis-à-vis *idanna mama* (that is, 'it is not mine'). The implication of this notion is that what I offer to others or to any supreme force was never mine to begin with. How then can I have a feeling that I am the giver? I am not a giver. I am only a receiver. But, we can just share what we have. Everybody else can feel that they have received something without anybody really giving that to them. How does this happen. It is often the feeling of gratitude experienced while giving which gets captured in the concept of anonymity of an altruistic act. Our culture says that when the left hand gives, the right hand should not come to know of it. When the 'giver' feels more grateful for the opportunity to share, the gift becomes a celebration of gratitude. It is not the 'giving' that we celebrate but 'receiving' of grace that becomes the basis of creating a web of social good.

This selfless way of serving society is evident among several of our grassroots innovators. One such innovator, Ganesh Dodiya, had developed a motorcycle-based sprayer. When GIAN approached him for further development, Ganeshbhai replied that he had done his bit and offered the GIAN to take the project in any direction it wished. There are so many innovators who have put their knowledge in public domain for the larger social good. When Amrutbhai had developed the modified pulley for drawing water from the open wells, he also generously decided to put it in public domain. The tens of thousands innovations and practices that the Honey Bee Network has put in public domain could not have been possible without such generosity of the knowledge providers.

But how have we treated such feelings of generosity?

Feelings can transmute our sense of being. George Santayana, the great philosopher, notes in his treatise called *Reason in Science*, 'a memory is a rumour'. Thus, our concept of the past changes. Even Gandhi has recalled different events differently in his various recollections. It is not because he was being untruthful, but because the context of what he remembered metamorphosed over time. If our meanings of 'past perfect' do not remain constant, will our meaning of 'future indefinite' ever remain static? We construct our past, we unfold our future and the present sometimes slips away. It is by living in the present that we can be detached and thus share our knowledge more easily and with more awareness.

It is well established that we would become deeply depressed if we were empathetic towards all the problems and sufferings and wrongdoings of the world. A little bit of schizophrenia becomes inevitable. How else can the imagination flourish, if the worlds of action and reflection are always in balance?

This subject has engaged researchers worldwide. There are, of course, many creative people who have had no history of suffering or mental illness, even minor ones. But they also have had the ability to imagine beyond the constraints of the real world around them. A disconnect from the world, which can be touched and felt, is the minimum condition for fertilizing imagination.

Scott Barry Kaufman (scientific director of the Imagination Institute in the Positive Psychology Center, University of Pennsylvania, USA, and co-founder of *The Creativity Post*) observes:[13]

What's more, only a few of us ever reach eminence. Beghetto and Kaufman (2007) argue that we can display creativity in many different ways, from the creativity inherent in the learning process ('mini-c'), to everyday forms of creativity ('little-c') to professional-level expertise in any creative endeavor ('Pro-c'), to eminent creativity ('Big-C'). Engagement in everyday forms of creativity (Richards, 2007)—expressions of originality and meaningfulness in daily life—certainly do not require suffering. Quite the contrary, people who engage in everyday forms of creativity—such as making a collage, taking photographs, or publishing in a literary magazine—tend to be more open-minded, curious, persistent, positive, energetic, and intrinsically motivated by their activities (Ivcevic, 2007; Ivcevic and Mayer, 2009). Those scoring high in everyday creativity also tend to report feeling a greater sense of well-being and personal growth compared to their classmates who engage less in everyday creative behaviors.

But then in the same blog post he notes:

> One aspect of creativity is obviously novelty or originality. Schizophrenic thoughts are more likely to be unique or new. So, by its very nature, schizophrenia disposes one toward satisfying one requirement for creative thought: namely originality . . . Schizotypal traits can be broken down into two types. 'Positive' schizotypy includes unusual perceptual experiences, thin mental boundaries between self and other, impulsive nonconformity, and magical beliefs. 'Negative' schizotypal traits include cognitive disorganization and physical and social anhedonia (difficulty experiencing pleasure from social interactions and activities that are enjoyable for most people). Nettle (2006) found that people with schizotypy typically resemble schizophrenia patients much more along the positive schizotypal dimensions (such as unusual experiences) compared to the negative schizotypal dimensions (such as lack of affect and volition).

Finally Kaufman concludes:

> Nevertheless, recent research suggests that creative cognition draws on both the executive functioning

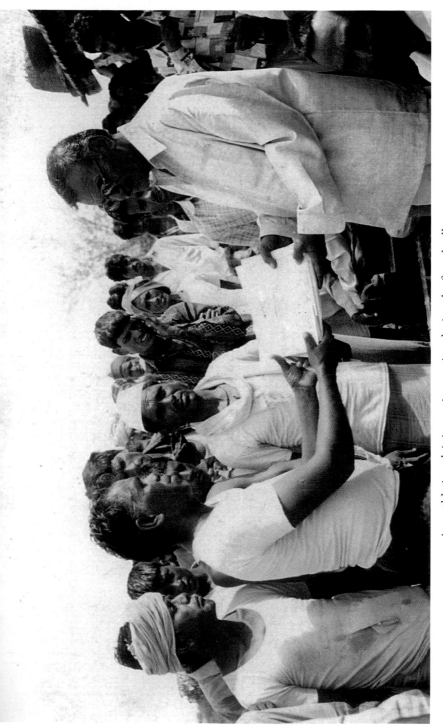

Amrutbhai explaining an innovation during the first shodhyatra.

New (top) and old windmills, developed by Mehtar Hussain and Mushtaq Ahmed from Assam. It was originally intended to pump water for irrigating a small paddy field. Through GIAN it was later adapted for pumping brine to fill salt pans in Gujarat to save on the cost of diesel.

Natural double-decker root bridge, Cherrapunji, Meghalaya.

Interacting with shodhyatris during the Meghalaya shodhyatra.

Dharambir, from Yamunanagar, Haryana, with his
old, multipurpose food-processing machine.

Mallesham's mother, from Andhra Pradesh, working on a conventional asu machine.

Mallesham, with his new programmable asu machine,
at the FOIN exhibition held at the Rashtrapati Bhavan.

Dr A.P.J. Abdul Kalam interacting with creative children
at the IGNITE awards function held at IIMA.

Ms Pratibha Patil, former president of India, honouring Arkhiben.

Autopoiesis: a self-correcting, self-designed and self-governed innovation akin to auto repair of error by this tree.

Scholars-in-residence with the President of India in 2015.

Nattubhai Vadher with his cotton-ball plucking machine.

Shodhyatris marching to the next village (shodhyatra in Purulia, West Bengal, 2007).

Children draw their creative ideas (shodhyatra in Tripura, 2015).

Artwork on a clay grain bin by Ram Tamari Devi, who knew no other way of making an ordinary bin (shodhyatra in Champaran, Bihar, 2008).

Terracotta horses under a tree: creating open-source standards of excellence (shodhyatra in Purulia, West Bengal, 2007).

Kanubhai got pithora paintings drawn on his wall by an artist named Babubhai, when his prayers for healing a sickness in the family were answered (shodhyatra in Panchmahal, Gujarat, 2009).

Chhaya Thakore, Class VII, presents her idea of an inclined drinking-water pipe to enable children of different heights to drink water easily (Gandhinagar, Gujarat, 2014).

The designing of a circular kiln to bake some clay pots by Mansukhbhai was not just a 'jugaad' (Gujarat).

Mitti Cool products by Mansukhbhai Prajapati include the clay fridge and numerous other pots, bottles, etc.

Sadhana Gupta felicitating a lady who brought a special food dish with some uncultivated ingredients in it (Rajasthan 2002).

A woman brick-maker (shodhyatra in Wardha, 2013).

Chandrasekhar, a brick-kiln worker from Andhra Pradesh, invented a brick-making machine that led to a fifty-fold increase in productivity. He is also a winner of the NIF national award in 2015.

Khimjibhai designed a device that shifts the load from the head to the shoulders (Gujarat, 2002).

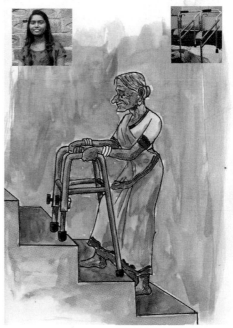

Modified walker, a universal design suggested by Shalini, a prototype of which was made in the NIF 'fab lab' in 2012.

Arthi, Vinotha and Laila, from Tamil Nadu, suggested a mechanism by which the motorcycle will not start unless one wears a helmet. The Bluetooth-based system was designed by the NIF team with the help of fabricators.

To prevent hand injuries while cutting chaff, Kamruddin Saifi invented an auto-clutch system with a pedal break, discovered during the shodhyatra in Uttar Pradesh in 2006.

Sajid Khan, a young innovator from Ranchi, presenting his rice cleaner during the shodhyatra in Jharkhand.

Gurmel Singh Dhonsi with his invention, the tree pruner.

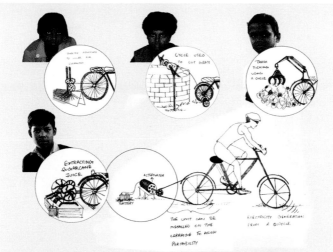

Multiple uses of a cycle suggested by children in the creativity workshop held at the Rashtrapati Bhavan during FOIN, 2015

An innovation to benefit the public in Jharkhand.

Ralte with his incense-stick making machine.

James Cameron keenly listens to Rai Singh Dahiya talk about the biomass gasifier.

A potter's family showcases their crafts and skills.

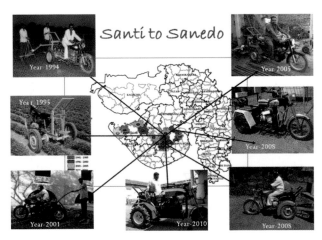

Santi, a motorcycle-based ploughing machine innovated by Mansukhbhai Jagani.

Wood lathe (shodhyatra in Dhemaji, Assam).

Roshanlal Vishwakarma working on the sugarcane-bud chipper that he created.

Kanak Das's cycle that generates energy from bumps.

An inquisitive girl trying the tree climber
(shodhyatra in Anantnag, Jammu and Kashmir).

that is tied to Intellect and the associative divergence that comes with Openness. Being susceptible to schizophrenia spectrum disorders may enhance Openness, increasing the likelihood of ideas that are original. To develop ideas that are creative, however, one also needs protective intellectual factors (and autistic-like traits) to steer the chaotic storm.

Therefore I reiterate, some distance from reality is needed, I feel, for innovators to deal with frequent rejection, neglect and, sometimes, hostilities. Our local community ecosystem has not been always appreciative of local innovators till outsiders have recognized them. Our contention is not with the negative side of the schizotypal condition but only the positive side, which also leads to more openness, as mentioned above. Without being open to new ideas and feedback from the outside, how can one expect an innovation to go forward? And yet, many innovators who remain stuck with their work in progress are those who refuse to take external feedback easily. When too deeply embedded, a person cannot adequately distance himself from reality. The conditions around himself may be constraining sometimes and outright frustrating at other times. Yet, deepening of the imagination takes place through detours; those fanciful visions which lead an optimistic innovator to see hope which most people suffering from inertia are not able to see.

The question we must bear in mind is which imperfections around us trigger specific feelings and make us impatient enough to take action. And moreover, what conditions sustain inertia while which conditions help one overcome it? It has to be realized that not all things can change at the same time, especially if meaningful breakthroughs are to be achieved. In which functions, form or features of a device or contraption, will one choose to maintain inertia, and in which aspects will change be attempted is a crucial decision for the success of an innovation.

Even passionate people are not passionate about everything. Some things really bother them and they cannot live without changing them, or at least trying to do so. On the other hand, the same people cannot find time for many other things which don't seem as important to them. A *passion* does not lead to performance automatically; it may need purpose, persistence and platform to facilitate the transition. I know of so many artists, teachers, innovators whose life got new meanings when their talent was recognized at an early stage. They did not have much of a clue about their own potential. The Honey Bee Network became a platform which connected such people with earlier achievers. Many of these achievers had many interests but they knew that they couldn't be outstanding in all their faculties. They had to specialize. They had to make a choice.

Calibration of one's sensitivities is thus essential. For example, the public sanitation standards are very different in India compared to private standards of individuals and households. The same people who keep their homes very clean are responsible for dirtying public places. Naturally, such people have not developed the same feelings towards both the contexts. In any organization, empathy is fundamental to trigger designs that engage one with them long enough to make a significant impact. We cannot win on all fronts, as said earlier. We should learn to lose on some fronts graciously. But, while engaging with a multitude of problems, one inevitably has to disengage with some of them.

One's feelings even about the same thing don't remain constant. The parents without whom we cannot live at one stage in our life become dispensable, so much so that one may not meet them for months and sometimes for years. It is not that one's affection has reduced over time, but that certain other affections may have taken priority. Feelings about work and other priorities in life also change. Maybe that is okay. Maybe not. Most scriptures advise us that excessive attachment to people, places, things and ideas can come in the way of pursuing new paths. This feeling, I will, however, leave to each person to resolve in his or her own way, without suggesting which way is better than others. We need to accept these trade-offs.

So long as this change (in our views about challenges we face or the ways to treating the social inertia around us) doesn't become a kind of opportunism, one can live with it, but when opportunism takes over, the definition of what should change and what should remain constant undergoes a shift. In such a case, one cannot be sure whether one's feelings truly reflect one's consciousness. The mind can play tricks on us in this way. Kinship networks do not always support the innovators in their efforts. Dharambir was neglected by his family. In fact his father and elder brother separated him from the family because he was seen to be spending too much money on his experiments, as explained earlier. Gopalbhai Suratiya from Bharuch, Gujarat, used to work at night on his four-wheel sprayer fearing that his family would become upset over what they might think of as wasting money. Mustaqeen, in western Uttar Pradesh, made an experimental helicopter keeping it hidden from his family and community. He and his friends were afraid that his family may not permit him to take up such gigantic task. Of course, it did not work much and the police did not let him try it out without testing and clearance since it could have posed threat to other people in case of a mishap.

When we convert our feelings into actions, we are conscious of the fact that not all actions are persisted with. Certain actions we take and forget; some are remembered, and some turn into habit. Once habits are formed, one no longer needs triggers of feelings. How we generate feedback from our actions depends upon the criteria we use to evaluate our actions. Many innovators persist with their experiments for decades and suffer a lot of losses. Still, they continue with their mission even if success is partial or sometimes elusive. But there are also innovators who take feedback from different quarters, fight with their feelings and accept changes, which may not have occurred to them in the first place. If they take feedback too often, they may miss their goals. If they don't take feedback at all, they may miss potential of improving their existing design. The middle path is not always clear. With oscillating extremes the middle cannot be constant anyway, but it *is* possible to be aware of such conditions. There are many innovators who remain stuck in the conception stages even if the operational significance of that is minimal. One such innovator had visualized using compressed air to pump water. Of course the pump did work with the air being compressed in a chamber using an electric compressor. A suggestion was made to try the same in a cycle rickshaw to help rickshaw pullers in navigating climbs. But then, to have sufficient air pressure, one needed a bigger tank, high-pressure air and stronger material. Several of these constraints could not be resolved. Other innovators had used compressed air to run a scooter or a car over a few kilometres. But none of them could completely succeed because they could not get the feedback they deserved or have access to new materials, and mentoring, to make this happen. Nor did they receive feedback to find a middle ground and develop a hybrid model to use multiple sources of fuel. When a major auto company imported such technology from France, we faxed the availability of these model technologies with the NIF to them but somehow the company concerned did not show interest in scaling up these grassroots innovations. In such a case, it was not lack of feelings on the part of innovators but by the company, which came in the way.

Disempowering Feelings

Often by chance, sometimes by design, we come across instances that reinforce our insignificance. We choose a small pond in which we can be a big frog; or do the opposite, choose a big pond in which we are a small frog. We can assume a lot of importance in a small pond or expand our peer group and recognize our relative unimportance.[14] But it is not necessary that humility[15] should breed disempowerment. On the contrary, humility is often a trait of empowered people. Like most actions then, disempowerment can also be deliberate. In many asymmetrical power situations, controlling one's power and behaving in a dominating way can be counteracted by invoking feelings of disempowerment in oneself. This seems paradoxical. But doesn't the famous hymn by the poet Kabir suggest that branches of trees which bear the most fruits always bend down? Another hymn tells us that there is no point in being as big as a date palm which doesn't give any shade to travellers and even the fruits are born after a long time.[16] It is not always the case that innovators are humble, but when they are, they go very far, as the following examples unequivocally show us: Dharambir, who made a multipurpose food-processing machine; Rajsingh Dhaiya, who developed a biomass gasifier; Gurmel Singh, who developed many machines including a tree pruner; Amrutbhai Agrawat, who developed more than a dozen innovations including the modified water pulley and tilting bullock cart; Paresh Panchal, whose machine for making bamboo stick became popular even in tribal areas; and Maltiben,[17] one of the most pioneering small-scale entrepreneurs of dairy in the Mehsana district of Gujarat.

Submission and surrender do not always evoke weakness. They can also imply an ability to be enormously compassionate. It seems that some others may take advantage of this trait of a person, but then, in the long term, one is always richer in one's spirit. The unwillingness to be humble also comes in the way of seeking opportunities to learn from unexpected quarters.

Recently, in a community course[18] I taught at IIMA on the Art of Knowing, Feeling and Doing, I invited a twelve-year-old girl named Chhaya, who was in Class VII, from a village in Gandhinagar, as a guest faculty member. Her father worked in a shop and her mother tended to a small farm. As mentioned earlier, Chhaya is the same girl who had been honoured for contributing an idea about an inclined water pipe with taps set at different heights to enable children of varying heights to drink water easily. When I first met her, I asked her why she had thought of this idea. She said that the teacher had given the class an assignment and asked everybody to contribute an idea about a problem that they were facing at a very practical level, which prompted her to think of the idea. Now if SRISTI had not organized the competition in 600 villages of the Gandhinagar district, we would not have created a context whereby Chhaya would have had an opportunity to generate and contribute her idea. Out of the 5000 ideas we received, her idea made it to the top. *Context*, therefore, is important in influencing the *content* of our consciousness. Chhaya was the winner and was invited to attend my lectures because she not only identified a problem, but also found a solution and actually had it implemented through her network teachers and community members. I wanted my students to learn by seeing: If a young child could overcome her inertia, could not they also do so? I had been to hundreds of schools during our field visits and shodhyatras, had seen numerous such drinking fountain built with standard-design water taps but it had never occurred to me that children of different heights could face a problem in drinking water. For all of sixty-seven years after Independence, nobody before Chhaya had bothered about this problem in the country. That does not reduce my guilt of not having recognized this problem earlier and thus having failed to be more sensitive. It is not enough to be humble and open to learn from unexpected quarters but we also have to admit, self-critically, our acts of commission and omission. It was important for my students to learn that an innovative solution by a rural child could change the learning context of other senior students and participants at IIMA. And that it had not occurred to me despite my extensive shodhyatras around the country.

The context of feelings thus defines the content of our action and also whether we feel empowered or disempowered. If one has a sense of responsibility, even a hopeless situation cannot be disempowering and provides one with courage to strive for change. On the other hand, a cynical person will convert the most hopeful situation into a hopeless one because of doubt and denial of any and all possibilities. The disempowering feelings may also be influenced by the company we keep. Lack of challenge and provocation in our environment may further create complacency. For the last sixty-seven years, people had seen the problem of same-height taps for short and tall children at school. They knew the problem and its consequences for the children. If they had tried, they could have found the answer. Their initial solution might have been costlier and less elegant, but eventually, by listening to the feedback of other people, users and non-users alike, a solution would have probably emerged. But it didn't. People with much greater knowledge may not always have the corresponding sensitivity to develop strong feelings that push them to look for innovative solutions. The fear of rejection, the possibility of being mocked, unsure assessment, lack of intrinsic motivation, lack of awareness about the solution, lack of confidence, and many other reasons could prevent the conversion of knowledge of a problem to a feeling of impatience that drives one to search for solutions.

Let me illustrate with another example of how children sometimes overcome their inertia much faster than adults, and thus, if only we can let them do that more often and learn this art from them, the world can change faster and for the better. Affan was one of the participants in the children creativity workshop organized by SRISTI as a part of the Festival of Innovation, in collaboration with the United Nation Children's Fund (UNICEF). When the children visited different slums in Delhi, they noticed that many localities had only one common municipal drinking water tap and people had to queue up for filling their personal water pots. What Affan suggested was to have a pipe with several distribution taps to allow say at least six to seven people to fill water from one tap at the same time (like a tanker has several taps). It does not matter that he did not know that a public innovation project in Jharkhand

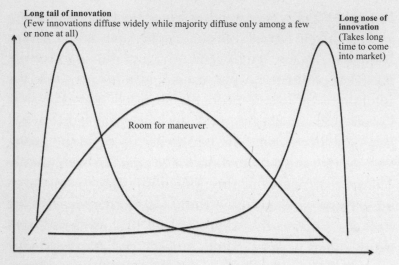

5.1 Long tail of innovation

had actually worked out something very similar, with a handpump in a primary school to enable more children to drink water.

The Answers for Taking Action Rest Inside

With the topic of innovative thinking thrown wide open in the multiple contexts in which it could occur, it is but natural that many innovators have imperfect beginnings. If they waited for a perfect understanding, they would possibly never begin. Many people who procrastinate possibly do so because they wait for the perfect moment or the perfect amount of information. Over the years I have realized that the opportune moments for doing and taking action is not an external circumstance. The answer is not *outside*; it is *inside*. The seeds of impatience have to sprout in the soil of subtle expectations. Another famous story comes to mind: There was a drought in a region. People were suffering as a due result. In a village located in a nearby interior area, all the community members gathered one day and decided to pray for rainfall at a temple located outside the village. The next day, everybody gathered again at the fixed time and started walking towards the temple. A little boy, who was carrying an umbrella with him, joined the group. Some elderly people asked him, 'Why are you carrying an umbrella?' The little boy replied, 'Aren't we all going to pray? Isn't it of course going to rain?' One may call the boy's response naivety or tremendous faith. The other people clearly lacked both. Expectations can do wonders. For want of a better word, I will say that only by expecting miracles can we really manifest them in our life. To me, a miracle is not something imaginary or magical. A miracle is the possibility of something happening when the chances are very remote, and the dice is loaded against us. Except faith and a little bit of ingenuity, what else can one do?

When birds weave their nests, they are very careful about what kind of sticks they collect and how they create a structure that is sure to hold the weight of the eggs, the chicks and the parents. Among a certain kind of weaver birds, when the male makes the nest and the female bird does not like it, she destroys it. The male has to weave the nest again. One could look at this phenomenon and say that maybe she is trying to bring out the best in the male bird; perhaps it can be considered as a form of feedback. Maybe she has a better assessment of what kind of strength is needed in the nest. Maybe he has the *skills* and she has the sensitivity of feeling. Both together, complete the story.

Impatience for Action

While walking through villages, we come across many innovations, but we also came across areas of inertia, where change had not taken place. Obviously, the inertia is not uniformly distributed across the country. Why some people feel impatient for action and others don't has been a constant question for us. But recently, while walking in the Mahendragarh district of Haryana, we came across several examples of cycle- or wheel-based weeders to remove weeds from the crop fields. These were being developed de novo, though some versions do exist elsewhere. In each case, the design was different and the way the problem was defined was also different. And yet, each solution was an active response to a local definition of the problem. In almost every case, communities outside the village were either not aware of what was going on, or if aware, hadn't really tested out the new solution. In such cases, one cannot wait for recognition to arise before interest in replicating the solution gathers mass. Individuals who have taken the initiative to solve problems may not go house-to-house parading and promoting their ideas. Even when action takes place, sufficient diffusion often does not. Perhaps the societal hunger for new ideas is weak. It may also be that the extreme specialization of the design to a particular solution as per precise local conditions prevents its diffusion in dissimilar contexts. Or—and I much prefer this approach—maybe the localized nature of diffusion is the right approach to problem solving. Why should we deny the legitimacy of those solutions which have neatly addressed local problems as illustrated by the long tail of innovations?[19]

The long tail implies that while a few ideas may diffuse widely, a very large number diffuse only in limited numbers and some not at all. Many small innovations remain localized to their embedded niches Will the goal of social, ecological and cultural diversity—which are vital for sustainability—be served well only if we developed solutions which diffuse *widely*? Will not the niche-specific problems remain unattended? Even in the agriculture industry, climate change risks are compounded with mono culture (that is one crop/variety occupying a large area); thus a few crop varieties occupy millions of hectares. Similarly, locally distributed manufacturing, whether through 3D printing or otherwise, may not flourish if the old model of centralized manufacturing and decentralized consumption continues to rule the roost. The time has come when scale cannot be made the enemy of sustainability. We cannot expect that a solution to a local problem should always be envisaged through scaling up and affecting a larger population, so that the innovation can be thought of as successful. The location- or niche-specific problems will need to be addressed. If scientists and technologists are promoted only on the basis of the area occupied by the technologies developed by them, then they will have no incentive for addressing problems of smaller communities. Some of these neglected and underserved or unserved communities may then feel alienated. It is not surprising that in many such neglected regions, we find much more incidence of insurgency or social unrest.

Let me illustrate the above paradox with an example of a problem we came across during the twenty-fourth shodhyatra in the Dhemaji district of Assam in 2009. The drinking water in the Dhemaji district had very high iron content. The local community members innovated and created simple water filters in canisters that contained gravel, pebbles, sand, etc. The resultant filtered water seemed completely clean. But when the yatris filled up this water in bottles and resumed their walk, the water turned brown after a while due to oxidation of the iron that was still present in the water. So, in this case, local innovation was not adequate in solving the problem completely. Conventional filters might not be the ideal purification mechanism and as the size of the market was small, large companies would not be compelled to innovate and manufacture easily affordable water filters for such regions. In such situations, do we wait till the problem expands before we begin to address it? Should we ignore the needs of communities whose own solutions may not be optimal because the scale is limited? It is at this cross section that the blending of formal and informal knowledge and innovations can help.

Now let's explore this paradox further to understand the differences between seeing, observing, abstracting, understanding and assimilating.

Many times, while walking or driving on the road, we *see* millions of objects, but we don't *observe* a majority of them. What we observe or notice may depend on a prior experience or interest or a future concern or curiosity. Having noticed something, we then try to summarize or *abstract* it in our mind. This step helps in subsequent recall. We may consequently *understand* some of our observations/notices partially or more fully. Only then does the observation and its meaning *assimilate* with our prior individual knowledge system. Many times, what we assimilate at one point in time is reinterpreted in the light of subsequent experiences and therefore re-assimilation takes place.

During the twentieth shodhyatra, from Purulia and Patamda to Bankura, in West Bengal in 2008, after finishing a noontime meeting, I was left behind, along with a few other yatris, because of an extended discussion in the village. We were a small group in the rear with a folded banner walking towards the next village. There, a few people were standing on the roadside, keenly watching us. As is our wont, we invariably ask in every gathering about any new innovation or oddity observed by the people we meet. An eye for oddity makes the Honey Bee Network (even sometimes referred to as) a network of odd balls!

We stopped and asked these people, 'Have you come across someone who has tried something new or different?' They denied having seen anyone of this kind. I persisted and asked whether they had tried anything different. The answer was same that they hadn't. I was not going to give up easily. Suddenly, I observed that one of the bystanders had a sparkle in his eye. I turned towards him and said, 'You have done something new, surely, have not you?' He smiled and then said yes, he had done a successful experiment. He had two cucurbit vines of bottle gourd and round gourd. One of the vines flowered early and the fruit set a whole month before the other one. To precipitate the other's ripening, he fused the two vines together by making a small section of air layering. His assumption was that the vine that flowered early would take nutrients from the second one and later, the second one would take nutrients from the first. By that time, the first one would have finished fruiting. Therefore, both vines would receive additional nutrients during their flowering and fruit-bearing stage. We would have missed learning about this very interesting example had we not paused and looked for the sparkle in the eyes of the strangers. Just an intense curiosity can trigger the search and discovery of creativity. Maybe, if we are not surprised often and discover more such examples, it is merely because we are not curious and patient enough.

The faith, that there are such people everywhere who experiment, triggers the search for a sparkle. It is not that we have succeeded every time on every mission, but we have succeeded enough times to carry this resounding faith. How else would the database of the Honey Bee Network grow to be so large?

During the shodhyatra in the Malnad region of Karnataka, we were having a village meeting and listening to the examples of different kinds of traditional knowledge practices which had recently been implemented in one case or another. In particular, there was an old healer who had developed many practices to cure dog bite cases. Seeing us pay so much attention and respect to that old healer, a young boy got up and asked loudly what was so special about him and his practice. The boy claimed he also knew which plant administered the same cure. Everybody became quiet on sensing the boy's anger. I said, 'All right. Let us figure out the reason for our actions.' We asked the people sitting there to raise their hands if they had had a dog bite case in the last three months. There were three people. We asked them who they went to when faced with the problem. They all pointed to the old healer. We asked the young boy if he understood the underlying message. By then, many people had realized the importance of our point. When people had trouble, they went to the old healer and not to the young boy, the latter not being perceived as an expert. Knowing the name and a few characteristics of a medicine was not enough. To know what precautions and supplements are needed, and under what conditions a medicine will work or not work was a complex skill. No healer could be successful by only knowing the specific uses of each plant. He or she would also have to know how to diagnose the problem and accurately decide the dosage and the method of dispensing the solution (sometimes the application varies from person to person). The young boy did also not claim knowledge in most of the functions associated with the actual treatment. It was clear that people in the community respected not just the unique set of knowledge but also one's ability to link that knowledge with users' needs. Local knowledge systems and institutions often have rules embedded in them that ensure that knowledge and skill are used by experts in creative and compassionate

ways to solve local problems. The community respected
the old healer but neglected the young boy who had
knowledge because he did not have the necessary
diagnostic skills to understand patients' needs on a case
by case basis. In this sense, local knowledge systems are
reasonably complex. Yet, there are a few clear patterns
that emerge. Very seldom, mere awareness of a specific
bit of knowledge evokes respect from the community
members. Reduction to practice is one trait that many
societies seem to have a greater respect for

When we were walking in the Araku Valley region of
Andhra Pradesh, we came across a village resettlement
which had been relocated to higher ground after the old
village was completely destroyed by a massive landslide.
A lot of people died and many houses were damaged.
We organized a biodiversity competition in the village
where, as you may recall, each child was asked to bring
samples of different plants growing around them and
explain the usage of those plants. Most of the children
went to only one side of the hillock and brought only
around ten to fifteen plants each, that too of a very
similar variety. On the other hand, Jyoti, who we later
learnt had lost her mother in the landslide, brought
about twenty-five plant samples, all of different varieties.
Immediately we recognized that this girl had a special
eye for diversity. When we asked about her parents, the
girl started crying. Somebody then told us that Jyoti's
father had remarried after she lost her mother. She was
being brought up by her grandparents. It became clear
that the elderly generation's careful grooming, attention
and distinct approach to her upbringing had opened her

eyes in a way that she could observe the world around her in ways that the other children didn't pay much attention to. While it was painful to hear her story, it was gratifying to see how she had evolved into such a strong individual because of it. We gave her a few books and few other gifts before moving to the next village. Everybody was flabbergasted as to how greater interaction with her grandparents had brought so much sensitivity in the eyes of Jyoti towards diversity. We have observed that nature-dependent communities and families invariably have a rich repertoire of knowledge about how to classify plants, mushrooms, even animal parts, and then find contingent uses for different parts of the same. If one looks at the words a language has for different waves, clouds, soils, ferns, creepers, wood, etc., one can figure out how that society has evolved over millennia. Human survival requires dependence on various resources vulnerable to climatic and other human-induced vicissitudes. If the Eskimo community depends on snow, they have to classify the variance or fluctuations in its different forms. One way to do so is through labelling, i.e., coining a word or phrase for it. That is how Franz Boas triggered a more than 100-year-old controversy on finding more than a dozen words for snow. Now it is supposed to be fifty kinds of descriptions of different conditions for snow through a variety of words and combinations thereof.[20] Farmers have more than a dozen different words for soil, coastal fishermen have the same for waves and so on. This ability imbues among such communities and the children among them to acquire unique insights about nature which urban children may often lack. Unless we value such knowledge, so critical for coping with climate change in the future, we will lose this precious knowledge.

The relationship between grandparents and grandchildren has generally been a one-way street. Grandparents want to give, give and give and the grandchildren expect to take, take and take. Of course, in the process of sharing their love, knowledge and ideas, grandparents also get joy and happiness. With the trend of nuclear families increasingly gaining traction, the time children actually spend with their grandparents has been significantly lower. I always ask my students at IIMA when they last talked to or visited their grandparents in the past year. The importance of this particular relationship lies in the transfer of certain values and traditional knowledge that takes place from one generation to another. I believe that more traditional knowledge has been eroded in the current century than perhaps ever before in the history of humankind because of weakening inter-generational links and the breakdown of joint family system. Grassroots innovations involve improvements on traditional practices, resources or skills, and traditional ways of knowing and experimenting. But often, these are completely unrelated to traditional knowledge systems. Jyoti could identify twenty-five different plants while other children went to exactly the the same places and collected the same plants. Innovations require going on the path less travelled after all.

In the Alwar district of Rajasthan, a similar biodiversity competition was organized and a boy got a small prize for having made a list of seventy plants with their uses. For some reason, it occurred to me that he was probably capable of documenting much more information; so I asked him why he collected only this much when he could have done better. The boy replied he could of course have, if only he had more time. He then asked us for more time to prove his credentials. I said all right and told him to meet us after a few days with a list of at least 500 plants. Ten times higher expectation in just three days. Other shodhyatris felt that the boy wouldn't come. After three days, he took a bicycle and found us during our walk through the villages. He knew the route plan of the shodhyatra. He had a notebook which had a list of 500 plants with their uses. We had never met anybody with so much distinction. It was easy for us to be satisfied with the seventy plants he had brought to us in the first instance. Whether it was his innate talent, or our excessive expectation or the combination of both that did the trick, it is difficult to say. But it was clear that expectations matter. I cannot restrain myself from repeating what I must have said a thousand times, 'One cannot commit a bigger crime than expecting less from oneself and lesser from others.' Are we not trapped in a culture of low-expectation–low-achievement syndrome? In order to trigger more innovations in any system at any level, we should begin by expecting more in the first place. And when an innovation does indeed arise, we should pay attention to it and not hesitate to appreciate it.

The story of techpedia.sristi.org is similar. As briefly mentioned, it is a portal created by SRISTI that has summaries and titles of more than 1,90,000 engineering projects from over 500 institutions. Hiranmay at that time was a third-year student at Sardar Vallabhai National Institute of Technology (SVNIT), Surat. He had come to invite me for a lecture at his college. I replied, 'I am Shylock, I want my pound of flesh.' He was confused, and I had to elaborate. I said that I needed a fee; a pool of at least 5000 engineering projects pursued by the students. Within fifteen days, he came back to me after accomplishing the task; so I had no choice but to go. After my talk, he asked what I needed next. I said maybe 10,000 projects. He went on to pool 20,000, 60,000 and 1,00,000 more projects within nine months. All of this was done through volunteers, with a very small token honorarium to cover the expenses. With a small letter of instructions from my side, they followed a simple heuristic process. Each student volunteer went to different faculty members from all over the country and asked if they would like their students to do original work. The responses were generally positive. Then, the students asked, 'How can we do original work unless we know what other students have done elsewhere?' The faculty concerned accepted this argument because it seemed very logical. Then the students will ask the faculty for the abstracts of their students' projects. And thus the pooling took place.

There are several lessons that can be learnt from this endeavour. By asking Hiranmay to collect only 5000 projects, I had underestimated his potential by twenty times at least. Truly speaking, there is nothing more criminal than that. Thus, the first lesson is: Expecting less from others as well as from oneself is a crime

(Dr Kalam also stressed this point often in his talks). I had inadvertently committed that crime. If ideas alone matter, during the years 2002–09, I should have been able to achieve the pooling target. As I mentioned in the beginning of the chapter, I had first talked about the vision for techpedia.in back in 2002 in a meeting organized by the Department of Information Technology. However, the idea remained just an idea until Hiranmay came around. The second lesson is: Ideas matter, but their execution matters more. The third lesson is: Authorization from higher institutions such as UGC (University Grants Commission)or AICTE (All India Council of Technical Education) was not necessary to accomplish this. Institutional inertia can hold back the progress of society only to a limited extent. After that, positive ideas find a life of their own. The fourth lesson is: In a democratic society, a good cause can find horizontal support, and, provided a humble, transparent process is put in place, where due credit is given, change begins to happen. So long as public goods are created that add value in a transparent manner and without any individual agenda, initiatives in a public space can be sustained. It is true that for a long time, there were not many resources available for this purpose, and even after that, only little support was available from the Department of Science and Technology (DST), Government of India. The voluntary contribution of thousands of students and the faculty members more than compensated for the lack of institutional support. Still, there is no doubt that there is considerable scope of improving the platform and its functions. The fifth lesson is: Imperfect beginnings are the key to make progress. If we had waited for all the pieces to fall in place, the puzzle would have never been resolved. The support provided by Gujarat Technical University (GTU), by way of joining hands to experiment and in linking MSME with the final year projects of the students, proved that these ideas had merit. GTU received many awards for the results achieved through this cooperation. Thousands of third-year students went out into different industrial clusters to identify the problems of small entrepreneurs and to write a synopsis on the same. Later, many of them based their final year projects on their findings. The result was a project by the students that some cases led to concrete solutions of the problem of a MSME. Though the process still needs much more systematization, better documentation and more rigorous analysis, a framework has been evolved. Small entrepreneurs cannot hire a professor from IIT or IIM as consultants but, if they don't become more efficient using other resources, they cannot be competitive players. And if they are not competitive, they will not grow and generate jobs for more young people. This linkage, tenuous as it is, between academia and the industry, achieved one of our major objectives of societal development. There were many other initiatives that were taken up through this partnership which have become a point of reference for other institutions as well. We also learnt a great deal in the process. Several other universities are trying to improve upon this experience. In many meetings, where college principals and MSME entrepreneurs came together, initial distrust soon gave way to willingness to cooperate. I remember there were small firms that used to put a board outside their gate that students were not welcome inside the premises. The same industries today welcome students, even seek them out. Hiranmay and many other volunteers, part of the SRISTI team, played a pivotal role in all these initiatives. GTU even granted adjunct faculty status to many grassroots innovators. These innovators were then invited by various engineering colleges in Gujarat to share their experience in fabricating frugal innovative solutions.

Punjab Technical University (PTU) had made it compulsory for students to upload their projects on to the Techpedia platform as part of getting their degrees for at least a year. Several other initiatives have been taken up through this platform. What is important to appreciate is that young individuals can take initiative, experiment, innovate and help in institutionalizing change. One does not necessarily require decades of experience to develop a certain legitimacy to bring about change. The country needs more and more such change agents who can subjugate their self-interest and elevate their social interest to a level that makes it their life mission. Not easy though, but one has to hope that such social change agents will keep emerging to channelize the energy of youth who have vitality but lack direction. While difficulties in the way of a change agent are not uncommon, the goodwill generated often outweighs the memories of the stumbling blocks faced in the process. Meeting such change agents while walking through the villages has been one of the hallmarks of the shodhyatras.

Some of the encounters during the shodhyatras leave me with a very high feeling of inadequacy. During the eighteenth shodhyatra, from my village Gangagarh (Bulandshahr) to Daula (Baghpat), during 26 December 2006 to 3 January 2007, we came across many innovations when one didn't know the reasonability of the limits of one's responsibility.

There were needs which we could not meet due to mandate constraints, but we have tried. We were walking on the main road and a lot of vehicles were passing us by. There were trucks, cars, tempos and, in a few cases, even cycles. In the afternoon, after having walked more than 15 kilometres, we paused under a tree to let those yatris who were left behind catch up with us. Suddenly, a middle-aged person got down from a tempo and asked us what we were up to. Before we could answer, he mentioned that he had observed us walking many miles before when his tempo had crossed us earlier. Then we noticed that many people were getting down from the tempo. Apparently, it had encountered some sort of a glitch. The man who had approached us introduced himself. He was a doctor and also owned a printing press. When we told him about the shodhyatras and their purpose—to look for creative people, learn from them, honour them and share their experience with others—he became very interested. He asked us about the village where we would be staying the night. He recalled someone who had invented a new device and had come to him to get the advertisement pamphlets printed some years ago. He offered to bring that person to meet us in the morning.

The next day, an innovator named Kamruddin Saifi—a mechanic who had a workshop outside a local police post in Muradnagar—came to meet us with the doctor's introduction. Kamruddin said he had seen a lot of people who had lost one hand in farming accidents. While operating the motorized chaff-cutter, people mistakenly trapped their hands in the cutting gear while pushing the fodder. By the time they switched off the chaff-cutter, irreversible damage had been done. Often the hand had to be amputated. Kamruddin had developed a clutch and a locking system operated by a foot valve. The moment one feared an accident was about to take place, one presses the foot valve and immediately the chaff cutter will get disconnected from the motor and the lock will stop the movement of the cutter. Thus, the damage was minimized and a major accident could be averted. This was a problem that scientists at IIT Delhi had been working on for years. Hundreds of people had lost their limbs. But somehow, Kamruddin's innovation, effective as it was, did not get much traction. He had written to the agricultural scientists in Delhi but somehow nobody visited him despite his proximity to Delhi. He and his idea remained localized. Since he had worked in a company earlier, he would not be eligible to get support from the NIF which supports only innovators from unorganized sectors, without any experience in organized sectors, and are without professional qualifications. But SRISTI decided to popularize his idea and also confer the SRISTI Sanman on him. This is a case where slower is faster: The slower we walk, the higher the chance of discovering random innovations and meeting. If we were moving in a vehicle, such encounters were most unlikely.

In every village we subsequently walked through, we asked whether there were people who had met with similar accidents. Almost in every village, there were a few people who had lost their limbs operating such machinery. As a part of our promotions for Kamruddin's device, we asked the people to put a price tag on a limb. The question seemed absurd. How could one put a price on a hand? We followed up on our question asking how could a device costing Rs 5000, that could prevent such an accident, be considered expensive? Did they know that such a device existed? But the response was mixed. Most people had never heard about this innovation, nor were they sure that an investment of Rs 5000 was fully justified.

It seemed to be a paradox. The hand was precious; nobody wanted to lose it. But despite knowing the risk and the real-life cases of those who were affected, they still didn't want to invest Rs 5000 to prevent a so-to-speak unanticipated accident. As is human nature, they probably thought that it wouldn't occur in their case. We were not happy with the situation but there was little one could do. Unless insurance companies subsidized the device or regulatory agencies made it obligatory in farming practice, the future of the innovation seemed uncertain.[21] Perhaps we could evaluate the project to see whether the cost of the device itself could be reduced drastically. Meanwhile, the innovation is stuck and life goes on. New cases of lost limbs continue to become a small two-inch news column and then they are forgotten. Why are we not more deeply concerned about such basic safety and well-being issues? Is it that we tend to believe that accidents will occur only to others, not to us, though we may be committing similar neglect of safety precautions? Widespread neglect of helmets by motorcycle-driving youth illustrates similar neglect.[22]

From another angle, the limitation of the NIF also emphasizes the gap in the innovation ecosystem. A small entrepreneur having professional exposure and experience is excluded because there are many less privileged, connected and resourceful innovative people who deserve priority. But, for other innovators who do need systematic attention and support, a small innovation-funding facility like SRISTI's sif.sristi.org is a very tiny step in this direction. The government has not yet been able to find a window to support such socially valuable innovations by self-employed people who have some exposure to the organized sector as well as work at the grassroots level. Maybe, with renewed focus on innovation and entrepreneurship, such innovators in small towns and villages will get quick support.

Our inadequacy in making a difference to Kamruddin's case is apparent. I have no hesitation in admitting our failure in making a breakthrough in this regard. But, there is hope. Someday, regulators will realize the merit of devices like this. Similarly, the Bureau of Indian Standards will change the standards of chaff-cutters and insist on incorporating such safety features. The Indian attitude to safety will have to change eventually. Under the Grassroots Technological Innovation Acquisition Fund (GTIAF),[23] the NIF acquires rights to grassroots innovations and then makes these innovations available at no cost or low cost to small entrepreneurs and users. Such public interest innovations, like the design of a breaking mechanism in a chaff-cutter, should be acquired and made available at lost cost to users. The acquisition will also require regulatory support so that both demand and supply side interventions help in diffusing such safety-inducing solutions.

During the same shodhyatra, we came across a very interesting temple that was dedicated to a dog. We were told that there are only two such temples in the country. The other one reportedly is in Karnataka. Let me tell you the story.

There was a poor farmer who had taken a loan from a trader-cum-moneylender to support his farming practices. However, due to crop failure, he could not repay the loan. Now the farmer had a dog that was famous for his loyalty and intelligence. The moneylender asked the farmer to give him the dog if he couldn't pay the loan. The farmer very reluctantly agreed to do so and told the dog to obey all the instructions of his new master. The dog seemed to have understood that. After many years with the new master, the dog noticed some thieves stealing jewels from his master's house. He quietly followed the thieves and figured out where they had hidden the booty. He went back and forced the master to follow him to the site. On recovering his treasure, the master was so pleased with the dog's loyalty, he decided to free him. He wrote on a piece of paper, tied to the dog's neck, that he was liberating him from bondage in appreciation of his loyal services. The dog promptly walked back to his original master—the poor farmer. When the farmer saw the dog coming, he was furious. He couldn't believe that despite his instructions, the dog had come back. Without thinking twice, he hit the dog hard and the dog died. And then, he saw the piece of paper and realized what he had done. It was too late when he realized his mistake. The dog had betrayed neither his old nor new master. His return was misunderstood. For retribution, the farmer built a small temple in memory of the dog and ever since, people come and worship at this temple. There is a small lake alongside. It was believed that because of the blessings of the dog, people who have skin diseases were cured by bathing in the lake.

Disregarding the belief about the lake water curing the skin infections, the spirit of loyalty and the service of the dog could not have been better celebrated. I offer salute to such spirit and culture, which can repent for its follies in such a gracious manner. In all my years I've noticed that compassion for animals, not just humans, is rampant at the grassroots level. Moreover, the concern for animals also influences institutional innovations. For instance, designs of bird-feeding platforms in north Gujarat and Saurashtra, hanging pitchers outside near roof in West Bengal, Jharkhand and several other informal institutional arrangements have been made for taking care of birds. More than two decades ago, Maltiben had innovated and been awarded for a simple water level maintaining device for her cattle. Using a simple flush valve, she ensured that the water remained at the desired level in drinking water troughs for her cattle.

Once, the GIAN tried to license four pesticides sprayers developed by four grassroots innovators to an entrepreneur. The entrepreneur wanted to test these in the field before finalizing the deal. These included a cycle-based sprayer, hand-held sprayer, bullock-drawn sprayer and one knapsack sprayer which produced fine mist. After the field testing, the entrepreneur came back. He said that he would pay the licence fee as he had agreed but would license only three out of the four sprayers. The reason was that the bullock-drawn sprayer was quite effective but had only one snag: the pesticide spray could affect the animal skin also. Given his religious beliefs, he was adamant about not hurting animals. Despite the obvious gain to his process, this is one of the rare cases where an entrepreneur did not license technology because of the likely effect on animals. Thus, grassroots innovations cannot be seen only through anthropocentric lens, that is, concern for only human being to the neglect of moral rights of other life forms.

Feelings are bridges that connect knowledge and action but not always in a straightforward manner. Sometimes they become a pivot on which a see-saw of knowledge on one side weighs against action on the other. Despite a lot of knowledge, the initiative to take action awaits the right trigger. Feelings are not always able to tilt the scale. What do we do to overcome our inertia, to become impatient, not just for our own feelings but for other fellow creative and innovative people as well? But we need to be accountable towards other non-human sentient beings as well.

The world of innovations at the grassroots is not delinked from the institutional context in which we make sense of our life, situate it in specific socio-ecological contexts and take refuge under our cultural belief systems when we are not sure about what to do.

I have argued that one of the existential dilemmas of our modern age seems to be our weakened ability to convert our knowledge about unmet social needs into evocative feelings for change. But when we do not feel uneasy enough to take some action, our search for additional information sometimes may become a reason for justifying our inertia. I am saying that imperfect beginnings make a reasonable way to start our individual journeys for looking for creative and compassionate souls, and support them to meet many unmet social needs innovatively. Language of 'learnt helplessness' will need to give way to language of negotiating complexity and uncertainty of the world through exploratory walks through unknown territories, among strangers. Immersion in the world of creative innovations, institutions and cultural crucibles may help us become a little apologetic about our imperfections, inadequacies and fallibilities. Thus maybe we can humanize ourselves a bit more.

SIX

Fulcrum of Frugality: A Circular Economy

M ost ancient cultures have had a long tradition of frugality. This stems from the inherent values of simplicity; a culture of living within one's means, not wasting resources even if one had enough, and also partly due to the compulsions of having to live through a prolonged period of scarcity of resources caused by droughts and floods and consequent famines.

The habit of aiming for more while parting with less also triggered an innovative culture. Material constraints, instead of limiting the imagination, fertilized it. Those who wanted to pursue better, more and surer outcomes in the wake of all the uncertainties and scarcities did not succumb to the constraints but transcended them. That's how traditional technologies like Virda evolved, in which fresh water was stored in wells in saline soil to produce saline groundwater in the coastal Banni area of Kutch in Gujarat.[1] When the use of milk for viral disease control was discovered by local communities in India and other parts of the world, it seemed to be a simple, low-cost, sustainable and frugal solution. When Amrutbhai developed a simple lever that did not let a bucket of water go down even when rope was let loose when drawing water from a well, he had, in a very frugal manner, addressed a problem that had remained unsolved for over 2000 years. Growing ladies' fingers around a cotton field was another frugal solution which could prevent so many farmers' distress and suicides in the Vidarbha region in Maharashtra of and other cotton, growing regions. Frugal innovations of course emerge at the grassroots level but not just there. Even small or large public or private organizations can develop frugal solutions for grassroots applications. The mission to Moon and Mars by the Indian Space Research Organization (ISRO) cost less than 80 million USD, whereas no country had accomplished these missions by spending less than one billion USD. These modular-design missions were highly frugal.

What Makes Grassroots Innovations Frugal, Flexible and Friendly[2]

Unfortunately, many thinkers and corporate leaders have completely misunderstood the meaning of frugality by focusing only or mainly on the affordability dimension of products. Therefore, their search for fortune at the bottom of the economic pyramid has led them to design products and services that, though affordable, often externalize a huge environmental cost. For example, a one-rupee sachet of shampoo, detergent or mouth freshener is affordable, but the repercussions of collecting the plastic pieces littered everywhere is enormous. Though frugal, the future generations will not forgive us for such unsustainable innovations.

In focusing too much on price, policymakers and institutions are missing out on a vital aspect of the innovation process: scope (design and need potential) and sustainability. How do such policy and institutional blunders take place? What gives legitimacy to such approaches? Every time we legitimize and celebrate such solutions, by using improper definitions of frugality, our search for eco-friendly product and service dispensers becomes more sluggish. When just the conventional meaning of 'frugality' takes precedence in design, we produce packaging that adversely affects the environment. Unless circularity (cradle to cradle) is brought into picture, what is affordable for humans may not be affordable for nature.

Let me go back to the roots of the frugal philosophy and try to answer these questions with the examples I learnt early in life and also the ones we came across during our shodhyatra over the last few decades.

Aparigraha: When Less Is Actually More[3]

More than 2500 years ago, the core of Jain philosophy enshrined the value of not accumulating more than one's basic needs. Frugality was imperative because minimalism was optimal. It was realized that happiness

is not found in *things*, but in *thoughts*. A rich collection
of things with poor thoughts is a recipe for disaster. One
can experience lifelong pain, frustration, dissatisfaction,
anger and purposelessness despite a lot of material
possessions. I recognize that we are all human and very
ordinary ones at that. Unlike saints, we are greedy,
feel the need for comfort and the desire to make our
children's lives better. Having lived through scarcity in
early years, practices like that of hoarding often follow.
It is a different issue that those who provide the most for
their children may get the least respect and affection. It
is the scarcity of things or lack of attachment to things
that one has, that might breed surplus of thoughts and
values, feelings and fortitude. The point is that when we
fill our lives with things and material possessions, where
do we get the time to reflect, to share ideas and even the
things that we have? So many innovators have shared
their knowledge with us without expecting anything in
return. Their generosity is partly owed to their simplicity
in life too. They use local materials to solve societal
problems in a manner that local community members
can afford their inventions and use them often without
producing much waste.

When I was a child, my *nana*, his brother, *nani*,
mama and other maternal aunts and uncles lived
together in a very small room in Daryaganj. It was
common for several tenants to live in small buildings in
narrow lanes, with small rooms and shared toilets with
an amazing assumed frugality. When we used to go to
the market to buy certain provisions, the shopkeepers
would not often give things in bags since polythene bags

were expensive at the time. Instead, the shopkeeper would wrap the items in a piece of newspaper and then tie them with a thread hanging from the roof in the shape of a ball. When we came home, my grandfather would ask for the package to be untied, then proceed to unfold the piece of paper and put it under the bed, on a wooden cot, after straightening it out. The piece of thread, hardly a metre long, would be hung on a nail on the wall. Both of these things would be reused whenever something was to be given away to someone. Even a small piece of thread was not thrown away! These prudent values have been a part of millions of people's lives. How is it then that we have become one of the most wasteful and thus dirty countries in the world? Every society goes through value transformation with the passage of time. But in our society the cleavage between accumulators and those who prefer simple living has increased a lot in recent years. The result is that simple solutions seem less viable to many and thus causing serious public health and other social problems. More than 50 per cent women[4] suffer from anaemia in India. There are many reasons for this problem, not only among the poor but also the middle class. The remedy is a simple, age-old, frugal practice—that is of cooking at least one curry or vegetable in iron vessel.[5] The introduction of iron pots or improving their use in communities in developing countries for the preparation of food may be a *promising innovative intervention* for reducing iron deficiency and anaemia. Further research is required to monitor the use and effectiveness of this intervention.

When I visited the University of Guelph in Canada, on the invitation of Sally Humphries to deliver the David Hopper Memorial Lecture, Professor Summerlee, former president of the university, shared the very interesting work of his student Christopher Charles on the use of cast-iron fish to ameliorate the condition of the people suffering from anaemia in Cambodia.[6] He gave me a fish to carry home. His work is an example of good science combined with extreme affordability, circularity and democratic access. But why is it not popular in India and majority of other developing countries? The policymakers would rather wish to introduce fortified biscuits and other inputs but not a simple solution, for example, a ladle or a vessel of iron in the Midday Meal scheme to overcome significant trends of iron deficiency among children.[7] Frugal solutions often generate a unique frame of mind.

Obviously, with the culture of consumption there was no simultaneous growth of a sense of responsibility among the designers of products and services. Irresponsible policymakers made certain materials cheaper but did not take into account the real effect of those products on the environment. There is nothing natural or accidental about it. Such decision making is a part of a very systematic strategy that has been implemented through a willing partnership between consumers, providers, policymakers, investors and, of course, corporations. The way we calculate the cost of any product or service does not take into account the cost of internalizing the externalities. This implies that manufacturers of a product price it by not including the cost of collecting wrappers, recycling them and putting them towards environmentally safe outcomes. They do not internalize the cost imposed on the environment and externalize out of their balance sheet on those who do not benefit from their decisions. Thus, when selling a detergent in a small sachet, we don't calculate the cost of collecting the wrappers from the thousands of consumers and then safely disposing them of. This structure of costing considers only direct inputs and excludes all the adverse environmental costs, leading to terrible problems of social sanitation and waste management. The national sanitation campaign will further have to deal with this mindset and focus not only on the end-of-the-pipe solution. We have to, of course, clean up the waste in public places but wouldn't it be more sustainable if we try to avoid practices which generate littering in the first place? We have to correct the mindset which encourages use of plastic water bottle at every public function instead of use of glasses and refillable jars. Otherwise we will not be able to solve the problem of sanitation at its root. Many institutions have started distributing metallic bottles to students and faculty so that they refill them from water points rather than using plastic water bottle every time they need water.

I had requested the prime minister in a column[8] in early 2015 after a shodhyatra in Sikkim that if he uses a bamboo cup in his office, the message may go all around the country about new aesthetics and efficiency methods besides circularity ('cradle to cradle' instead of 'cradle to grave' approach) and sustainability. So many jobs will be generated in tribal areas, apart from solving a wastage problem in at least one supply chain. But frugal solutions do not always diffuse. During the Third International Conference on Creativity and Innovation at Grassroots held in January 2015 at IIMA, in collaboration with the NIF, SRISTI and the Honey Bee Network, we had used edible cutlery, completely avoided plastic bottles and plastic use. Similarly, for the last few years, Sattvik, the traditional food festival organized by SRISTI in collaboration with the NIF and the GIAN and other members of the Honey Bee Network, no plastic bag is used for dispensing things by organic farmers. But the dominant direction in which the world is moving is waste- and junk-oriented progress. The fact that majority of grassroots innovators use second-hand parts helps in minimizing the problem, apart from making their solutions extremely affordable and environment-friendly.

The culture of frugality—once part of several traditions, for example Buddhism and Jainism in our society and considered a natural way of life—is now called an alternative social movement or trend. Traditionally, some of these frugal cultural traditions also implied responsibility for the whole earth, calling it the Gaia system. Gandhi's synthesis of these values was a recent reminder of frugality in the famous quote about the world having enough for everybody's need but not enough for their greed. Ecologists insist that the integrity of our ecosystem must be at the centre of discourse while deliberating any issue of future or current consumption. Jains, Buddhists, the Amish and many Native Americans members of tribal/aborigine cultures have advocated a frugal lifestyle. In a famous lecture series titled 'The

Gospel of Dirty Hands' (1952),[9] the former minister of food and agriculture, Dr K.M. Munshi, said that community cultures which dominated the environment completely vanished from the earth and those which were overawed by nature remained as primitive tribal. He stressed that the only time his granddaughter dirtied her hands was when the ink of the fountain pen leaked. He referred to the fact that she did not have to work with her hands since there were servants at home. He, in a self-critical tone, exhorted extension workers to link with people who worked with their hand. Frugal thinking, by empathizing with the working class at the grassroots level, was quite apparent in his writings and speeches.

One has to find a middle ground. The central focus of social discourse has shifted and we celebrate the name of Gandhi without ever imbibing the values he stood for. Let me recall an episode in our history when a policymaker used his moral capital to bring about a large-scale behavioural change through a call for frugal behaviour.

Lal Bahadur Shastri was appointed prime minster of India when the country was in the grip of a drought. Soon after, Shastri had to deal with a major war with Pakistan (1965). Severe shortage of foodgrains followed in the wake of cessation of food aid from USA. (Under PL 480, the Public Law of US, it gave food aid to various developing countries, including India. The money generated by selling those grains was used for developmental projects.) The last time people died on the streets as a consequence of famine was in 1966–67.

Fortunately, India has managed to ward off destitution-
triggered death on a large scale after that. But hunger
and large-scale infant malnutrition still persists.[10] The
consecutive failure of rain had imposed a serious burden
of meeting the food needs of the nation. Shastri was in
a dilemma because the existing limited supply of grains
had to be distributed more widely, given, widespread
failure of rains and consequent hunger. He addressed
the nation on the radio and asked fellow countrymen to
forgo grains during dinner on every Monday evening.
Through routine fasting, he encouraged people to save
grains. It is commendable that a vast majority of Indians
voluntarily decided not to eat grains every Monday
evening. Shastri's creative solution is the epitome of
understanding how frugality can in fact be an instrument
of public policy. Frugality cannot be forced, but it can
be fostered.

Let me go back to another event some 2000 years
ago. A monk was known to teach in a very metaphorical
and unorthodox manner. He had many disciples
whom he tried to teach individually, according to their
sensibilities. One day, a particular disciple started to
argue with him about the need for conservation. The
monk asked the student to bring him a glass of water.
The disciple brought the water. When the monk drank
the water, the disciple took away the empty glass, and on
the way back to the kitchen, threw away the remaining
droplets in the glass by inverting the glass a few times.
The monk asked him to explain what he had done. The
disciple said, 'Nothing, I just brought the glass of water
as you advised and then took the empty glass back.' The

monk asked, 'Is that all? Try to remember everything.' The disciple narrated the entire sequence of steps of how he went to bring the water and then went back to keep the glass in the kitchen. He was asked the same question again and the disciple kept repeating the same answer till he realized his mistake. He finally recalled the entire event. When the teacher asked him to bring a glass of water, he went to the kitchen and brought the glass of the water. While going back with the empty glass, he added, 'I threw away *just* a few drops of water.' The monk said, 'What! Just . . .' The disciple achieved Zen by concentrating or focusing on the word 'just' and realized that even a drop of water could have multiple destinies. Throwing those drops away purposelessly was certainly not a responsible act. Maybe these drops could have been put forth into a flower bed or a nursery or a watering pot for birds. The realization that even a few drops should not be wasted, though there was *no* apparent scarcity of water then, was the source of enlightenment.

Two thousand years ago, there was no shortage of water. For another 1900 years there was not likely to be a major shortage of water. In this parable, why did a teacher then inculcate consciousness about saving even a drop of water? And yet, instilling the prudence value to save even a single drop of water shows how deeply the culture was embedded with the notion of frugality. If we had maintained this value, we probably would never have had seen water shortage, or any other shortage for that matter, in subsequent generations.

Frugality is not important only for poor countries, communities or companies. It is important for everyone.

Nature itself is very frugal; it never wastes anything. Konrad Lorenz, a Nobel laureate from Germany was a famous ethologist. He has done pioneering work in understanding patterns in nature. Rupert Riedl (1984)[11] refers to Lorenz's work and asks a simple question. He notes that the entire occurrence of diversity in nature may have some simple rules underlying it. To illustrate, he suggests that we look at feathers of all birds, fins of all the fish and branches of all the trees. And then, Riedl asks, 'What is the range of the angle at which the feather, the fin and the branch is set to the respective trunk in each case?' When we see the narrow range of angle, say between fifteen to ninety degrees within all the shapes of trees influenced by branching angles, the relationship between fish and birds can be explained; we can see the simplicity of rules that nature observes. He concludes then, 'Nature is very parsimonious. It has a few designs and it plays with them all the time.'

Frugality requires affordability, circularity and durability or renewability. The cradle-to-grave model assumes wastes, which in some cases may be reduced, reused and/or recycled. The concept of rejuvenation does not count for much. The concept of rejuvenation refers to when the property of a used material is repaired or re-seasoned such that its life increases to more than its original life. For example, when certain iron gears are heated with coal or other carbon sources, their hardness and durability increase. This was one of the most ancient discoveries, which has shaped human history.[12] This practice is still relevant, of course, and blacksmiths and grassroots innovators who have never gone to any school or technical institution know it through inter-generational transfer of knowledge. They innovate when they find materials that have fatigued for one purpose, say autocars, which may still have life for low-speed, high-torque application like motorcycle plough—tens of thousands of which, called santi, are used in Saurashtra, Gujarat, thanks to the original innovation by Mansukhbhai Jagani in 1992 in Amreli. Several versions of santi have evolved through derivative innovations by hundreds of mechanics in Gujarat.

Industrial ecologists define waste as material for which use has not yet been found. The concept of frugality, in terms of economic, environmental and social costs, has sustainability at its core. Short-term affordability with adverse long-term consequences will not do. However, a new model of design and manufacturing can be conceptualized to make affordability compatible with sustainability. In various machines or products, not all components age or fatigue at the same rate. In a car, the age of the engine may be different from the age of the axle, gearbox, steering wheel or other components. Grassroots innovators are aware of this process of differential aging of different components of any manufactured product. It is not surprising, therefore, that they tap the unfinished life of various components when designing innovative solutions. Ninety per cent of engineering products at the grassroots level have second-hand components. The innovators, generally, do not compromise on safety. I am not arguing that all grassroots innovations are frugal, but the majority of the ones scouted by the Honey Bee Network so far are.

However, I am not implying that frugal grassroots solutions are always sustainable. Most solutions are, but indeed there are exceptions. When fishermen use dynamite to catch fish in the water, they kill small as well as big fish. It is very economical and affordable but a completely unsustainable practice. When small fish die, the population dynamics is adversely affected. And the total amount of catch will also start to go down with the passage of time. Such concepts of affordability must be avoided. Thus we should avoid extensive generalizations.

Reverting to mechanical products, many companies are beginning to realize that they can delay the entropy[13] by tapping into the unfinished life of the components or fixtures. The movement from order to disorder implies gaining entropy. The disorder is also implied in dissipation of heat or energy in many cases. An axle of a car or truck may have a life, say of forty years, but the vehicle itself may not have a life of more than fifteen years. Since different materials depreciate at different rates, it makes sense to discard only those components that become useless for one purpose, but to retain those that may very much have use for another—and not waste all of them. The life of a car or an airplane may be between fifteen to twenty years, but certainly not each component or fixture can be expected to share that lifespan. But one of the European airlines realized that the life of an airplane seat was perhaps more than a hundred years. They facilitated a subsidiary company which took out the seats, refurbished them, and asked another company to sell them as household furniture. In the future, while designing products, the plan for renewability should not only be thought of as a whole but of each component as well.[14] Each component should have the fatigue factor[15] mentioned on it. Moreover, there should be roadside labs which will be able to conduct stress tests on each component, and specify the remaining life of the same. The whole economy surrounding a particular product should become more creative, innovative, circular and sustainable. It is also possible that the users will discover diverse innovative uses of each component beyond what the original designers intended.

More than forty years ago, there was an unfortunate plane crash in the Sujangarh area of Rajasthan. Different parts of the plane were scattered all over the place. A creative artisan looked at the tyre of the plane and noticed that it hadn't flattened even after crashing over sand. He decided to use it for a camel cart and it' became a great hit in the region. Local entrepreneurs started buying the old tyres of planes from various air force stations. Subsequently, the largest dump of such tyres was created there. An environmental problem of disposing the old plane tyres became a viable, economic and environmentally compatible market opportunity, solving the problems of economically poor people in a more efficient manner than had been done in the past. This was a very frugal solution because the life of the tyre may have finished for the plane but was still to be tapped for the camel cart. It also was not a makeshift solution but a systematic optimal choice.[16]

Pareshbhai had designed a kite thread winder many years ago. While kite flying, when the opponent cuts your kite, it floats in the air for a few moments before dropping to the ground or being caught by someone. The kite flyer has to wind the remaining thread manually around the spool, which takes a lot of time and energy. To address this issue, Pareshbhai fitted a small tape recorder motor inside the wooden winder and essentially repurposed it, thus adding a new life to it which in a defective recorder, it had exhausted.

Repurposing objects has been a worldwide phenomenon, not peculiar to India. But at the grassroots level, it provides a strong antidote to the junking mindset, and fosters further creativity. On a shodhyatra in Dhemaji, Assam, we came across three different designs of wooden lathes in a single village. The various interpretations of lathes used different kinds of wheels, including cycle rims, power-wooden lathes to shape-legs of cots, chairs and other furniture. These wheels might not have had further use in their original context.

Where repurposing objects may become a stumbling block is when it reduces the desire to make durable, long-term solutions and thus creates a mindset of living with makeshift or temporary solutions for long-term problems, also what is popularly called as jugaad mindset. In this case it may sap the creative energy of a society.

In 1994, I along with my former colleague and an active volunteer in the Honey Bee Network, Kirit Patel, visited several Latin American countries in a kind of international shodhyatra. In Kali, we organized a workshop with the help of Professor Mario Mejía-Gutierrez to enable local youth workers in different developmental voluntary organizations, we asked participants to think of different creative uses of tyres and learnt:

(a) Most uses of new materials are guided by the spirit of recycling the resource. Waste is abhorred.

(b) The variety of uses is not just functional but also conceptual. The material is classified for a given set of uses and the category of use precedes the actual search and use.

(c) Many uses are discovered serendipitously as a part of fun and frolic. Not every use is preceded by a systematic search.

(d) At times, similar uses evolve cross-culturally through simultaneous innovations and not always through diffusion as is often assumed.

(e) Some of the uses are guided not merely by cost-reducing compulsions but also to facilitate easy reparability, replicability, etc.

In other words, functional flexibility is a watchword for most of these innovations. There could be other motivations for innovating, but it was clear during our visit to Costa Rica, Colombia and Ecuador that once professionals were introduced to the Honey Bee philosophy, they are never disappointed in their search of new sources of creativity at the grassroots level.[17] The reason that many of them did not see many of the same innovations was lack of faith in people's ability to solve local problems endogenously.

The search for sustainability in different parts of the world has triggered discovery of green, circular innovations which produce nil, or rather very low quantity of waste, or utilize the waste material in other supply chains. When a frugal solution is developed— say using lemon juice to help in controlling a pest like aphid—it fails to enthuse agricultural departments, research organizations and other bodies precisely because it is so simple. To this I ask: Should the complexity of a solution be what makes it worthy of attention from scientific minds or policymakers?

In 1994, we observed the practice of lemon juice being used to control the pest aphid—a phenomenon also recommended in the US and elsewhere by organic producers. Ramesh Patel, now secretary of SRISTI, then a young researcher, reported that a farmer Samantbhai Dholakia, from Surendranagar, Gujarat, also follows the same practice locally to contain aphid populations, more commonly known as 'molo' in Gujarat. Farmers claim that 'molo' are generally not found during the monsoon. Aphids normally appear on four-month-old cotton crops and attach themselves to the undersides of the leaves and suck the sap. A black sticky substance is also found on the aphid-infested leaves and this particular condition is known as 'galo' (meaning sweet). Generally, yellow and green aphids are found in cotton crops. If unattended, the condition persists till the end of the cotton season. It is believed that if an indigenous variety of cotton is grown as a rain-fed crop, aphid infestation does not occur. Samantbhai thought about using the juice of lemons to control aphids. He mixed approximately 100 to 200 millilitres of lemon juice with 15 litres of water, and sprayed it over the crop—between eighteen to twenty pumps over 1 hectare.[18] He repeated the treatment at weekly intervals. Last year, Samantbhai sprayed his cotton crop thrice and was successful in controlling the pest. If an extremely frugal solution of using low-cost lemon juice is not popularized, farmers have to use costly chemical pesticides which may also develop resistance among pests due to prolonged use. A treadmill effect follows. That is, more pesticide has to be used every year due to resistance of pests and killing of predators (the natural enemies of insects, or pests which eat pests). Frugal solutions many times are also more efficient and sustainable.

Numerous farmers have committed suicide due to their inability to pay debts incurred for pest control by chemical methods, yet despite the expected easy diffusion of frugal innovations, many other practices similar to the lemon juice have not reached farmers till recently. Frugal solutions are not always seductive for scientists and policymakers and extension workers; perhaps these are not reassuring ideas for many either because of their inherent democratic nature and ease of use without expert help, or these do not provide any incentives to extension workers which sellers of marled inputs might provide. Lack of institutional support thus comes in the way of diffusion of such low-cost, easy-to-use innovations amongst those who need these most but may not have discovered them themselves.[19]

Thus, the challenge is: How do we make open-source, democratic, frugal and simple knowledge widespread so as to increase the self-reliance, sustainability and circularity of outcomes? The Honey Bee Network is attempting various experiments in this regard, which will be discussed a little later.

When products are designed in a frugal manner, the supply chain for distributing them should also be frugal. Accessibility, affordability, adaptability and availability—all the four characteristics have to be combined. For example, there is no point in a primary health centre being accessible and dispensing affordable medicines if it cannot make essential medicines available when needed. People who are dependent on fair price shops for foodgrains have a first-hand experience of the malfunctioning supply chain in terms of availability.

There are many more examples of affordable, accessible, available, durable and renewable innovations at the grassroots level. In another instance, Roshanlal Vishwakarma from Madhya Pradesh developed a sugar cane bud chipper, a device which can cut just the bud or eye of the sugar cane set such that instead of sowing the sets, farmers can just sow the buds. The remaining parts of the sugar cane can be used to extract juice. Hot water treatment of buds disinfects them. Since buds take much lesser space than the sets of sugar-cane (that is small, six to eight inch pieces), these are easier to disinfect before sowing. The chipper is very affordable and the amount of buds required goes down drastically. In the process a lot of canes are saved. Overall, the device is productive, efficient, affordable and sustainable.

However, even the consumer may not always value only the frugality of the function of the innovation; the aesthetics and packaging may make a difference. The question is: Can new aesthetic sensitivity be developed as an alternative trigger for green and grassroots-oriented consumerism? For example, can a new style of packaging be evolved without the predominant use of plastic? It is not necessary that every product solution needs to be long-lasting, say beyond three to six months, or that its outreach needs to reflect consumption 1000 kilometres away from the source. Given the unorthodox (yet effective) approach I suggest with regard to sustainable low energy ways of problem solving, such frugal-solution-based ideation will surely require us to change our mindset.

In 2013, the SNCF—Société Nationale des Chemins de fer Français, or the national French railways—sent twenty fast-track senior executives to India to learn from grassroots innovators, amongst other things.[20] When we had a brainstorming session about how the railways could rethink their business approach, many different proposals for a better user environment emerged. Roles for new vendors, new ways of using platform space, giving opportunity to young people to interact with distinguished passengers with their consent, separate coaches for children or others to celebrate their birthday, etc., were some of the ideas generated in our discussion. Many new services can be added without extra cost but to much greater consumer satisfaction. Frugality is not only relevant to products but also to services. For example, it does not require a great deal of logistical management to incorporate some space on platforms for organic producers to sell their products to commuter traffic. Even in Europe, frugal solutions are sought to increase consumer choice and behaviour for making the transition towards sustainability outcomes. They met two innovators, one of whom was Ratnakar,[21] who had fitted a large number of hydro-turbines to generate decentralized energy in coffee-growing plantations in Karnataka. Another innovator they met was Vinod Mahadeviah,[22] who had designed a machine to make cold tender coconut water available to consumers besides numerous sweets made of tender coconut. The frugality of these attempts made a deep impact on these executives. It might become difficult for them to miss frugal options henceforth.

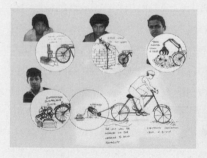

6.1 Multiple uses of the cycle as suggested by children in the creativity workshop held at the Rashtrapati Bhavan during the FOIN in 2015.

How do we shape consumers' minds to create a market for such frugal grassroots innovations? It is not enough to have these innovations but also showcase these to them through multiple media channels including social media. Ralte and Sailo, two friends in Mizoram, designed bamboo-splitting and incense stick-making machines. Initially, they made two separate machines for the two different functions. Later, by slightly altering the design, they combined the functions into a single machine. Consequently, the cost decreased, affordability increased, the waste reduced and sustainability was enhanced. There are a few other versions of bamboo and incense stick making machines to meet the requirements of niche segments. Each one of them has some special characteristics. But in the north-east, with vast areas under bamboo plantations, it can help in generating a lot of jobs and that too in just a payout of Rs 5000 per job. Linking the incense stick-making industry with distributed production will help. Maybe an Amul kind of model could be developed by the state government to have decentralized production, procurement, processing and marketing. When consumers directly experience products made through frugal innovations, their support for such a cause might increase.

It may be worthwhile to mention here that five grassroots innovators who were hosted by the president of India as Innovation Scholars in Residence this year included Shri G.K. Ratnakar from Karnataka (innovation: Mini Hydro-turbines), Shri Mushtaq Ahmed Dar from Jammu and Kashmir (innovation: Walnut Cracker), Shri Lalbiakzuala Ralte from Mizoram (innovation: Bamboo Split Making Machine), Shri Mallesham Laxminarayana Chinthakindi from Andhra Pradesh (innovation: 'Laxmi' Asu Making Machine), Shri Amrut Lal Bawandas

Agrawat from Gujarat (innovation: Aaruni Bullock Cart and Innovative Pulley), besides a student Swapnil Talukdar and a college student Anuradha Pal.[23]

So far there have been three rounds of innovation scholars-in-residence at the Rashtrapati Bhavan, hosted by the office of the president of India.[24] It shows the respect for the frugal grassroots innovations at the highest level. But is that enough to change the mindsets of common people?

No, We Do Not Need Jugaad

The use of the term jugaad to characterize majority of these innovations is not only inappropriate but also an outcome of lazy intellectualism. The jugaad mindset essentially reflects a makeshift approach in which one tries to get around the problem rather than solving it systematically and for longer term if possible. When faced with a problem, finding a temporary solution sometimes makes sense, but if it becomes a habit, it could be extremely harmful for the growth of ideas and diffusion of innovative culture. Mitti Cool, the clay refrigerator, requires seven different machines to perform different functions in the value chain. Mansukhbhai Prajapati has meticulously designed those machines, including special purpose kilns, moulds, press machines, etc. To call this elaborate manufacturing process a result of jugaad[25] is a despicable use of the term. Unfortunately, many Indians have lapped up the term not realizing the dangerous consequences of this kind of mindset.

The word 'jugaad' became popular by the Indian habit of finding some way out of persistent problems using whatever means available. Some of these solutions were short cuts and in fact not always very safe. For instance, if we did not have a plug, an electrician at a function will use two matchsticks, tie them to wires, and then insert them in the socket. Yes, it will work for that moment but it is indeed hazardous. That is why we have so many accidents due to loose connections causing sparks or other such reasons. Similarly, given the poor conditions of the road, farmers had put stationary engines over carts and thus made a makeshift traction vehicle. Tens of thousands of such vehicles can be seen in rural areas helping in short-distance transportation. The regional transport officers could have taken action against all of these local mechanics and farmers though they did not give them the benefit of registration. It somehow did not lead to a low-cost rural traction vehicle, which could have met local aspiration and yet remained affordable and safe for local communities. But in Gujarat, motorcycle-driven ploughs, invented in 1992 by Mansukhbhai Jagani, went through a lot of systematic improvements as mentioned earlier. Efforts are under way to get standards developed with second-hand parts so that 10,000 santis, now with four-wheel chassis with ten to twelve horsepower new engines do not remain illegal, though socially legitimate.

Many readers might have faced the unfortunate situation of not being able to use a standard plug with different sockets in the same building or room. Inability to manufacture multipurpose products with high precision design is another consequence of the jugaad mentality.

The attitude of living with inefficiency is a precursor to the jugaad mentality. No country can ever progress with such a mode of action. Mentioned in a previous chapter, the example of the steel almirah whose door did not close properly, and the user accepting the limitations of the product, demonstrated a case of not only personal inertia but also a tendency to compromise with inefficiency. Since the mason who made the floor of the house levelled it unevenly to provide a slight slope for cleaning water to drain easily, it aggravated the almirah's design shortcoming in the process. The problem can be solved by putting a small packing under the front legs of the almirah, but if we don't fix the problem permanently then jugaad solutions will prevail. This is the problem: If manufacturers do not pay attention to fine-tuning the product specifications, or take user conditions into account through deliberate design thinking, pursue precision engineering, and generate flexibility for the user to adapt the product to local variable conditions, the need for jugaad will unfortunately emerge. Thus, jugaad solutions often are an indicator of what we lack in design, manufacture, supply chain and user-driven redesign processes.

Let me provide another example of how this mindset perpetuates itself in our daily life. If you notice the grill on a window, a tree guard or fencing made of iron wires welded together, you will observe that it has been put together without attention to detail and roundedness of edges. The joints are rough because they are welded with excessive material such that multiple cuts on the wire pose serious hazards. Yet, despite these reasons, such grill designs can be seen in all parts of the country, including top institutions like mine.

I took photographs of several of these joints and gave it to a student of mine, Abhinav Jha, then a master's student in the UK and an intern at SRISTI, with instructions to question the welders about their quality of work. Later, about thirty welders were invited for a discussion to IIMA. We showed them the slides illustrating jugaad mentality they had inadvertently used in making those grills. Some of them were actually involved in executing the order at IIMA. We showed them tree guards, fences, and other grills in the campus. What we learnt was astounding. The measurements used by the welders were in inches and feet, and not centimetres and millimetres. There was a difference of 2.54 (1 inch=2.54 cm) in the simple measurement, such that their measuring was that much less precise. They also mentioned that the clients took a long time to decide what needed to be fixed when broken, or fabricated when a new fitting was needed, but did not give welders enough time to make the modifications or complete the order. The irregular quality of the welding rods was also cited as one of the reasons why excess material was put into the structure. They, however, conceded that the compromises they made on quality were a result of bad habits. They worked hard to do a shabby job. Ironic, isn't it? Better quality of work would have required less effort, material, labour and time. Fixing things anyhow, not smoothening edges, not ensuring uniform welding quality leading to unequal load distribution and thus possible faster wear and tear, are all a result of jugaad mindset. India has to come out of it. International companies which are getting on this bandwagon are forewarned; they cannot avoid their doomsday too long if they follow such an approach.

Many times, when one goes to a five-star hotel and uses the washroom, one can see the gap between the edge of the washbasin and the wall. This gap is packed with some filling material to give the appearance of smoothness. We compromise not because we cannot make precise joints or attachment of fixtures on walls, but the habit of living with lesser quality—less precise joints, and less accurate fixtures—has permeated even highly sophisticated environments. There is no justification for inertia, inefficiency and inaccuracy—this thinking can and must be changed.

There are several dimensions of frugality which have a bearing on impact on the environment, society and institutions: (a) material, (b) multifunctionality, (c) repurposing and rejuvenation, (d) flexibility and location-specific adaptability, (e) availability, affordability and accessibility. These dimensions have been explored in detail below:

Material

One of the universal goals of frugality and sustainability is dematerialization and/or predominant use of biomaterials. Dematerialization refers to the reduction in the amount of material used, and increase in the amount of relevant knowledge and innovation applied to get the output. The drug sector was one of the first sectors where knowledge intensity of final product became evident. The value of the material quantity in a pill or capsule may be of much lesser value, but the knowledge embedded in the drug through research and development became larger. The use of biomaterial—that is composites or other substances which use natural fibres mixed with chemical polymers or resins to make new materials, or through other methods—achieves the same end by moving from non-renewable to renewable forms of outputs. Since biological materials are decomposable, they have a much less negative effect on environment. A large number of disadvantaged communities have used biological materials to manage their livelihood, and thereby identified sustainable and affordable options. Herbal medicine for humans, plants and animals is a major area of health management at community levels. Even here, there are several rituals and taboos to prevent excessive extraction of these raw materials. Though with market penetration, self-regulation is becoming weaker besides a heavy market demand that is taking its toll.[26] Many innovators are now making use of bamboo, straw, wood, clay, etc.

The double-decker root bridge in Meghalaya described earlier made use of renewable material, like roots and stones, in its construction. The confluence of technology, institutions and culture is the pivot of sustainable design. If technology is the word, institutions are the grammar and culture is the thesaurus; we need all three for articulating or generating sustainable solutions. In this particular example, the materials are so frugal and renewable that this solution meets practically all conditions of affordability, accessibility, availability and durability. Circularity (the cradle-to-cradle approach) is embedded in the design since everything is recyclable—every material launches into another life cycle instead of getting wasted; used stones go back into the river, worn out roots can be recycled as manure.

The design of the bamboo windmill is another example where materials like bamboo make the solution not only affordable, but also renewable instead of using metal rods or pivots.

Multifunctionality

In nature, all species are multifunctional. Every tree, shrub and herb can potentially provide multiple ecological and economic services, and thus, perform multiple functions. It is possible that some of the functions may seem less important from an anthropocentric perspective as they are from an ecological perspective. Likewise, many grassroots innovations are frugal because they are multifunctional. The argument is not that a single device or product cannot be frugal, but that multifunctionality makes frugality more easily achievable. A motorcycle-based ploughing machine like santi, as discussed earlier, is a multifunctional device. It can perform tillage, planking and laddering, sowing, spraying, etc., with a lot of flexibility. Given the user-driven manoeuvrability, the functional, flexible and affordable characteristics of the motorcycle-based plough and multipurpose tool bar (santi) make it user-friendly and flexible.

In a traditional economy that is dependent on nature,[27] there are very few things which are used only for one purpose. Many of us have used a metallic lock not only to secure the door of our house, but also for cracking nuts, fixing a nail on the wall, as a paperweight and for other odd jobs. There is an innate tendency on the part of most Indians to use things for multiple purposes, sometimes beyond the imagination of the original designer. Yet, furthering this analogy, we are likely to find multiple marks of nails on the wall because such a way of fixing nails should not be expected to produce a precise solution. In other words, a jugaad approach cannot spawn an attitude of precision in design. But, multifunctionality is not bad per se. It simply implies that we don't have separate devices for different functions. That is why food-processing machines have multiple jars and pots for grinding different kinds of ingredients. The jugaad approach differs from multifunctionality as the former reflects a preference for a makeshift solution that is temporary in nature, and delays the search for permanent or durable systematic solutions; while the latter widens the consumer choices on an ongoing basis.

Moreover, multifunctionality gets enhanced when we create platform technologies, i.e., those intermediary conditions which make development of different solution possible using those basic conditions. Imagine that a cycle is affixed with a multipurpose platform, or pivot, or base. Using the energy generated from the pedal one can operate an attached mixer, grinder, cutter and numerous other devices fixed on to this platform. If one goes a step further, the cycle can also be used to power a washing machine, to remove cobwebs from walls, to irrigate hanging flower pots, etc. It is a pity that cycle manufacturers have not paid attention to this style of attachments for the cycle. In millions of homes, a cycle is an aspirational good. For the poor, the cycle is often their only durable asset. Yet, the design of the widely used cycle has not been greatly improved or augmented. In a UNICEF–SRISTI children's creativity workshop organized as a part of the Festival of Innovation at the Rashtrapati Bhavan, children were asked to come up with different uses of the cycle other than transportation of goods and persons. They came up with a wide variety of uses in a few minutes.

Repurposing and Rejuvenation

While discussing the fatigue factor of different components, I mentioned earlier that the repurposing and rejuvenation of each component must be planned at the time of designing the original part or device. The designers of cassette players, before the flash drive-based music systems came about, did not plan alternative uses for the motor. However, many grassroots innovators have used the motors taken out from the cassette player for designing numerous applications in agriculture as well as their household chores. For example, some have used these motors for scattering seeds in the fields. The tapes have been used to tie these around the fields. Reflection from these tapes in the sunlight keeps birds away. When the wind blows, these tapes hanging on the four sides of the field move and the reflections also move scaring the birds. Compact discs have also been used for similar purpose to reflect the light. Plastic buckets are stitched when torn to elongate their life.

The entire network of various fabricators inspired by Mansukhbhai's invention in 1992 of a motorcycle driven santi—a multipurpose toolbar in Gujarat—is a good example of this. More than 200 fabricators made a whole range of derivative innovations—that is, innovations with some modification in form, features or function using the concept developed by the primary innovator—and in some cases parallel or simultaneous innovations as was the case when the four-wheel santi was developed; several innovators developed similar designs. The crux was that the innovators used different components from different auto-vehicles, and made both three- and four-wheel traction machinery for farms. Small tractors made by several big companies could not compete with these local innovations that recycled auto components. The large number of farm machinery, particularly, multipurpose ploughs could not have been designed without availability of second-hand parts. The durability, safety and integrity of the device, of course, are not negotiable. The imagination of local communities would not get fertilized without access to a large variety of second-hand components.

The multifunctionality, affordability, local reparability, easy availability of components, etc., of local traction devices scored over standardized small tractor made by big companies.

Flexibility and Location-specific Adaptability

Multifunctionality may make a design more flexible, though arguably even a single-purpose device can be flexible. Let us continue using the example of agriculture for a moment. Because of the variability of soil conditions, various tilling devices have to be fixed at different angles and the invention of the multipurpose toolbar—a kind of hollow pipe with holes on the sides—made that easily possible. Hundreds of thousands of farmers earlier used bullock-drawn santi and now use either motorcycle-based or reconfigured, locally powered tilling devices instead. Flexibility was needed in changing the inter-row distance which varies from location to location. Similarly, the device could be easily used for spraying pesticides or weeding, sowing, planking, laddering, etc.

When Rozadeen converted a pressure cooker into a coffee maker, he added a new functionality to the device in a very flexible manner. By adding a pipe connected to a switch, he could use steam pressure from the cooker to froth cups of coffee.

Physical location or socioecological production environment influences the quality of raw material and the way it is processed. The machine devised by Dharambir for food processing can be easily adapted to process various kinds of fruit, and even the same kind of fruit with varying thickness or hardness. It is true however, that not everything is adapted to locational needs. Often, the lack of adaptability means specific needs remaining unmet. Higher the fit between the design of an innovation and local needs, lesser are the chances of its replicability widely. The only way to resolve this paradox is to have solutions that are flexible, and fit many diverse user conditions.

Let us look at the long tail of innovation. There are some technologies which are likely to sell in millions because the need for them is pervasive. But contrastingly, there are also likely to be some solutions that meet the needs of only a few hundreds or thousand people. Taking the example of an online bookstore, we know that while some books are best-sellers, some sell less, and some none at all. If the store only carried best-sellers, as it often happens at railway stations or airport bookstalls, a potential book buyer may not spend too much time browsing because the choice is so limited. Paradoxically, best-sellers are sold using an 'almost yes', not with some 'maybe yes'. We almost know what kind of literature we know, so we have a quick look and then move on. Our initial bias gets confirmed most of the time and thus we stop trying to search for a book of our choice. Those who have read a review and wish to buy it or have a favourite author and thus go for it more or less, will stay longer. Those who have not bought many books and do not have strong preferences may browse many options and then may or may not select any. The point is that we had books which only one or two may read or buy, some which a few more may browse and so on. The ecosystem will be much richer, more sustainable and engaging. A good library will have books which only a handful of readers might have read in a few decades but then who knows what thoughts this book might trigger in those readers' minds? It will serve the need of readers of popular books but also less popular books.[28]

To be able to provide a rich ecosystem, one needs to provide solutions for the localized needs as well. If these needs are not met, it may lead to alienation. And with alienation comes anger, frustration and, sometimes, protests. The irony is that we are willing to spend millions in fighting our own disgruntled citizens in many tribal and other regions, but not spend mere thousands on developing location-specific solutions. I am not implying that all those who are fighting in the name of tribals are genuinely interested in the development of the region. But the sustained neglect certainly breeds alienation. To illustrate the degree of systematic neglect of tribal regions, let me take the case of forest produce. Rarely ever, even one gram of forest products, particularly non-timber ones like fruits, herbs, medicinal plants or pods, etc., are processed for value addition in situ. That it, all the raw material goes out of the forest and gets processed elsewhere. The tribal communities get a very low share of the value chain. Unless we deploy small-scale technological innovations in these regions to add value in the places from where these materials are collected (in situ value addition), alienation will not be overcome on a sustained basis.

It is not surprising that some of these locations constitute the economicallypoorest regions of our country. Wherever attempts have been made to reverse the trend, the results have been spectacular. For example, in Udaipur, a regional forest officer by the name of Mr O.P. Sharma bought two grassroots innovations from the Honey Bee Network and made it available to the local tribal community. One of these was the machine with which they could make incense sticks out of bamboo, invented by Mr Panchal and the other was the multipurpose food-processing machine invented by Dharambir from Yamunanagar. With proper packaging and marketing support, the income of the tribal people went up manifold.

Still there have not been too many such experiments by the forest department as yet. One way to treat this situation is to provide a food-for-work programme or what is now called MGNREGA (Mahatma Gandhi National Rural Employment Guarantee Act). The idea seems to be: Treat tribals as 'unskilled' labourers, ignore their knowledge systems and just pay them wages for collecting forest produce. How do we disrupt this mindset? Compared to the pure entitlement-based[29] approach, an entrepreneurial approach is not only more sustainable, but it also reinforces self-respect and dignity. Maybe we need to blend both: entitlement to basic means to start an enterprise, such as risk capital,[30] access to fabrication facilities and markets, etc., with individual- and community-level initiatives to take risk and link them with the unmet needs of customers through an entrepreneurial approach. In the past, by relying on the entitlement-based approach, we had treated poor people as a sink for aid, assistance and advice rather than as a *source* of ideas, innovations and enterprises.[31] Location-specific adaptability and flexibility in engagement models will inevitably promote entrepreneurial solutions. It must however be remembered that majority of grassroots innovators do not make good entrepreneurs. We may need different entrepreneurs to join hands with innovators and investors to take an innovation to market through social or commercial channels. The problem is that innovators generally find it difficult to make two things that are exactly alike whereas an entrepreneur has to make batch by batch consistent design and ensure delivery of the same.

Availability, Affordability and Accessibility

Frugality is not only sufficient in product design, but also needs to be extended to supply chain management. Sometimes the cost of supply chain management may be the largest contributor to the price at which a product or service is provided to the consumer.

Let us assume that there is a generic medicine, made by a reputed manufacturer, and procured by the Public Health Department to provide the medicine to the public at an extremely affordable price, say through a public health centre located within the village. Here the medicine meets the accessibility and affordability criteria but it does not meet the availability criteria if the dispensary does not have sufficient stock when a patient comes looking for it. Obviously, in such cases, the needs are not met.

Similarly, in the case of machinery or a value-adding device, the invention may meet all three criteria—i.e., availability, affordability and accessibility—but may lack after-sales service or efficient and flexible maintenance support. In such cases also, the problem will not get solved. Attention to detail is fundamental when it comes to providing sustainable solutions.

Environmental management of the waste produced in the processing or during disposal of any malfunctioning components is very seldom paid attention to. There are hardly any waste collection systems for electronics, batteries and numerous other devices and their spent components in rural areas. It is not surprising then that the improper disposal of the unrecycled materials is ultimately harmful to us as they enter the ecological or food chain in a potentially hazardous manner. Unless we build an exchange for such waste in every city, as well as online, a derivative innovation system may not emerge which will think of recycling or reusing these items. Many countries already have fixed points where disposing such electronic waste is obligatory. Else, if such waste is mixed with other wastes, as in India, its recycling and rejuvenation will become very difficult, if not impossible.

In any change process, we can have primarily two kinds of transaction costs—ex ante and ex post. Frugal innovations also require institutional arrangements through which sustainability impacts are discussed at ex-ante (before a technological exchange) and ex post (after a technological exchange has taken place) stages of the technological change. If various transaction costs are not met explicitly, they are invariably transferred to the weaker partner. How do we measure, and then eliminate these transaction costs? The first set of costs is incurred before the terms of exchange or a contract is arrived at between the provider of solutions and the consumer of solutions. The ex post costs arise when implementation starts.

Before I take a real example of a grassroots innovation, let us assume that you want to watch a film. Before, the ex ante cost will unfold as follows: First you will have to decide which film you want to watch. This constitutes the search cost. Having decided which film, you need to find out in which theatre this film is being shown. Some may be far, some may be close, some may have better quality of sound or better ambience, and after various considerations, including the cost of reaching there, you decide on the theatre. This is called the cost of finding the supplier. Now, you reach the theatre and want to buy the three or four tickets for the back row corner or aisle. You have to negotiate with the counter clerk about the acceptable location, price, sequence, etc. This is the cost of negotiation. And then the cost of getting the ticket, after paying the price, becomes the cost of arriving at a contract. The ticket is the contract between the cinema viewer and the ticket provider at the theatre. Thus, ex ante transaction costs include searching for information, finding a supplier, negotiation and drawing up the contract.

Now, let us move to the ex post transaction cost. With tickets in hand, you take the help of the usher inside the theatre who uses a torch and guides you to your seat. This is the enforcement or compliance cost. Sometimes, when you go to the seat you find someone else may be sitting there, and if this someone happens to be the friend of the theatre owner, the usher may have difficulty asking him to move to his place. This is very unfortunate, against the rules and not fair to the person who has actually paid for the ticket on those seats. Dissatisfied consumers are offered various deals ranging from seat upgrades to an extra ticket for a later visit and so on. These are called side payments. When the terms at which the original contract was signed become difficult to implement because of the changes in market condition, or technical, manufacturing or supply chain difficulty, the original terms may be modified to include other possible lubricants to make the deal go through. But there are times when as potential viewers, we don't want to forgo our entitlement. Your ticket is in your hand and you want it to be honoured. A conflict takes place, and the cost and time involved in dissolving the conflict comprises the conflict resolution cost. If the conflict is not resolved, that is, you don't agree to sit somewhere else, you may either demand compensation for the inconvenience or you may redraw the contract on mutually agreed terms. This component is called the cost of redrawing the contract. The ex post transaction cost thus includes the cost of enforcement and the cost of monitoring the implementation of the contract, side payments—i.e., the cost of modification in the terms because of the changes in the environment, which could not be anticipated at the time of signing the contract— the conflict resolution cost and, finally, the cost of redrawing the contract if nothing else works. I don't approve of bribing as a side payment cost because it is not only unethical, but it also disenfranchises the poorer people who, of course, cannot meet such costs.

Let us now see the implications of this framework for traditional knowledge holders and grassroots innovators:[32]

Searching for information

How do traditional knowledge holders or grassroots innovators find out the potential applications of their knowledge for which a third party may have some use. In the absence of this knowledge, they may sell something very precious at a throwaway price to middlemen, as they often do. There are hardly any databases of traditional knowledge in local languages.[33] How do they search for information while aspiring to a better future if such databases are not available locally in schools, tribal council offices or other common service centres. Likewise, the entrepreneurs who want to set up businesses around innovative products and services have to find out about the potential leads. Now they may or may not be Internet-savvy. In some cases, they may not even be educated. The method of searching for information has to be compatible with the existing knowledge, capacity and willingness to pursue on the part of seekers of information. At the same time, the format of information and the language can also make a difference in influencing the reduction of transaction costs. The potential investor may not know both the entrepreneur or the innovator. The available information may not confer sufficient faith in his mind to motivate him to invest. How then would such investors develop a partnership with the innovators and/or the entrepreneurs?

This cost cannot be met only by providing information on the web, and that too, in the English language. But access to multimedia and multilingual databases may make it possible for people to learn from each other and also interact with other stakeholders. In the case of herbal knowledge, the transaction costs of the potential investors, entrepreneurs, and R&D players in seeking knowledge about the scientific names of plants found in the local communities is enormously high. In the absence of scientific names (which can only be ascribed after taxonomic authentication), the modern scientific institutions, drug, dye, and nutraceutical companies may not be able to make offers of possible cooperation.

Tracking usurpation of one's knowledge rights

Local communities and individual innovators also need to track the usurpation of their knowledge by unauthorized intellectual property (IP) seekers. They will have to have access to and the ability to scan the patent applications around the world, interpret and then inform themselves and the patent offices about any suspected violation.[34] Otherwise they will remain dependent on the benevolence of the state or other civil society organizations. The bringing of their knowledge into the public domain without their authorization by national and international scholars and institutions has been the single most important instrument of exploitation and unfair treatment of their knowledge rights. In fact, no research council in the developing world or developed countries has yet characterized such behaviour on the part of the scholars as inadmissible and unethical conduct. The publication of people's knowledge and thus bringing it into the public domain reduces the transaction costs of potential users in the Western and educated segments of Eastern society. Their search costs go down without conferring any advantage on the local communities and grassroots innovators. However, providing synoptic information that is brief, only abstract, without giving technical details) is extremely useful and can generate a large number of queries for the knowledge holder.[35] The NIF received queries for various grassroots innovations from more than ninety countries entirely because it shared the synoptic information on the web. Therefore, we should balance the advantage of open-source, multilingual databases with the disadvantage of disclosing unique knowledge. While the advantages are obvious, the disadvantages are: (i) copying strategies in different regions, (ii) lookalike products entering the market, (iii) people maintaining quality and thus bringing a bad name to a category of innovation, etc. However, given the larger public interest, sharing seems to be a better alternative to holding on to information.

In the case of a multilingual database put up by SRISTI on its website, about 10,000 innovations or traditional knowledge practices were put up in the public domain so as to generate wider interest in this knowledge system of grassroots innovations and outstanding traditional knowledge practices. It remains the largest database of its kind on the web even after so many years. It is also expected that various intermediate users will share this resource with local communities, otherwise the search cost of the communities will not go down. This is one of the reasons why SRISTI, along with the NIF, organizes shodhyatras twice a year, so that existing knowledge base can be shared with local communities at their doorstep. However, this is a very costly way of diffusing knowledge though it has its own advantages in terms of cultural and ethical impact on the learners' values. Further initiatives to have the Honey Bee Network connected on mobile is under discussion with some telecommunication service providers so that almost 800–900 million cell phone users can be reached, depending upon their need and preferences, by the network.

Finding suppliers

Having found the sources of information, one has to find providers of information, services and other support systems. For a local healer or conservator of genetic resources, or an innovator, to take a sample of their material to a public or private sector R&D lab to get it analysed for potential negotiations, is well-nigh impossible. It is important to create capacity through training, counselling, institution building, so that they can deal with the institutions and their norms of providing knowledge, processing and managing at their own terms. For an innovator, to find a supplier of facilities for fabrication of machinery, testing, design, packaging, and marketing and distribution is not easy. That is why a lot of grassroots innovations remain undeveloped and localized. The cost of finding innovators has been reduced drastically for all stakeholders because of the Honey Bee Network's contribution over the last more than two decades and a half. The NIF maintains a database and is able to connect people almost instantly, even if just for a call. The mobile revolution has meant that farmers from different parts of the country and the world can simply call and get information. In due course, once we are able to generate the Honey Bee Network resource on mobile, we will be able to make a lot of the information retrievable through voice protocol without human mediation. In general, suppliers of information, commodities or services may not become authenticated or apparent while searching for information, such that somebody has to authenticate information before a lay person can rely on it. Transaction costs involved in finding supplier should not be confused with just making a website or a database. It also includes the cost of confirmation, (if not validation, which takes many years) and authentication of the knowledge in database. There is a whole lot of vouchsafing to be done before a bit of information becomes worth engaging with. Similarly, for an investor or entrepreneur or a corporation finding the right kind of innovation meeting their specifications may require prior art search (that is, reviewing prior literature and doing market research to find uniqueness) and benchmarking.

Negotiating a contract

Having found a supplier or potential user of their knowledge, the grassroots innovators have to and do use a combination of IP and/or contractual instruments as a basis for negotiation. The tension between individual and collective knowledge, organizing proper representation and nomination for negotiation and having internal as well as external negotiations are other dimensions that come into play. Negotiations between a rural innovator and an urban entrepreneur or investor can involve a whole range of ethical issues of prior informed consent (PIC),[36] capacity to negotiate, honest brokering, etc. SRISTI, the GIAN and now the NIF help innovators in this regard when opportunities for licensing their technologies arise. There have been cases where entrepreneurs have licensed technologies for which patents were not even granted. The entrepreneurs paid money because they appreciated the spirit of the negotiating platform, i.e., the Honey Bee Network. Therefore, negotiation is not just a matter of finalizing the terms of exchange but also involves influencing the ethical framework in which the stronger party does not necessarily take advantage of the weaker party.

Drawing up the contract

To be able to exercise PIC, and then arrive at reasonable terms of agreement which are acceptable within the community and as well as to the negotiating partner involves tremendous complexity, cost and resources. Without meeting these costs and enabling the communities to participate from a strong standing, the contracts may remain asymmetrical and sometimes difficult to enforce. Moreover, the language of the contract may not always be comprehensible to school-dropout innovators. Under such conditions, the responsibility of the Honey Bee Network becomes very critical. Negotiation on behalf of the innovators is a delicate matter. As they get more information, it is natural that their expectations will change. One may have to restart the negotiation as the expectations change. Since nobody ever paid heed to their intellectual property rights, it is not easy for them to understand initially that they should be paid for giving others the right to manufacture. We have developed a concept of 'technology commons'[37] which implies that people-to-people copying of technology is not only allowed but also encouraged, but people-to-firm transfer of technology should be done through licensing. Some of the interesting aspects of the contracts negotiated by us in the last twenty-five years are:

   a. The first contract SRISTI entered into with a company involved pooling of traditional knowledge in public domain and was licensed with a small upfront payment.
   b. Licensing of the rights to manufacture and market on district basis. This was perhaps the first time in the country when a technology of tilting bullock cart[38] was licensed to three small entrepreneurs for the right to sell in earmarked districts. The fee was hardly USD 500 to 1000 depending upon the number of districts. This way of licensing on non-exclusive basis

can help in democratizing the technological innovation and at the same time bring small actors into the market who may otherwise be deterred by the complexity of negotiations and terms. There was no patent granted on tilting bullock cart in this case. However, media attention and awards to the innovator influenced the market for technology.

c. The licensing to entrepreneurs on exclusive basis with the condition that if they did not sell pre-specified number of products in a year (on which royalty depends), the licence would become non-exclusive.

d. Incorporating the privilege of marketing the value-added product developed by the entrepreneur in his own district. In addition to the royalty and upfront payment, the innovator also gets dealership for a district.

e. The licensee is enabled to access funds for adding value to the product.

f. Non-exclusive licences to many manufacturers and marketing agents with or without upfront signing fee and with royalty per piece to the innovator.

g. Setting up companies jointly with the private sector to ensure value addition and marketing the products of innovators with fair and just benefit accrual to the innovators through the Technology Business Incubator (TBI) of the NIF.

h. In a model-benefit sharing agreement, a share for nature conservation, community, women's innovation promotion, and risk or contingency welfare fund for innovators has also been provided for.

There are many other conditions which have been negotiated to safeguard the interest of the innovator, including the right to revert the licence if the licensee does not commercialize a technology within a given period.

Enforcement of the contract

Having entered into a contract, keeping track of the licensing and sub-licensing of technologies by the primary contractor becomes an obligation of the communities. It is possible that the contracting party, in this case, a company or a state agency, may not work with the licensed IP from the communities directly. They may even sub-licence it to a third party who may generate revenues, which may or may not be shared with the innovators. It is important to keep track of such happenings. The enforcement of the conditions therefore requires tremendously important skills, and capacities have to be built for acquiring and using those skills. There are cases where the licensee not followed all the terms diligently. So far, the Network has avoided legal recourse for settling such problems. However, it is very clear that in the absence of any power to enforce, a small grassroots innovator may feel handicapped unless helped by platforms like the Honey Bee Network and other well-wishers.

Side payments

It is not always possible for communities or individual grassroots innovators to wait for benefits to accrue and be shared with them. Upfront sharing of benefits may be necessary in some cases, but not always. Such concessions may have to be negotiated. Sometimes offering concessions beyond the terms of the contract generates confidence amongst the innovator as well. Recently, a firm in south India to which SRISTI licensed twelve herbal products developed in its lab, displayed the names and photographs and sketches of the innovators on the package of these products. This was done as a side inducement so to speak. Likewise, innovators can offer some additional leads if the deal on the earlier contract goes well to induce the contracting parties to go beyond the terms of the contract. The opportunity exists on both sides for making terms of the contract mutually favourable by offering concessions, discounts or other considerations if the agreed terms of contract are not generating desirable outcomes.

Conflict management

During the benefit-sharing process, conflicts may arise. Such situations require capacity building of the community of innovators to settle the disputes in an efficient manner, without damaging their interests and welfare. Hence, the capacity of the community and innovators to negotiate, to identify the right platforms, and to engage public interest lawyers and supporters becomes crucial for achieving the ends of justice. Here the role of the Network and the NIF becomes very critical. There have been cases where innovators entered into contracts with a company on their own and later, when the terms were not upheld, they sought the help of the NIF. Sometimes local collaborators, in their anxiety to help the innovators quickly, may take recourse to short-circuiting the negotiation and the contractual process with the best of the intentions. But, given their lack of experience, the innovators may suffer and consider the Network responsible. It is a matter of where careful attention has to be paid by all the stakeholders to avoid conflicts from getting out of hand. So far, the policy of the Network has been to avoid acrimonious exchanges and thus try to leverage the power of persuasion instead. The results of this approach have been satisfactory by and large.

Renegotiating the contract

If despite all persuasion, the existing terms don't work, and conflicts cannot be resolved satisfactorily, the renegotiation of the contract with the attendant costs is the only alternative. In some cases, this may even be desirable. Some of these issues are described in more detail elsewhere.[39]

The implication here is that grassroots innovators face enormous transaction costs which, if not reduced, will come in the way of collaboration between various stakeholders. This message is universally applicable. No amount of pious sermons will help their cause without the creation of an institutional environment in which these costs are reduced, if not eliminated, so that the journey of 'Mind to Markets' is completed. India will otherwise remain a country of prototypes, as Laurent Perrier said in a meeting at the S.T. Microelectronics (STM) office in Noida after I delivered my talk on their Innovation Day (2015). It was organized by Varambally, senior leader and head of research and development at STM.

Inclusive development does not only mean provision of appropriate solutions, innovative products and services which are frugal and environmentally sustainable. It thus also means minimizing the transaction cost so that the people, who deserve to benefit from a particular scheme, policy or a window of opportunity, do not get excluded. Very often, the eligibility criteria in various programmes are designed to eliminate the chances of participation of the most needy and deserving. In 2010, the National Innovation Council shared a proposal for creating an India Inclusive Fund of a hundred crore rupees. As a member, I suggested that the team of people working on this Fund look at the experience of the Micro-Venture Innovation Fund which is much smaller in size but implemented with a very low transaction cost. Of course, people didn't bother. They refused to critically analyse how this Fund managed to provide in situ incubation support to grassroots innovators all over the country, with a very small team (just two or three people) of staff, but with a very active help of volunteers. And while doing so, the Fund managed to recover more than 70 per cent of the amount. Several of the recipients became very successful entrepreneurs. However, after interacting with the stakeholders they felt 'relevant' (excluding MVIF team or funded innovators). The then National Innovation Council came out with a proposal which would not invest in the early-stage, proof-of-concept ideas of the engineering students. They were of course aware of various recipients of the Gandhian Young Technological Innovation (GYTI) Award given by SRISTI through Techpedia.Sristi.org at the hands of Dr R.A. Mashelkar—recipient of the Padma Vibhushan and Fellow of Royal Society—and also the chairperson of the governing board of the National Innovation Foundation. *It is paradoxical that a Fund aimed at promoting inclusive innovation excluded the neediest and the most deserving candidates i.e., the young students of our country.* The result was that not even one young inventor received support from public funds to take his or her idea to the next level of prototyping, product development and dissemination through market or non-market channels.[40] We have highlighted the transaction costs involved in scouting such inventors, documented their experience, got them critically reviewed by the experts and then honoured them with citations so as to take them to the next level. Since a proper dialogue never took place, I gave a note of dissent and wrote to the then science and technology minister and other members of the Council. I have not yet given up though the minister then and later have listened to our plea and understood the situation.[41]

One of the most promising developments has been an agreement between SRISTI and the Biotechnology Industrial Research Assistance Council (BIRAC)[42] under which a project management unit will disburse fifteen grants of fifteen lakh rupees to young biotechnology/ medical-device students or just passed out innovators who have received the GYTI award. Another 100 promising students will be encouraged to work on grassroots innovations through a grant of one lakh rupees each. This is perhaps first time a bold investment is being made in the ideas of young creative thinkers and innovators.[43] Fifteen winners of the second round of BIRAC–SRISTI GYTI award were honoured at an award function at the Rashtrapati Bhavan organized as a part of the Festival of Innovation on 13 March 2016.[44]

The earlier decision in 2012 to fund only companies illustrates how the seeds of exclusion of needy grassroots innovators or of the tech-savvy youth/students are sown at the time of design itself. Such efforts may lose legitimacy in due course. If one invests only in the companies, then 90 per cent of the ideas will get aborted and may never reach the point by when their technologies mature, team gets formed, investments are received and thus they can establish companies. Bias seems to exist to some extent even in 2015–16 though the hope is that it will be tempered soon. What is missing in the marketplace is financing for very early stages of innovation. Nobody provides funding except the BIRAC, when even the proof of concept may not be fully frozen and ideas are at an early, formative stage, but the potential of innovation is apparent, though risk is high. This kind of insularity in policymaking systems needs wider public debate and dialogue. The accountability of institutions that try to escape from answering the questions about the exclusion of deserving and the needy ones has to be enforced. That also shows why frugal and sustainable solutions have received such little attention in the public policy system so far.

Exclusion can take place by neglecting five major constraints people face—spatial, sectoral, seasonal, skill, and those related to social segments. The policymakers can ignore ideas as well as constraints faced by people living in marginal drought- or flood-prone regions, forests or mountain areas. Spatial exclusion is often very systematic. So much of unrest in several economically backward regions is largely because of poor public and market infrastructure. Paradoxically, the probability of discovering innovations is higher in such regions as compared to the well-developed regions where markets respond to most of the unmet needs of society; people have to find their own solution here. Sectoral neglect or exclusion is typical when certain activities don't command as much demand as they did in the long past. For example, handloom and khadi are two such sectors. After agriculture, the weaving sector employs the largest number of people. But it has been so grossly neglected that after farmers, the weavers are the largest category of people committing suicides.[45] Neglect reigns also because weavers are in the clutches of moneylenders and yarn sellers who often also buy their products. They are exploited in the entire chain of production. The NIF has many innovations in handloom design but none have been disseminated widely yet since public policy support is quite weak for this sector.

Seasonal exclusion takes place when large parts of the country get cut off due to floods or other natural calamities leading to forced migration of pastoralists and other workers. The amphibious cycle by Chaurasia and Saidullahji are examples which help reduce climate-impact-induced exclusion in flood-prone regions. Those people who cannot afford boats can use these alternative solutions. Ironically, despite floods being a recurrent problem, even these innovations could not diffuse for lack of demand from state and market agencies.

Skills, which have lost markets, are another source of exclusion. When houses were made of mud or local materials like lime and stones, the workers trained in making the structures with those materials were in demand. We have to find new applications for these skills and new products using those skills to revive the prospect of these communities. Mansukhbhai Prajapati, who invented Mitti Cool, the clay refrigerator to keep vegetables fresh for five to six days, trained many more potters in making non-stick clay pans. Increased demand for his goods and services has revolutionized the pottery business and workers' skill sets. Erosion of skills of clay workers was stemmed in his village at least.

Social segments of numerous kinds are neglected on the basis of caste, economic and cultural grounds. Sometimes the place these communities dwell makes their exclusion doubly complex. Tribal communities have low literacy, very low purchasing power and are excluded by markets and the state alike. One can incorporate them in the innovation value chain by building upon the potential of traditional knowledge for developing value-added herbal products. Linkage with modern science and technology, protection of their IPRs (intellectual property rights) and creating the 'mind-to-market' journey can generate a path of hope and assurance for these marginal communities.

There are several new platforms that we need to create to facilitate the emergence of frugal and green innovations. A clearing house backed up by a database of various materials and components, including second-hand components with identified leftover life, can stimulate innovations around using these materials for solving various social and industrial problems. Many small entrepreneurs don't know about new materials or processes, and thus energy-saving technologies don't get adopted widely. A large number of MSMEs do not have access to new materials. Even their search for old components remains restricted to the nearby recycling centres.

A do-it-yourself (DIY) culture has to be promoted by sharing open-source solutions, advice, circuits, designs, etc., combining the Instructables (http://www. instructables.com/) with a library of material, component and design.

Platforms for collaborative design across disciplines, sectors, spaces and institutions are needed to promote lateral learning. A library of open-source tools for design, distributed fabrication labs, mentoring and a co-creating culture can help trigger a lot more innovations than has been the case so far.

SEVEN

Mobilizing Social and Ethical Capital for Supporting Innovation

In 1996, the planning for the first International Conference on Creativity and Innovation at Grassroots (ICCIG) had started at the IIMA with the support of the Honey Bee Network and other sponsors with the aim of bringing the best of formal and informal science together. Never before did innovators in education, technology, institutions, culture and marketplace had come together at one place to explore the emerging options for grassroots innovators and supporting actors. Before the conference was inaugurated on 11 January 1997, there was considerable interest within IIMA and outside about the activities of the Honey Bee Network. Delegates from forty countries got together to look at different ways in which a bridge could be built between formal and informal knowledge, science and technology and institutional systems. Srimati Elaben, the founder of the globally acclaimed SEWA bank and the Self Employed Women's Association (SEWA)—a new social movement and a trade union—was invited to speak at the inaugural session. Srimati Elaben had started a microfinance movement many decades ago and also struggled for the right of pavement dwellers, and created the first women's bank. She had set up SEWA as the trade union for poor women vendors in 1972. To support the women workers financially, a Shri Mahila Sewa Sahakari Bank, or SEWA Bank was set up in 1974. Thanks to the efforts of SEWA, the Indian Parliament passed the Street Vendors (Protection of Livelihood and Regulation of Street Vending) Act in September 2013. This Act prevents arbitrary eviction and regulates fines, besides other protections.

Despite all my supposed sensitivity on gender issues, I committed a major blunder at the event. The dais was appropriate for the male speakers but not for the female speakers who are generally shorter in height. We had forgotten to put a small bench so that the lady speaker could be seen properly by the audience and establish proper eye connect. Srimati Elaben made a mention of this inadequacy of ours. We deserved this reprimand. In the next issue of the *Honey Bee Newsletter*, we narrated this story to show that mere commitment to a cause was not enough. One has to convert one's concerns into a carefully crafted, diverse range of actions. We acknowledged that we had failed in doing that.

Conceptually, the natural capital was the first to come about with the evolution of human civilization. The hunter-gatherers societies started drawing boundaries

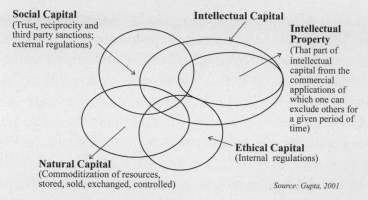

Social Capital
(Trust, reciprocity and
third party sanctions;
external regulations)

Intellectual Capital

**Intellectual
Property**
(That part of
intellectual
capital from the
commercial
applications of
which one can
exclude others for
a given period of
time)

Ethical Capital
(Internal regulations)

Natural Capital
(Commoditization of resources,
stored, sold, exchanged, controlled)

Source: Gupta, 2001

7.1 Interaction among natural, social, ethical and intellectual capital resources

around natural resources asserting their rights to collect, store, exchange or gift resources drawn from nature. Conflicts were inevitable and the development of strategies for safeguarding accumulated natural resources followed. The emergence of rudimentary common property rights led to the assertion of one's dominance over others. The arguments began: 'I will graze my animals here, you do it there; I will harvest the fruits of these trees, you do it elsewhere.' On one hand, humankind started inventing ways of harnessing natural resources and on the other, inventions for safeguarding one's rights over the resource boundaries, besides accumulating stocks of the same, also began to develop. One did not live only from day to day. If one got a good harvest of fish or fruits, not everything could be consumed the same day. The technologies for storage, institutions for protection, and culture for sharing began to evolve. Sharing of resources led to evolution of communities, not always harmonious, not always respectful of the rights of other communities. Not all social groups had similar skills or tools to harvest natural resources for the common good. Moreover, the private property rights had not yet evolved. But the urge to express individual perceptions of nature through art, architecture and other artefacts began to take shape. Cave paintings, as mentioned earlier, made 40,000–50,000 years ago are an example.

Peaceful coexistence was not always the rule. Battles for domination began, so did the innovations in the means of fighting, whether using stone tools, archery or other kinds of weapons.[1]

When mere hand tools did not suffice, and the stocks of natural resources needed to be stored, moved, or processed, there was a need for new processes and techniques to evolve. For example, the seeds had to be stored for many years so that despite drought- and flood-induced losses, the new production cycles could be launched when weather favoured the situation. Many decisions by individual farmers cannot be made independent of the choices of constraints faced by others. Institutional context and cultural values invariably shaped technological choices. When gender differences affected roles and thus technological choices as explained in Chapter 5, the cultural values also started reinforcing these choices, though not always through consensus. Creative tensions from factors based on gender, status, clan or location did not always remain fair or just in their disposition. That is how domination and unjust exploitation became part of society. However, local communities did try to explore collective win-win solutions, which led to social capital accumulation for any community. We have perhaps noticed anomie more than the order social capital creates in our society.

If in semi-arid regions, one farmer grows crops but all neighbouring farmers leave the fields fallow, the prospects of damage by grazing animals increases manifold. But technological developments had to be complimented by new institutional designs, new rules or norms. In many dryland regions, striga is a major weed causing loss of productivity in the sorghum crop. It is a parasitic weed. Various ways of controlling it had failed. Then scientists at the Central Research Institute of Dry Land Agriculture, Hyderabad, learnt from farmers and worked with them to identify a very creative way of coping with this problem. They noted that in places where the entire village decides not to sow crops like sorghum before a particular day of the lunar cycle, the weed infestation was high. But where farmers sowed the crop ten to fifteen days earlier, the weed infestation was low. If sowing is done fifteen days in advance, the crop grew up early, shade from the leaves did not let the weeds like striga to flower, and the seeds are not set. In the next season, the weed infestation goes down because of lesser seeds set and left in the soil during the previous season. However, such practices did not work at an individual level. Everybody had to cooperate. Similarly, many of the indigenous breeds of cattle and other animal species could be preserved mainly because the community collectively decided to maintain good-quality breeding bulls. They were not allowed to mate with its daughters to prevent inbreeding and the loss of vitality. Such practices with far-reaching consequences for productivity of farming systems over millennia could not have been possible without indigenous common property institutions (see an open-source database of such examples from different parts of the world: sristi.org/cpri). Individuals in such cases did not take private decisions ignoring group norms. Thus social norms started shaping individual and social imagination. Groups cannot take decisions independent of what they think is the compliance capability of the members of that group. Yet, a creative tension among centripetal and centrifugal forces defined the imaginative space.

The emergence of respect for collective norms leads to formation of social capital. It evolves through iteration and interaction of trust, reciprocity, and third-party sanctions. There is often an implicit faith that if social capital is harnessed for a common or public good, people reciprocate by increasing their trust in the institution and moderating their expectations accordingly. With very little resources and a small team, the Honey Bee Network had mobilized around 5000 ideas, innovations and traditional knowledge practices by 1997. Most of these were shared in local languages not only with the provider of the knowledge but also with other community members. Perhaps the Honey Bee Network has shared the largest pool of open-access knowledge based on people's creativity for strengthening sustainable livelihoods in the world today. We have had our share of ups and downs in the performance of the network. But it is important to understand the interplay of social, natural, ethical and intellectual capitals to appreciate how the Network has succeeded in harnessing so much goodwill and voluntary support.

Let us take the case of a fishing community to understand the evolution of social and ethical capital. Some fishing communities have a norm that nobody will use a gill net of less than four inches mesh size. This practice will ensure that only big fish are caught and small immature ones are spared. If somebody is caught catching small fish, the community may sanction his behaviour (confiscate the net, damage it, fine the offender and in the case of repeated offence, may even order social boycott). Such a norm is decided upon collectively, compliance is ensured through trust and reciprocity and in the case of default, there is social penalty or sanction. The role of social institutions is very important in providing the context in which technological innovations evolve at all levels—at the grassroots or even in formal organizations. The shared understanding of what is acceptable to a group may define the boundaries of what rate, scale, scope of technological change is tried.

New norms are evolved by communities which make tools, technologies and social institutions compatible with advances in the human civilization journey, but not always in fair and just manner. Many paradoxes pervade this journey. For example, women were prevented from accessing various skills and tools freely. Just as women were prohibited from ploughing the land, there were many restrictions put on their occupational choices. The kind of skills in which girls were required to be adept were focused more on their domestic roles. So far as learning opportunities were concerned, there were great many women debaters and scholars in the same period when such occupational restrictions were put. But by and large, they were culturally denied carpentry and blacksmith tools in India. By force of exclusion, they could not develop certain kind of solutions even if they had ideas. But they learnt to cope with, rather than transcend, the stresses in many cases. Similarly, certain Dalit communities were denied access to specific skills, roles and institutions. Different kind of exclusions paved the path for those who tried to defy various norms. Similar restrictions, as those put on women, were also put on Dalits, traces of which still exist in many parts of the country. But then innovators are a kind of deviant researchers, as I have argued earlier.[2] They overcome these barriers by collaboration across community and gender boundaries. (We have come across numerous examples where communities have created social norms for collaborative learning. Karimbhai, a Muslim potter, serves community members of different faith including tribals with his herbal tradition of healing. Similarly, Rehmatbhai treats all the community's animals as well as others, around without any reservation. Khemjihai was once approached by women of Gadhada village in the Sabarkantha district. They complained of a lot of pain in their neck due to the heavy loads they carried on their heads, particularly water pots. Khemjibhai, a retired teacher, observed in a lighter vein that the head was not meant to carry load; it was designed to think! The womenfolk felt he was not taking them seriously.

But Khemjibhai later designed a load-carrying device which shifted the load from the head to the shoulders.

There are similar creative people across different cultural and social identities and yet stock of social capital gets affected by sectarian or amiable pursuits of interested parties. If an innovator works in isolation, and the innovation does not address a community-felt need, social respect and trust may not follow in the same way if the case was otherwise. In Morigaon village, Kanak Das was one such individual innovator engaged in developing a cycle that generated energy from the bumps on the road (though to a limited extent only), and many other ideas such as charging a battery by shock-absorbing energy. The community did not identify much with these ideas and social capital was limited. Later, when he addressed the needs like paddy-threshing devices or other farm solutions, his situation changed. The expression of creativity in technological fields is not always very distinct from its expression in other fields.

How art, culture and social institutions not only stifle but also nurture social innovations and creativity through norms, rules and taboos is worth looking into. The oldest cave paintings discovered, as mentioned earlier, date back 40,000 years in Europe and Indonesia, and about 25,000 years in India. The existence of art and the need to express experiences or insights demonstrates very early evidence of human creativity. The primitive art forms generally deal with expressions of hunting or chasing animals or human forms with various kinds of embellishments/ornamentation. The moment sharing became the dominant ethos of human society, the evolution of trust could not have been far behind. There are two kinds of reciprocities that generally dominate our day-to-day transactions that influence the evolution of trust. Specific reciprocity: i.e. 'this' for 'this', or for example, you paid for my tea yesterday, I pay for your tea today. Sometimes young people even say, 'We are square'. Now the experience over tea yesterday cannot be compared with a chat over tea today. So we can never be square really. Still, an impression is gained that we are. Generalized reciprocity, on the other hand refers to 'this' for 'that', or for example, I helped you in thatching your hut, so you help me in ploughing my land. It is very difficult to work out the exact equivalence of the two acts. How vulnerable one is if a roof leaks for want of repair can be felt by one who suffers from this problem. Likewise, the criticality of pooling bullocks by small farmers to till one's land in critical time zones in view of climatic change because of sudden rain in dry regions is another obvious example. Many times it rains on one side of the village and not in the other in semi-arid regions. In such cases, those who get rain one time will not be able to sow crops in time if not assisted by other farmers whose fields may not be ready or may not have received rain. Such exchanges or 'I owe yous' (IOUs) invariably create trust when they remain unredeemed. That is, many obligations are not encashed or settled in the hope that these will trigger goodwill reciprocities when the need arises without asking for them.

When written languages were still not developed adequately, many civilizational tools evolved to create settlements, social bonds and other forms of social organization. In these situations, trust and reciprocity must have been the primary driver of the first few communities that emerged. Thus, social sanction became imperative to ensure compliance with collective norms. The collaborative creations in the form of managing pastures, grazing lands and waterbodies, and conserving forests became a social imperative. The social capital was thus an outcome of reliable and somewhat predictable exchanges among community members generating trust in the process. The reinforcement for trust came through reciprocity. The fairness and trust in the institutions was achieved through third-party sanctions. Not necessary the superior authority, even peers or strangers could sanction one's behaviour. Norms in society cannot be enforced unless people have a peer culture and people feel responsible enough to sanction each other's behaviour when required.

Ethical Capital

Let us assume that you are visiting a new city for some work. While walking to your office, you pass by a small roadside garden where children are playing. You notice two children fighting on the roadside pavement. You fear that one of them might hurt or push the other on to the road with heavy traffic. What would you do? Most of us will not think twice. We will go and separate the kids and might even offer advice to them to be careful and not play so close to the road. But who gave us the right to separate the kids? What is the probability that these children's parents might pass through the

city where we live and might separate *our* children
in a similar situation? Even when there is no chance
of a direct reciprocity, we still hope that somebody
responsible would someday respond similarly to our
children if anything untoward happened. We let our
children play on the roadside without supervision all
the time. All of us have borrowed from the social and
ethical capital of our society in the form of unsupervised
fun, learning, and explorations. There will be no
childhood if every moment was supervised. In this case
the right to sanction the behaviour of children was
assumed because of social, ethical and moral values.
These values in fact reduce transaction costs a great
deal because of the trust they create or reinforce.[3] When
we get back the things we have lost by forgetting or
leaving them somewhere only because of the honesty of
the person who has found them, we see ethical capital
in action. When an innovator develops sound-related
or other devices to scare away the birds in summer, but
would not kill them, it is an example of ethical capital.
It would have been so easy to scatter poisoned seeds for
killing the birds and thus save oneself the trouble under
the hots scorching sun. But millions of people do not do
that, thankfully.

Unlike social capital, ethical capital involves sanctions
from within. We feel guilty when we break a rule and
feel enriched when we punish ourselves for an act that
we don't feel very good about. Trust and reciprocity are
vital in ethical capital too. But, in the absence of external
regulation, by peers or superiors, the reciprocities are
implicit and not explicit. Trust acts a kind of contract

between oneself and one's conscience. Let us take the case of the same fishing community we talked about earlier. Among the fisherman, there may be a taboo on using a gill net having a mesh size of less than four inches. The community may also have established norms of not catching fish during spawning periods: This is the time when fish are very dull, they go upstream, spawn their eggs in shallow waters, move very slowly and are easy to catch. But, to maintain the reproductive cycle, there is a taboo on fishing during this period. There is no external regulation and there is no third-party sanction. Compliance to this norm is observed through ethical capital. Why would a society evolve a norm not to catch fish when they are *easiest* to catch? Otherwise, sustainability is not possible. Foregoing current consumption for future assurance in supply for our and future generations is deeply embedded in the indigenous institutions evolved by people at the local level.[4]

The higher the ethical capital of a society, the lesser is the need for external regulation, and greater is the trust, peace and rule-bound behaviour. The norms may be cultural, social or moral; the enforcement can be through external or internal regulations. Even in companies where ethical capital is higher, quality control expenses will be low and self-regulation will ensure much higher productivity and quality. Ethical capital in such a case implies an institution-building process thus relying on one's own sense of right and wrong rather than external inspections, and constant oversight. Self-regulation is not a substitute for a lack of systems, norms and standards. Rather, it provides an efficient way of achieving adherence through internalization of the enforcement of these norms. External enforcement is not needed but through tracking of exceptions. In highly specialized groups, where tasks are not easily substituted, higher ethical capital is the only way to achieve excellence and relevance. At the grassroots level, when farmers deliberately do not use electrical fencing in order to avoid hurting wildlife, even if they can afford it, they are augmenting ethical capital. Likewise, setting land aside by growing crops preferred by wild geese, waterfowl, etc., for natural damage by wildlife, is a way of coexisting with nature through natural and ethical capital.[5]

Intellectual Capital

The intellectual capital, of course, is the sum total of the knowledge of various transactions in society. In different parts of the world, notwithstanding the efforts made to exclude certain sections of society from access to collective pool of knowledge, there has been a tradition to share much of the knowledge openly. It is said that the hands of the workers who built the Taj Mahal were cut once they finished building one of the seven wonders of the world so that they could not make another structure like it. Whether this is true or false, the point remains that societies have tried to restrict the sharing of some part of intellectual capital with others in one way or the other. In ancient literature, certain low-caste communities and women were denied the privilege of listening to or learning from sacred texts. This was a mechanism of securing special rights for certain privileged classes. The concept of intellectual property is not new. That part of the intellectual capital, from the commercial application of which one is excluded for a given period of time constitutes intellectual property as we understand it now. I will not get into more details except to recall a few more examples of how restrictions on the spread of knowledge as a public good have been erected by people in power but in some cases, communities as well.

It is said that there was a particular mango variety which was sent in a basket to the viceroy in Calcutta by the farmers in Murshidabad. However, the farmers didn't want that this variety should be grown anywhere else. Before sending the mangoes, they would take a thin needle and puncture the stone (seed) inside the mango so that there was no chance of growing of a plant from the seed again. In this way the community maintained a control over their genetic property.

Among the Zuni tribe members, located in New Mexico, USA, there was a tradition where even the brothers and sisters could not copy the ornamental designs made by one without the other's permission on various kinds of ceramics.[6] This indigenous community has many other unique traditional knowledge practices, some of which have contemporary relevance. For instance, when they wanted to revive old peach trees in the past, they had only the stumps of the trees cut. There were no other trees around. A group of elders then advised the young people to make a wedge on the stump and cover it with cow dung and other manure. After some time, new sprouts would come up. One could then take these sprouts and plant them elsewhere to grow the seedlings. This knowledge was shared openly among the members of the tribe.

But, there are umpteen instances when certain tribal healers may not share their formulations fearing that by telling others about it, they might lose their significance. There may be many reasons for drawing such restrictions around a knowledge system. In untrained hands, it might do more damage than good. If some of the ingredients are rare in occurrence, their excessive use might lead to extinction of these species. In some cases, the ingredients may be commonly known plants and by sharing that information, the intrigue and the mystique inherent in the formulation and its practice may disappear. The faith of the people in the viability of the solution may also weaken. I don't want to pass a judgement about the willingness, or otherwise, of people to share knowledge. But it would suffice to say that had intellectual capital been predominantly or excessively restricted at any time in history, so much civilizational growth would not have taken place. Open innovations and knowledge systems, twenty-six years ago, appeared the only way. In the Honey Bee Network, we have tried to protect the IPR of schoolchildren, farmers, artisans, tribals and others so that people-to-people learning takes place openly. But, people-to-firm sharing is mediated through licensing. This is what we call as Technology Commons.

The earlier example of the motorcycle-based santi, the multipurpose toolbar, is a good example. Mansukhbhai Jagani invented the attachment of santi for bullet motorcycle in 1992. Later a patent was granted to him in the USA in 2003 through SRISTI and in India through the GIAN. More than 150 fabricators over the last two decades have copied and adapted, improved and redesigned the same to make location- and crop-specific derivative innovations. During the doctoral thesis of Riya Sinha, the concept of Technology Commons evolved. It 'evolved based on the need to bundle lead technological innovations and their derivative innovations so that people-to-people learning, imitation, and replication would not only be tolerated but even encouraged. However, "technology commons" ensure that sharing of this bundle with firms is mediated only through licensing.'[7] The interplay of natural, social, ethical and intellectual capital provides unique opportunities for companies and other formal organizations to shape their agenda under corporate social responsibility (CSR) and other platforms for engagement with the informal sector or other social segments of development. The portfolio of various kinds of capital would influence how viable and durable the relationships between the formal and informal sector are. When we structure the mode of engagement between the formal and informal sector focusing too much on utilitarian exchanges, it may come in the way of institution building. An organizational relationship becomes institutional when external demands are replaced by internal commands. When external commands drive our behaviour, we are doing something because we are told to do so. Obviously, such work will never bring out the best in us. When we do what we wish to do because that is the right thing to do, we are driven from within. We are guided by our norms, some of which may have been influenced by social norms but not by any external authority, our behaviour becomes institutional in nature. Not all institutions are liberating and empowering. Many women accept to be in positions of disadvantage not because they are being forced to, but because they have internalized that to be their 'natural' state. Such a case of 'learnt helplessness' should be taken as an example of negative institutional behaviour, as against positive institutional behaviour where autonomy matches agency; that is, one has not only the freedom to do things, but also the ability to take decisions in the best interest of the task, the institution and the person or performer.

Many organizations help in building institutional norms of behaviour among themselves but also with outsiders. It is here that the synchronicity in values comes into play. One cannot expect that human preferences will always favour material over ethereal, immediate over distant, and definite over indefinite. The foundations of so-called rationality are not always very deep. How else will society work towards creating and redeeming inter-generational IOUs?

The idea is that when community members remember favours made by somebody's grandparents to one's own, there are debts incurred which take many generations to settle. This creates a long time frame within which the IOUs are settled. A longer time frame is not restricted to personal favours or exchanges; sometimes these extend to nature and social relations too. The grassroots innovators tend to take a larger and longer view of life and don't seem to be in a hurry to make a lot of money from their creativity—exceptions aside. Since they might have received help from others, they extend the same to budding innovators, and the generous Honey Bee Network, an open-source movement, is sustained. The more trust a society has, the longer is the time frame in which it appraises the viability of human choices. Many of the nature-dependent communities have longer time frames and preference for more diverse ecosystems. Truly speaking, development can be defined only as an ability to think in the long term and have a wide horizon of choices. A shorter time frame as well as narrow choices makes a system not only unsustainable but also vulnerable. During our shodhyatras in many villages, we have noticed poor people planting slow-growing species. It is generally assumed that poor people have a short time frame and thus may prefer fast-growing species instead. Paradoxically, people who were more prosperous are the ones who planted tree species which mature faster, such as the eucalyptus tree. And yet, we affix the terminology of underdeveloped to the former and developed to the latter!

The longer time frame often also leads to more diversified choices and thus a more compassionate view of life. When we are in a hurry, wanting to get returns quickly, we are less tolerant and far more utilitarian. But for most practical and useful connections, everything else becomes dispensable. None of us likes it, yet most of us conform to it. Isn't it strange that our preferences do not always reflect what we seem to inherently want? We tend to follow a scale to measure our satisfaction, which is calibrated by those people for whom short-term results are the only worthwhile things to care about. There is one more paradox that has to be appreciated. Long-term vision, on one hand, generates patience with the outcomes, but on the other, it makes us impatient to start things here and now. Recently, Professor Joichi Ito showed how the concept of now-ness, i.e., starting things here and now helped in achieving results in real time which otherwise seemed so improbable. After a tsunami struck the nuclear reactors in Japan, Joichi was concerned as a Japanese citizen whose house was not too far from the reactors. When he checked on the Internet, he found a lot of other people shared similar concerns. They were all doubtful about the ability or willingness of the government to share full information on the extent of the crisis. They were not sure how bad the situation of radiation leakage was. In their search for solutions, a community of the individuals concerned started emerging. Joichi felt that unless Geiger counters were fabricated quickly and easily, the people will not be able to measure the radiations correctly and thus take care of themselves and their kin appropriately. Joichi found experts on the Net who knew how to make Geiger counters; some who even knew how to communicate the designs to enable people to measure radiation levels themselves. Eventually, the Geiger counters could be made, disseminated and, in a democratic way, innovative knowledge could be generated and used. As professionals, they work on long-term projects with high uncertainty and complexity. But, in order to maintain their sanity, they have to act sometimes impatiently, for short-term, large-impact outcomes. I call this the 'theory of imperfect beginnings'. In our anxiety to do things well, sometimes we don't stress on doing it all. The best outcome becomes the enemy of the better alternative. Perfectionism is a virtue, but procrastination is a vice. The middle ground between the two extremes lies in the making of imperfect beginnings.

This desire to improve things despite all constraints has existed among all strata of our society, as mentioned earlier in the context of forgotten labourers. The social, ethical and intellectual capital of workers at the grassroots level has remained grossly underutilized. Let me refer to another instance from Jamaica referred by Clifford D. Conner:[8]

> Between 1760 and 1830, the Jamaican Legislature passed 49 bills granting patents for improved methods in sugar and rum production. Of these, 34 were for innovations in the infernal sugar crushing mills. It should be said that there were also many agricultural patents at the same time in the mother country, but they were mostly concerned with how to prepare manure or improve irrigation. Machinery patents were in the distinct minority. The most important patents in Jamaica were undoubtedly those that involved the application of steam power to the sugar mill. It would take at least 30 years for steam power to be as important in the British textile mills, a cornerstone of the industrial revolution.

The role of workers in developing these inventions is now well established and yet policies and institutions did not recognize the potential of creative communities the at the grassroots for years. Louis Proyect, in his blog, refers to Clifford Conner's 'People's History of Science', and specifically refers to Satchell's work which, 'reveals that many of the patents were the inspiration of artisans working on the mills, most of whom were slaves rather than scientists off in a laboratory. The slaves themselves occupied a sort of netherworld between abject fieldwork and free labour.'[9] As Proyect comments on Satchell's observation:

> Nevertheless, slaves were the principal artisans, and they worked in foundries. My considered view here is that the slaves actively participated in inventing new techniques and equipment pertinent to the sugar industry. My position is based on two premises. First (as stated before), slaves were the principal artisans in the island. In Jamaica there was a paucity of White artisans, so there developed an almost total reliance on the artisan slaves. Planters relied heavily on slave labour for all aspects of plantation life; it is for this reason that Douglas Hall concludes that the slave was a 'multi-purpose tool'. Barry Higman notes that at the time of emancipation in 1834 compensation was paid for 17,873 artisan slaves, representing 5.74 per cent of the total slave population. These included blacksmiths, millwrights, coopers, wheelwrights, masons, plumbers, carpenters, coppersmiths and engineers.

Many of these slaves are believed to have come from that part of Africa where a long tradition of metallurgy existed and arms and ammunition were manufactured for long. I recall another short study that one of my students and currently a faculty member at IIMA had done as a part of a Doctoral/Fellow Programme in Management (FPM) course on Institution Building at the Institute. Then a student, Vaibhav Bhamoriya, was interested in looking at some instance where common people had produced examples of outstanding excellence in their work without external help. I had known that puncture-repair mechanics on the roadside are often so adept that long-distance drivers can be sure that a puncture repaired by them would never leak from the same spot on the tyre. Keeping this in mind, I asked students about any incident when they had experienced a puncture leak in their car. A new puncture was always possible. Almost never did I get any example of that kind of leak. I thought of it as a six-sigma case of excellence. I advised Vaibhav to study this phenomenon. He dutifully did so, going around and talking to mechanics repairing motor and scooter tyre punctures, and in his research located a senior mechanic from Kerala who had trained most other mechanics in that region over the last thirty years. The mechanic had come from a background of rubber plantations back home. Most other workers who trained under him had also come from working on similar plantations. The mechanic mentioned that handling rubber was natural and instinctive to them. He had imbued in his trainees a sense of ethical responsibility towards the commuters who trust the mechanics to do an almost perfect job. Thus an individual ethical responsibility towards users gave rise to social and ethical capital of the entire community.

Excellence can thus be achieved through ethical capital. When the National Innovation Foundation had to file patents to get grassroots innovations validated, tested or fabricated, most partners did not charge for their time and only took minimal fees. Thus the NIF could make use of its limited resources for serving a much larger number of innovators and traditional knowledge holders, which, otherwise, it could not have done. Market players, much against conventional understanding, offered to extend significant support voluntarily or at concessional terms as well, thus adding to the financial, intellectual, social and ethical capital base of the Honey Bee Network and the NIF.

It is not just the actors from the formal sector who have added to the social capital base, but the grassroots community members themselves who have made the most contribution. They have shared their knowledge without demanding any reciprocity. They often join the shodhyatras requiring sometimes six to eight days of constant travelling, all at their own cost.

The vulnerability of the economically disadvantaged but knowledge-rich workers, whether as slaves in history or free workers in democratic societies, has not constrained their creativity.[10] Getting more out or less for more (MLM), as Dr Mashelkar puts it, is an imperative adage for grassroots innovators. How else could they manage with so little for so long?

EIGHT

Lessons for Learners

Technically, most readers should glean their own lessons from the stories narrated here based on the lives of creative, knowledge-rich, economically disadvantaged people. But then, given the compulsions of life, being busy with things, sometimes with thoughts, there may be some who would prefer to know what the key takeaways from this book are. As I see fit, here follows a quick summary of lessons for readers:

Looking for Ideas

Sensing unmet needs

Is there any bigger threat to democracy than making a lot of communities around the world feel that their unmet needs are of no concern to those who matter? A distributed, networked and shared economy requires a large number of spurs for sprouting ideas, inventions and innovations. Not all ideas may grow into useful products and services, whether for the local economy or global application. But some may.

Diversity is the essence of inclusiveness and creativity. Redundancy—not too much, lest it leads to inertia, and not too little, making life fragile—is helpful. Addressing these unmet needs also makes business sense for those who wish to invest, or want to be an entrepreneur or just wish to innovate for innovation's sake.

Ideas matter, a lot of ideas matter even more

Let us not nip ideas emerging at the grassroots level in the bud, and let us not claim that we know which ideas are needed by society in the now versus the future. The Honey Bee Network has used screens of varying intensity at the community, regional, national and global level. Sometimes the spirit of breaking out of inertia which is deeply entrenched in local mindsets is more important than the substance of the actual output.

Don't ethics influence the efficiency and economics of doing things?

When hundreds of intellectual property law firms, scientists in public and private sector labs and other volunteers support grassroots innovators without charging for their time at all, or only nominally, then it does seem that ethics influence efficiency. When an even larger number of innovators share their knowledge without expecting much in return, indeed a goodwill-based knowledge exchange system is established.

Patents are a small part of the knowledge sector as compared to what has been shared freely in the open, and this reveals the generosity of the informal sector. The formal sector still has to show many more good examples of reciprocity and reasonability in this regard. Should such people remain poor because their ethics are superior while the rest get richer?

Design is not a cyclical process but a zigzag journey

The oscillations of design alternatives in the sea of experience do not allow for a linear discourse. Therefore, a zigzag description is a more accurate narration of any design process in the life of a product or service. Back and forth movement of choices between users, non-users, onlookers and others reflects a more realistic iteration of the design journey of innovations at the grassroots level.

Learning New Heuristics, Not Just Solutions

Fertilizing the imagination: Slow and turbulent is the optimal pace and also more sustainable

Maximizing output per unit of time is not always better than the alternative. Likewise, smoother flow of throughput is not always better than turbulent or irregular flow. Working with frugal innovations at the grassroots level can teach us new or different ways of thinking, thereby fertilizing our imagination in the process. We should not forget that the wood of the trees that grow slowly is much stronger, lasts much longer and is more useful for making memorable furniture and sculptures than the soft wood of comparably fast-growing species. New heuristics or metaphors of gestalts are worth learning from frugal grassroots innovations—one should not dismiss them only because their artefactual value may not appear as relevant.

Learning requires listening, and a lot of listening

Many socioecological interactions at the grassroots level can only be understood when people trust outsiders to share both their agony and achievements. The pastoralists in a lion sanctuary understand the need for lions to remain closer to primary prey (deer) and secondary prey, i.e. cattle. Thus, at times, common people understand ecological principles much better than the managers of the system.

Building Bridges between Different Knowledge Systems: Design, Diffuse and Derive Innovations

Reciprocal, responsible and respectful bridges between the formal and informal sector need to be built

The belief that David and Goliath can work together should eventually propel social knowledge exchange and engagements in the future. Learning from grassroots innovators not only at the artefactual level, but also the metaphorical, heuristic and gestalt levels, will enrich the repertoire of corporate actors in the organized sector.

Elongating an innovation's journey to market by adding too many features may not help

The difference between the few who succeed and the many who don't sometimes lies in this ability to stick to the essentials in version one of the innovation.

What are the barriers to diffusion of open-source, extremely affordable solutions?

If a very large majority of women and girls are anaemic, then using iron ladles and vessels for cooking and short-term storage could meet the deficiency of iron in their diets. But then, public health programmes may not choose to diffuse such simple yet effective solutions. A bit of lemon juice will render the solution even more effective. If the many vessels used for cooking and serving mid-day meals could help millions of girls get their essential iron, it may hurt the iron supplement industry—but not the poor, will it?

Are we programmed to reject simple solutions? Is complexity a sign of credibility? Do public policymakers prefer purchased solutions over do-it-yourself, simple, scientific, innovative and/or time-tested solutions? New channels of communication have to be forged for democratizing such knowledge.

Learning from users can help, but just that?

Users of existing products and services can indeed suggest improvements in them. Lots of research and action has shown that those makers who listen to creative users benefit from and can generate even more new ideas, even if they seldom share the benefits arising out of these improved products and services with the idea providers. Yet, the examples where they actually work with grassroots innovators to co-create solutions to the problems of the knowledge-rich, economically poor consumers are very rare.

The issue is that not all potential consumers are alike. Some can give feedback on existing or proposed products and services while some can give feed-forward about new possibilities. And what about those who have never used these products and services; can their aspiration not guide us at all? Those who do not use the products may also have viewpoints which can be helpful to designers of new products and services. After all, an ecosystem includes not just consumers and providers, but also onlookers.

Why are national innovation ecosystems afraid of grassroots innovation?

Every country and culture has enough oddballs who wish to try things out differently and solve problems using their own genius. Every shop floor has workers who wish to *try*. Every school has children (and even those out of school) who are bubbling with energy to change things in the here and now. But we are afraid of accepting such unorthodox innovations. It will require much more openness to accept the fact that good ideas can come from the most unexpected quarters. It will require redesigning institutions, restructuring systems of governance and re-evaluating the evidence—which the Honey Bee Network has marshalled over twenty-six years. The vision requires the building of bridges between the formal and informal systems of science, technology, manufacturing, services, agriculture, and rural and urban development.

I hope there will be new beginnings to learn about the spirit, philosophy and structure of thoughts spawning frugal innovations. It does not matter whether rich or poor, every country, corporation and community needs to reinvent the ecosystem of frugal and green innovations at the grassroots level. Then the days of wasteful, consumption-oriented lifestyles will be over.

Do we need new standards for legitimizing grassroots innovation?

Standards play a very important role in promoting innovations and creating markets for innovations. Since manufacturing standards exist for products that are already known or can be anticipated, they are generally made compatible with global norms. But grassroots innovations are not regulated by such standardizations. Most fabricators change the design parameters according to variability in the agro-ecological conditions in which users work. It becomes more complex in the case of innovations that use mostly second-hand parts.

When an innovation has spread widely and has been adopted by many users, should there be a less cumbersome process for registering manufacturing standards? What kind of system will help grassroots innovations to reach and diffuse in the market?

In the Pursuit of Authenticity: I Learn, We Learn

Authenticity is the necessary condition for making a breakthrough

For making breakthroughs in life, there has to be synchronicity between the inner and outer being of the same individual. Without such synchronicity, can we really seek authenticity? A very simple way to test one's own authenticity is to ask if you will behave the same way in the absence of any external monitor.

It is also a truism to say that doing something repeatedly does not necessarily make us an expert. Practising some form of knowledge, craft or art makes us good at it but this is not always the case. Hence, authenticity also means being true to your cause and learning new things, questioning the status quo and daring to traverse the untrodden path. It also means that setting our own standards to gauge the progress of one's inner journey is a tough challenge. One might set the bar too low to enjoy a sense of achievement. But isn't it unfair to lower our expectations from ourselves?

Success counts only when you can share it

With most of our education centred on competitive learning rather than collaborative learning, we have forgotten the joy of sharing. I was reminded of the collaborative feel of success during a shodhyatra in Ladakh, when a student commented on how some students had gone further ahead leaving some behind to fend for themselves: 'Sir, today we realized that if you are on the top and you have no one to share it with—you are not there.' Many times we are so obsessed with excelling in our own chosen missions that we forget to interact with our peers, fellow passengers, fellow walkers!

Samvedana se srijansheelta

Mallesham not only addressed a personal problem of his mother's pain, but also removed the capacity constraint of the Pochampalli sari industry. Do we always need to experience societal pains ourselves to be able to find solutions for them?

Over the years we've found that children are often more receptive of others' problems than adults. Try organizing an idea contest or just a fest among children— they amaze us with their creative, compassionate and collaborative solutions.

Many grassroots innovators like Dharambir, Rajsingh, Mallesham, Mehtar Hussain, Arvindbhai Patel, Amrutbhai Agrawat, Maltiben, Arkhiben etc., have generated individual solutions and assets but have simultaneously contributed to community capacity building and upliftment. A team without strong empathy for the people to be served may achieve efficiency but may not make breakthroughs. Empathy invariably relies more on inner happiness as the driver of efforts rather than seeking external recognition and rewards. Empathy or samvedana is a major driver of grassroots innovations.

Expanding the network through voluntary spirit

No social movement can be sustained for long without mobilizing the voluntary spirit of its members. Managing volunteers requires paying respect to their differences rather than treating them uniformly.

Overcoming Inertia

Both drivers—guilt and gratitude—can evoke deeper feelings to generate the search for more knowledge, which can also be a prelude to inertia

When silence envelopes problems affecting millions in society through a kind of hidden conspiracy—a common mindset which legitimizes neglect of the problem for a long time—one needs whistle-blowers to battle this kind of inertia. In fact, many innovators are actually like whistle-blowers, since in a sense they are questioning the consensus on silence. Yet, the deepening of the imagination takes place through detours, those fanciful visions that lead an optimistic innovator to see hope, which most people suffering from inertia are not able to see. It has to be realized that not all things can change at the same time, especially if meaningful breakthroughs are to be achieved. In which functions, form or features of a device or contraption one chooses to maintain inertia, and in which aspects change is attempted, are crucial decisions for the success of an innovation.

Some people follow the practice of self-flagellation, i.e., self-punishment, whenever they realize a deep contradiction between what they do and what they think they ought to do. Inertia also comes in when one is not aware of the consequence of one's inaction on others. Or, even if one is aware, one is not too perturbed by the consequences. Inertia becomes inevitable when one's expectation from oneself goes down. The ability to adapt, adjust and accommodate constraints becomes the first step on the ladder of inertia.

Why does inertia persist more in technologies used by women?

It is very difficult to bring about change in every system or subsystem. To keep focus on the desired substrata of change, one should recognize the limitations of living with inertia in other subsystems. However, when inertia is too deeply entrenched in the psyche of a society, one doesn't even realize the need for change.

Such inertia is much more evident in activities performed by women, who are often denied access to tools for overcoming their physical constraints. Women workers are often denied access to carpentry and blacksmithing tools. Even if they had ideas, many times they could not implement them. The time has come to remove such barriers and invoke higher participation from women in the grassroots innovation ecosystem.

Institutional Strategies for Sustaining Frugal Futures

A change not monitored is a change not desired

In many of the ongoing programmes bringing about change or redirecting strategies are fraught with risks. It is not easy for people to change their habits. By asking different questions, we not only bring about change in mindset but also in outcomes. If a society does not track ideas in the informal sector or, say, those of students (as attempted by techpedia.sristi.org), it implies that in the national polity, such ideas don't matter. The only way values in vogue manifest is by looking at the monitoring system and the change it tracks.

Innovation is a process, not just an event

Nothing substantive is achieved by celebrating the specific innovative products and processes. The spirit, which triggers such innovations, has to constantly remain in ferment. Impatience with change, a hunger for ideas, a bias for action and respect for creative ideas constitute some of the elements of an inclusive innovation culture.

Open-source standards of excellence spur constant innovation

Societies which nurture innovations and continuous creativity often rely on open-source standards of excellence. The younger generation gets particularly motivated when such standards are shared widely. They feel challenged and the standards help in bringing out the best in them.

Product standards have to be regularly updated for expanding the space for innovation

The role of standards created by the National Standards Institution is extremely important for regulatory purposes. However, many innovations may not fit into existing standards. When small-scale producers use second-hand parts to modify the form, feature or function of a product, they may fall short of existing standards or may go beyond them. In the absence of regular tracking of such standards, no institution can remain cognizant of the potential of a team or a community. Quality and dynamic standards are at the heart of a sustainable future.

Poor people don't have only hands, legs and mouth; they also have a mind

The employment programmes have treated 250 million people as unskilled, despite majority of them having one or the other unique skill sets because they may lack a contemporary market. Innovations by workers will be noticed more when one purges labels such as 'unskilled labourers'. The democratization of knowledge, resources and skill-building opportunities cannot be expanded without treating such hidden skills as a precious resource for triggering innovations.

Say 'no' to the jugaad mindset

It is tragic but true that a large number of Indian and foreign organizations have done great injustice to Indian innovation systems by characterizing them as jugaad. They forget that jugaad is a temporary solution, a makeshift that gets around the problem but never gets over it. One should *not* celebrate the habit of not going to the root of the problem and focusing on the transient suboptimal solution instead.

Looking Within for Outside Innovations

Emptying oneself is a necessary condition for deeper learning

Our prior assumptions and beliefs about societal needs and expectations may prevent us from learning to innovate. Disempowering oneself requires humility and a sense of surrender to the purpose. Consequent yearning for change is accompanied by emptying oneself since the ego and the attendant desire to seek approval from others have to be subordinated.

Knowledge, feeling and action don't have to transpire in steep declining order

The irony of our times is that as knowledge has exploded, the proportion of things about which we have strong personal feelings goes down. The tragedy is that, within these feelings, what one actually acts upon or feels responsible for is even lesser. We have to constantly review the proportion between knowledge, feeling and action to modify our motivation for bringing about change.

When excellence becomes imperative, nothing more remains to be rewarded

Having come across many creative people who didn't know a mediocre way of doing things, I can claim that unless people find their own North Star pulling them towards their own goal, any lasting substantive changes are unlikely.

One can pursue the ideal of enlightenment even while suffering from acute deprivation of basic needs

Repeatedly we see how creative and innovative people have made breakthroughs, despite being economically disadvantaged and poor. There couldn't be greater evidence against Maslow's hierarchy of needs. The implication is that one should look for innovations from anywhere and in any social groupings, regardless of the degree of affluence in the community.

Finding a Way Forward

Maximizing uncertainties breeds an adventurous spirit

Risk-averse minds will seldom find innovative solutions to contemporary or historical problems. Prudence demands that when one is vulnerable, one avoids taking chances. And yet, many grassroots innovators did exactly that. They realized the value of uncertainty, randomness and persistence despite all odds.

Good ideas can remain dormant in the absence of energetic implementation

It is a truism to suggest that one should implement good ideas carefully. However, not everybody has equal strength, propensity or potential for implementing ideas. But this doesn't mean that implementers do not have their own ideas. Recognizing the merit of special skills required for implementation will help create a more viable and vibrant innovation ecosystem.

Deviant research must be encouraged in every organization to promote innovations

Remaining within the boundaries drawn by people who have reached positions of power, but may not have respect for genuine and deviant explorers, stunts innovative thinking. Even if such deviants are a pain in the neck, without their being around, one may not feel the pressure to bring about change with or without innovation.

Passion doesn't always lead to performance, but without it, there is never performance

Nine out of ten successful innovators are known for their passion. At the same time, the majority of those who fail to convert an innovative idea into a viable product or service lack the purpose, persistence or platform to execute performance. Passion is like a river; without strong banks, the energy of its flow gets dissipated and it becomes a lake. But without a river, there is no flow.

The long tail of innovation implies that not all innovations will achieve scale

There is a persistent fallacy of measuring the merit of every innovation on its ability to achieve scale. What is forgotten or ignored is the fact that a lot of needs that are localized in a niche require innovations with limited potential for diffusion. Without such solutions, the unmet needs of these niches or social segments will trigger alienation, a stage prior to anger and sometimes unrest. Inclusive innovation ecosystems should accommodate both scalable and non-scalable innovations.

The circular economy is imperative for a sustainable future

Treating waste through an end-of-the-pipe approach is not viable in the long run. Ideally, we should encourage innovations that don't produce waste at all or provide for multiple life cycles to ensure repurposed upscaling.

Early-stage funding for nascent ideas is still a weak spot in many ecosystems

Unless there is a hunger for innovative ideas, the funds will not flow towards innovators and good ideas will remain unimplemented. In every sector one has to provide for early stage seed funding for ideas to be tried. It doesn't matter if many ideas fail; only then will innovators who take risks come up. Unfortunately, public policy has neglected this aspect of innovation promotion, except in the field of biotechnology, and to some extent, in grassroots innovations.

While microfinance serves the need for ideas for which markets exist, micro-venture finance is needed for untested ideas

Isn't it strange that while risk capital is considered crucial for biotechnology, information technology and other sectors, the same has not been given its due place in public policy, globally, for leveraging grassroots innovations?

Technology Commons may be a future model for inclusive innovations at the grassroots level

People-to-people copying and sharing of ideas and innovations have to not only be allowed but also encouraged, and people-to-firm technology transfers may take place through licensing.

Can the Honey Bee Network philosophy help in fostering innovation at all levels in society worldwide?

As the global economy is under squeeze, even large corporations and countries are looking for more economical ways of conducting R&D and developing innovative solutions for meeting unmet needs.[1] The spirit of cross-pollination of ideas across sectoral, social and temporal boundaries reinforces the idea of learning from anyone, anywhere. Giving an identity to nameless, faceless creative persons/communities underlines the need for recognizing, respecting and reciprocating ideas from the informal sector as well as from the shop floor. Sharing back with due gratitude what one learns from creative people means that open innovation systems must become more reciprocal by sharing what the formal sector has done with the implementation of an idea as well. Such feedback will strengthen the self-respect of the idea provider who may take his or her own ideas more seriously and may become even more generous in the future. Inclusive innovation ecosystems build upon empathy, respect for frugality, circularity and extreme affordability to foster creativity, compassion and collaboration. Let us listen to the sounds of mynah!

ACKNOWLEDGEMENTS

With gratitude I acknowledge only a few to illustrate a very wide variety of friends and fellow shodhyatris whose debt the Honey Bee Network and I have incurred over the years. Without learning from them, this book would not have been possible.

I must first thank the railway coolie who in 1971 taught me the value of anonymous sharing. My grandfather, Shri Revati Prasad Vanprasthi, had once told me, 'If someone does you an inch of a favour, treat it as a mile; you will remain in debt but you will always be happy.' It is this spirit in which I thank three of my outstanding teachers, Dr S.N. Kakar, late Dr Y.P. Singh and Professor Kuldeep Mathur who have moulded my values and perceptions very significantly. I can't thank them enough.

All the directors and deans at the Indian Institute of Management, Ahmedabad, and chairmen of the CMA since 1981 deserve the deepest appreciation for providing unrelenting institutional support. Professors V.C. Vyas,

I.G. Patel, Narayan Sheth, Pradip Khandwalla, J.L. Saha, Samir Barua, P.M. Shingi, Bakul Dholakia and Ashish Nanda in particular must be thanked for the support they provided so generously for over three decades at IIMA.

Kirit Patel, who shouldered much of the responsibility of building the Honey Bee Network in the first decade, and Riya Sinha, who helped in fostering the DNA of the NIF and supporting the Honey Bee Network in the next decade, have a special place in my heart and the heart of thousands of innovators. Vipin Kumar has had to bear with my impulsive reactions and sometimes too critical comments. Despite that, he has contributed significantly and joyfully towards the Honey Bee Network in its third decade. Professor Vijaya Sherry Chand has been a great support in so many ways, apart from extending the frontiers of research and action on innovations by schoolteachers, particularly in government schools. The portal he created, www.teachersastransformers.org, is one of its kind—an open-source database of unaided ideas developed by the teachers themselves. He has also made a very valuable contribution towards institution building.

Ramesh Patel has steered SRISTI with a sense of humility and devotion that is difficult to find in many people today. He has organized dozens of meetings every year for experimenting farmers—the shodh sankals which were started by Dilip Koradia. Mahesh Patel took responsibility for taking the GIAN to its present position in very difficult times and with limited resources. Hiranmay helped in creating the techpedia.sristi.org database, besides triggering the GYTI (Gandhian Young Technological

Innovation) awards with enormous youthful energy. Anamika R. Dey has helped not only in sustaining various initiatives with children, students and innovators but also in bringing out the *Honey Bee Newsletter*. She has also helped in searching for difficult references and photos for this book besides providing new metaphors and artistic provocations. Chetan Patel's explosive energy has helped in managing shodhyatras, children workshops, pooling innovations by schoolteachers, etc. Ramasamy Baskaran could bear with me for almost three decades—a feat by itself extraordinary, given my idiosyncrasies, sometimes excessive work demands and never-ending expectations. From providing secretarial support in welcoming grassroots innovators to the institute to coordinating with the office of the last three presidents of India besides other policymakers is something that only Baskaran could have done. The Honey Bee Network owes a great deal to the devotion of numerous colleagues in the IIMA like him.

Several other colleagues have helped in different ways over the years, not listed in order of importance: R.P.S. Yadav, late Purshottam Patel, Nirmal Sahay, Unni Krishnan, Alka Raval, Vijay Pratap Aditya, Muralikrishna, Srinivas, Chiman Parmar, Pravin Rohit, Pooja Tole, Shailesh Shukla, Keyur Panara, Naginbhai, Mahesh Parmar, Jayshree Patel, Mukesh, Bala Ganapathy Mudaliar, Murali, Murugan, Sethumadhavan, Mahadevan, Hema Patel, Nisha Binoi, Rekha Shah, Subodh Bishnoi, Kinjal Popat, Ketki Desai, Bhoomi Shah, Nitin Maurya, Vivek Kumar, Ravi Kumar, Pawan Kumar, Rakesh Maheshwari, Hardev Choudhary, Debati Devi, Deepa Gogoi, Neeta Patel, Chintan Shinde, Devasi

Desai, Sumitra Patel, Ghanshyam, Balwant, Tejal Dabhi, Manish Doshi, Vijay Chouhan, Ramesh Taviyad, Pravin Vankar, Ramesh C. Patel, Bhavesh Dhrangi, Dashrath Thakor and Mukesh Chouhan.

Several colleagues in the faculty and staff have provided extraordinary support during the three international conferences on 'Creativity and Innovation at Grassroots' held at IIMA.

I am grateful to the honourable president of India, Shri Pranab Mukherjee, and his office for elevating the innovation exhibition to a national celebration in the form of the Festival of Innovation. It was a rare dream come true to link grassroots creativity with the patronage of the highest office in the state in this manner. He also gave away the first Dr A.P.J. Abdul Kalam IGNITE awards in 2015. Late Dr Kalam, former president of India, started the tradition of honouring grassroots innovations with biennial presidential awards through the National Innovation Foundation, and later, the annual IGNITE awards. He also taught a course, GRIIT, with me at the IIMA for three years and, even after that, continued to visit the IIMA to give feedback to the student projects and continually inspire them. Srimati Pratiba Devisingh Patil, another former president of India, initiated the tradition of grassroots innovation exhibitions hosted by the office of the President of India. She also co-invented the critical water irrigation systems in drought-prone areas—a rain gun mounted on a tanker—in collaboration with several innovators, particularly Dharambir. A model of the invention is kept in the presidential museum at the Rashtrapati Bhavan.

I must thank Ms Omita Paul, secretary to the President of India, for shaping and guiding the Festival of Innovation along with her entire team. I cannot thank Dr. R.A. Mashelkar enough for all that I learned from him and continue to do so. Thanks are due to Dr V.L. Kelkar, Ms Elaben Bhatt, Dr E.A.S. Sarma, late Shri M.L. Mehta, Professor Inderjit Khanna, Dr Ashutosh Sharma, Dr H.K. Mittal, Dr M.P. Yadav, Dr Gajendra Singh, Dr P.L. Gautam, Dr K. Vijayraghavan, Dr T. Ramasami, Dr V.M. Katoch, Dr V.S. Ramamurthy, Dr Girish Sahani, Dr Sameer Brahmachari, Dr S. Ayyapan, Dr Sanjeev Saxena, Dr Ashok Jhunjhunwala, Professor R. Kumar, Dr Dhananjay Tiwary, Dr Renu Swaroop, Dr Raghuveer Chaudhary, Dr P. Pushpangadan, Dr Anamik Shah, Dr P.K. Sinha, Professor Bakul Dholakia, Professor Sanjay Verma, Professor Mukund Dixit, Professor Pankaj Chandra, Abraham Koshy, Professor Ashish Nanda, Dr B.T. Patel, Dr Jayvir Anjaria, Dr Minoo Parabia, Dr Shashi Bala Singh, Dr Gautam Biswas, Dr A.K. Das, Mr Amrutbhai Patel; late M.P. Ranjan, Mr Piyushbhai Desai, Mr Suresh Yadav, Ms Manjari, Mr D.S. Sharma, Mr R.K. Prasad and numerous other colleagues who have helped in ensuring a star-studded sky for the grassroots innovators.

Scouting and documenting innovations from thousands of villages was not possible without the active help of colleagues like P. Viveknandan, T.N. Prakash, Balaram Sahu, Reverand Hubby Mathew, Shri Sundaram, Brigadier Ganesham Pogula, Arun Chandan, Sudhirendra Sharma, Dr B.T. Patel, Dr Ghanysham Patel, Professor Kalyanasundaram, Professor Janakiraman,

A.S. Reddy, etc. Shri Narasa Reddy, Professor David Martin, Sanjay Chaudhary, Dr Akshay Aggrawal, Dr N.M. Patel and several other colleagues have helped in realizing the dreams of the creative youth and others. The Ahmedabad Educational Society (AES) has been extremely generous with its help to SRISTI and the Honey Bee Network. I must particularly thank late Shri Shrenik Kasturbhai Lalbhai, Shri Sanjay Lalbhai, Professor Prafull Anubhai and all other colleagues from the AES who have helped us from time to time. Late Motibhai Chaudhary inspired us through his simplicity and integrity and spirit of service to society.

Support from Dr Motlabur Rehman, Mr Anisuzzaman, Dr Zainul Abedin, Dr Nurul Alam, Robert Chambers, Paul Richards, Professor Eric von Hippel, Professor Niel Gershenfeld, Professor Zhang Liyan, Professor Sanjay Sarma, Professor Chintan Vaishnav, Professor Brij Kothari, Professor Aseem Prakash, Professor Arun Agarwal, Professor Elinor and Vincent Ostrom, Mr Thomas Turano, Dr Sudarshan Iyengar, Ms Malti Mehta, Mrs Maltiben Choudhary, Shri Karimbhai Sumara, Shri Dharambir Kamboj, Shri Sonam Lepcha, Shri Tshering Gyatso Lepcha, Dr Debal Deb, and Ms Wei Wei is very gratefully acknowledged as well.

I also greatly appreciate the Department of Science and Technology (DST), NSTEDB, New Delhi, Government of India, the Ministry of Finance (GoI), BIRAC (DBT), Sadbhav Trust IDRC, Canada, and numerous other public and private organizations which have supported the HBN social movement. The board members of the NIF, SRISTI, and the GIAN cannot be thanked enough for their outstanding support to the movement.

My wife, Sadhana, thank you for being my rock even when my boat was wavering in turbulent waters. My children, Abhas and Prayas, and my parents, Gyan Prakash Gupta and Daya Gupta, for bearing with my absences from family functions (almost all) and missing out on so many things at home when I had to be at work, serving the cause. The peons in the IIPA who brought tea to me from the Express Building when I worked right through the night, and B.D. Singh and R.K. Hazari who fed me during those difficult days. My students at the IIMA, and the schoolchildren I encountered during the journey so far, have kept this professor young by proving time and again how little I knew and how much more remained to be discovered.

How can I thank my wonderful editors enough—Radhika Marwah for keeping me on my toes, and Dipti Anand for adding so many insights and ensuring that this book saw the light of day. Their enormous patience with me missing so many deadlines is something all my colleagues in Wing 13, IIMA, appreciate. I discovered so much about my own thoughts through their critical comments.

Usual disclaimers apply. I, and I alone, am responsible for all the inadequacies of this narrative. The credit for everything here goes to tens of thousands of grassroots innovators and outstanding traditional knowledge holders of India and many other countries. They trusted us and shared so much, often without making any reciprocal demands. I trust that we have been able to come up to their expectations.

NOTES

CHAPTER ONE
SEEING BEYOND WHAT IS VISIBLE

1. Mrs Sharifa Begum, widow of Mr Abdus Samad of Tatihara village, Narandia Union, Kalihati Upazila, Tangail district, at Palima, on-farm research site of the Bangladesh Agricultural Research Institute; personal communication with Nurul Alam, 11 September 2015.
2. Gupta, Anil K. 'Deviant Research'. 22 September 2007. *New Scientist*, 195:2622, p. 56.
3. Shri N.V. Satyanarayana's Micro Windmill for Generating Energy at the Second National Grassroots Technological Innovation and Traditional Knowledge Awards, National Innovation Foundation, 2002. http://nif.org.in/upload/innovation/2nd/198-microwindmill-driven-battery-charger.pdf.
4. George de Mestral designed the Velcro used so often on watch straps, shoes and school bags, etc., in the 1940s, after observing the shape of the cocklebur plant found in the mountains of Switzerland. Such examples are also used to illustrate biomimicry. For more, see http://hookandloop.com/invention-velcro-brand/ for more.

5. Personal communication with Angchok Dorjey, Defence Institute of High Altitude Research (DIHAR), Ladakh. 2006.

6. See Banerjee, K., Jhala, Y.V., Chauhan, K.S. and C.V. Dave. 'Living with Lions: The Economics of Coexistence in the Gir Forests, India'. 16 January 2013. *PLoS One*. 8:1.

7. In a blog post in 2009, Jeff Attwood observed that music and coding share 'rhythms and cadences of algorithmic flow'. See Atwood, Jeff. 'The One Thing Programmers and Musicians Have in Common. *Coding Horror*. http:// blog.codinghorror.com/the-one-thing-programmers-and-musicians-have-in-common/. Several other writes have echoed this thought lately. See also Johnson, Phil. 'Music to Get You into the Coding Groove) 11 December 2015. *ItWorld*. http://www.itworld.com/article/2892928/music-to-get-you-into-the-coding-groove.html.

CHAPTER TWO
EVOLUTION OF THE HONEY BEE NETWORK

1. To learn more about similar informal practices in the USA, see, 'Ripening and Harvesting Tomatoes'. *Garden. org*. Accessed 15 September 2015.http://www.garden.org/foodguide/browse/veggie/tomatoes_harvesting/374.

2. Many innovators often don't succeed in commercializing the fruits of their labour. They are satisfied with meeting local needs. But this should not imply that they don't keep track of what broader markets need. During the Pune Science Congress in 2000, a big pavilion was organized on the 'Mind to Market', under the chairpersonship of Dr R.A. Mashelkar. The grassroots innovators were given an opportunity to speak from the same dais as the Nobel laureates.

3. Van Asten and his colleagues note that intercropping between banana and coffee plants improves the productivity of coffee by almost 50 per cent in Uganda. As an interim crop, banana might help when temperature goes up due to climate change. It also provides shade and reduces the temperature by 2 degrees Celsius with its canopy. It reduces water evaporation through its deep roots and also adds mulch. I observed a similar combination in the Cali region of Colombia. In the case of the areca plant, the effects of additional shade and mulch also help in water conservation since areca is known to suffer due to moisture deficit. See, 'Coffee + Bananas: A Climate Smart Combination'. 21 January 2013. *Consortium*. Accessed 19 September 2015. http://www.cgiar.org/consortium-news/coffee-bananas-a-climate-smart-combination/.

4. The board was chaired by FRS, Dr R.A. Mashelkar; former director general, CSIR, and present national professor, Anand Mahindra; founder and present member of SEWA, Elaben; former expenditure secretary, E.A.S. Sarma; present representative of the Department of Science and Technology, V.L. Kelkar; former secretary of finance and adviser to the finance minister, Riya Sinha (also former CIO of the NIF and present representative of the Honey Bee Network); besides secretaries of several ministries such as MSME small industries, AYUSH under the Department of the Indian System of Medicines, etc. For current board membership, visit, http://nif.org.in/governing_board.

5. Use of bamboo stems in controlling termites: Termites cause a lot of damage in rice, maize, peanut and pepper fields by cutting through roots and stems. This damage occurs significantly in most parts of the fields. Mr Sekou Camara, aged sixty-four, from Guinea, has been pursuing farming in the village of Lamikhoure since his early youth. His field is located close to the village. Because of

the difficulties in accessing expensive inputs, Mr Camara resolved to find a low-cost solution. He cut bamboo pieces of about one metre length and planted these in the termite-affected plots at intervals of one metre in all directions. Four to five days later he saw that the termites abandoned the crop to lodge instead in the hollow bamboo pieces. He carefully removed them and shook them off into fire. He applied the technique to the peanut, maize and pepper and obtained the same result by using millet or sorghum stems as well. Mr Camara explained this technique to his neighbours, who also had problems with termites. These people confirmed the efficiency of the technique, and today the technique is used in all the surrounding villages. See, *Honey Bee Newsletter*, 19:1. 2008.

CHAPTER THREE
SHODHYATRA: A WALKING CLASS

1. The thesis was on the biochemical parameters of adaptation in wheat.
2. Watch Anil Gupta's videos as a TED speaker here: https://www.ted.com/speakers/anil_gupta, Mysore, 2009.
3. Rutledge, Pamela. 'Social Networks: What Maslow Misses'. 8 November 2011. *Psychology Today*. https://www.psychologytoday.com/blog/positively-media/201111/social-networks-what-maslow-misses-0.
4. Tripathi, Shiva Kumar. *A Garden of Deeds: Ramacharitmanas, a Message in Human Ethics*. iUniverse, 2004. Also see, Pandey, Gyan. 'Tulasi ke Ram'. 3 August 2011. SpeakingTree. Pandey quotes Tulsidas: *Swantah Sukhaya Tulasi Raghunath Gatha*, who implies it, and Karma Yoga also states '*Swantah Sukhaya, Bahujana Hitaya*', which when translated is understood as from one's own happiness, to the well-being of everyone.

5. See, Hofstede, Geert. 'Hofstede's Culture Dimensions: An Independent Validation Using Rokeach's Value Survey'. 1984. *Sage Journals*. jcc.sagepub.com/content/15/4/417. short?rss=1&ssource=mfr.

6. For more information on the 23rd shodhyatra from Dahod, Gujarat, to Alirajpur, Madhya Pradesh, in 2009, visit: http://www.sristi.org/cms/files/shodh-yatra-report/23_Shodhayatra_Book.pdf.

7. For more about the Gandhian Inclusive Innovation Challenge Awards 2015, visit, http://www.nif.org.in/giica.

8. Stanley, Autumn. *Mothers and Daughters of Invention: Notes for a Revised History of Technology*. New Jersey: Rutgers University Press, 1993.

9. Once when a colleague's wife sent in a submission for an innovation to the NIF's national contest, I was guilty of asking why the colleague had sent it in his wife's name. When we met the colleague's wife, I realized that she was, if anything, even more creative than her husband, though not eligible to participate because she belonged to the formal sector.

10. Gupta, Anil. 'Why Don't We Learn?' 1993. Ideas. https://ideas.repec.org/p/iim/iimawp/wp00618.html. In this the author claims, we make our learning contingent on learning and reform by others.

11. To learn more about Ranjit Mirig's innovation, visit: http://nif.org.in/innovation/manual-paddy-transplanter/511.

CHAPTER FOUR
LISTENING TO THE MINDS ON THE MARGIN:
SOUND OF A BIRD

1. Macdonald, Stuart. 'Agricultural Improvement and the Neglected Labourer'. *The Agricultural History Review*, 31:2, pp. 81–90. 1983. http://www.bahs.org.uk/AGHR/

ARTICLES/31n2a1.pdf. Also see, Gupta, Anil K. 'From Farmers First to Labourers First: Why Do We Still Know So Little?' *Future Agricultures*. www.future-agricultures. org/farmerfirst/files/Add_Gupta.pdf; and Gupta, Anil K. 'The Forgotten Labourer'. *SciDevNet*. http://www.scidev. net/global/biotechnology/opinion/the-forgotten-farm-labourer.html. 2009.

2. For more details, see, Dandekar, Kumudini and Manju Sathe. 'Employment Guarantee Scheme and Food for Work Programme'. 12 April 1980. *Economic and Political Weekly*, 15:15, pp. 707–13.

3. See, Gupta, Anil K. 'Mind! As If It Matters'. January–June 2006. *Honey Bee Newsletter*. 17:1 & 17:2. Also see, Gupta, Anil K. 'Managing Knowledge for Creative, Collaborative and Compassionate India'. October – December 2006 & January–March 2007. *Honey Bee Newsletter*. 17:4 & 18:1.

4. Mitch, David. 'Learning by Doing among Victorian Farmworkers: A Case Study in the Biological and Cognitive Foundations of Skill Acquisition'. Economic History Department, London School of Economics. London, 1994.

5. Nikula, Jouko and Ivan Tchalakov. *Innovations and Entrepreneurs in Socialist and Post-Socialist Societies*. Cambridge, Massachusetts: Cambridge Scholars Publishing, 2015, p. 415.

6. This idea was first suggested by a student of IIT Bombay where I had organized a workshop on creativity and innovation many years ago, sometime around 2005–6.

7. Personal communication with Dr Murali Sastry. 2007.

8. Radjou, Navi, Prabhu, Jaideep and Simone Ahuja. *Jugaad Innovation: Think Frugal, Be Flexible, Generate Breakthrough Growth*. New Delhi, India: Wiley Jossey-Bass, 2012, pp. 288. In this book, the authors consider

low-cost ECG machines, developed by General Electric (GE) through intricate engineering with Mitti Cool, an outcome of series of trials under jugaad, which essentially means a makeshift solution. Elsewhere I discuss why no society or company can ever progress by relying simply on a jugaad mindset. It is unfortunate the book uses our work and misinterprets it so grossly.

9. It is acknowledged that several communities following different faiths bury the dead bodies of both sick and healthy persons regardless of their condition. We respect such beliefs and the variations in them as per respective tribal traditions.

10. With $70 billion (or 4 per cent of GDP), India was one of the top recipients of remittances in 2014, said the Human Development Report 2015 of the United Nations Development Programme (UNDP). 'Officially recorded remittances to developing countries are expected to increase from $436 billion in 2014 to $440 billion in 2015,' the report also said. Other top recipients in 2014 were China with $64 billion, less than 1 per cent of its GDP, and the Philippines with $28 billion, almost 10 per cent of its GDP. See, 'Emerging Markets to Receive $440 bn in Remittances This Year'. 14 December 2015. *Economic Times*. Accessed 3 January 2016. http://economictimes.indiatimes.com/articleshow/50171465.cms?utm_source=contentofinterest&utm_medium=text&utm_campaign=cppst.

11. See a brief report of this shodhyatra: 'Bhikampura to Nilkanth Gadh'. December 2001. http://www.sristi.org/cms/?q=en/book/print/24.

12. *Ibid.*

13. Many other examples are available at nifindia.og/ignite. One can download the IGNITE Award books free of cost from this website.

CHAPTER FIVE
KNOWING, FEELING AND DOING:
EXPANDING THE DOMAIN OF RE¬SPONSIBILITY

1. See, Hawks, John. 'How Has the Human Brain Evolved over the Years?' *Scientific American*. 1 July 2013. http://www.scientificamerican.com/article/how-has-human-brain-evolved/. The article shares: 'The final third of our evolution saw nearly all the action in developing brain size. *Homo habilis*, the first of our genus, *Homo*, who appeared 1.9 million years ago, saw a modest hop in brain size, including an expansion of a language-connected part of the frontal lobe called Broca's area. As our cultural and linguistic complexity, dietary needs and technological prowess took a significant leap forward at this stage, our brains grew to accommodate the changes. The shape changes we see accentuate the regions related to depth of planning, communication, problem solving and other more advanced cognitive functions.' Also see, Young, Richard W. 'Evolution of the Human Hand: The Role of Throwing and Clubbing'. January 2003. *Journal of Anatomy*, 202:1, p. 165–74; and, MacDougall, Robert. 'The Significance of the Human Hand in the Evolution of Mind'. April 1905. *The American Journal of Psychology*, 16:2, pp. 232–42.

2. Auer, Arthur. 'Hand Movements Sculpt Intelligence'. Waldorf Research Institute. Accessed 5 January 2016. http://www.waldorfresearchinstitute.org/pdf/Hand-Movements-Create-Intelligence.pdf.

3. Tools were also developed perhaps collectively. See, Wilson, Frank R. 'The Hand: How Its Use Shapes the Brain, Language, and Human Culture'. New York: Pantheon Books, 1999, p. 397. In the book's review, David Paineau writes, 'In other words, cooperative tool manufacture could have provided a crucial precondition for the evolution of

language. An emerging language based in the growth of cooperative tool manufacture would have fostered the evolution not only of a more sophisticated tool manufacture but also of a more complex social culture and a more refined language.' See, Paineau, David. 'Get a Grip: Are Hands the Key to the Evolution of Human Intelligence?' *New York Times* 19 July 1998. https://www.nytimes.com/books/first/w/wilson-hand.html.

4. Thurston, Tina and Christopher T. Fisher. *Seeking a Richer Harvest: The Archaeology of Subsistence Intensification, Innovation, and Change.* London: Springer Science & Business Media, 2006, p. 274.

5. Dyble M. et al. 'Sex Equality Can Explain the Unique Social Structure of Hunter-Gatherer Bands'. *ScienceMag*, 15 May 2015, pp.796–98. http://science.sciencemag.org/content/348/6236/796.full.

6. Devlin, Hannah. 'Early Men and Women Were Equal, Say Scientists'. *Guardian.* 14 May 2015. https://www.theguardian.com/science/2015/may/14/early-men-women-equal-scientists.

7. 'Brain Connectivity Study Reveals Striking Differences Between Men and Women'. 2 December 2013. Penn Medicine. http://www.uphs.upenn.edu/news/news_releases/2013/12/verma/. See also, M. Ingalhalikar et al. 'Sex Differences in the Structural Connectome of the Human Brain'. *Proceedings of the National Academy of the Sciences*, Vol.111, No. 2, 14 January 2014, pp. 823–28. doi: 10.1073/pnas.1316909110.

8. See, Gigerenzer, Gerd and Henry Brighton. 'Homo Heuristics: Why Biased Minds Make Better Inferences'. *Topics in Cognitive Science*, Vol.1, No. 1, 2009, pp.107–43.

9. Dixon, William McNeill. *The Human Situation.* New York: Pearson Longman, 1939.

10. There are many studies and statements on the subject that we overestimate our chances of failure. Margie Warrell, in the article 'Take a Risk, the Odds Are Better Than You Think' in *Forbes* in 2013, observes: 'Because what we focus on tends to magnify in our imaginations, it causes us to misjudge (and overestimate) the likelihood of it occurring. Yet the reality is that the risk of something not working out is often not near as high as we estimate and the odds of it working out well, are often far better.' (Find the full article at http://www. forbes.com/sites/margiewarrell/2013/06/18/take-a-risk- the-odds-are-better-than-you-think/#5467c81e1d09). Mark Greer quotes Baron in an American Psychological Association publication in 2005, 'When intuition misfires, to say, without justification, people intuitively favor inaction.' (Find the full article at http://www. apa.org/monitor/mar05/misfires.aspx). But sometimes, we could also do the opposite. 'We overestimate our abilities and underestimate what can go wrong.' 'Instead of trying to anticipate low-probability, high- impact events (also called black swan events) we should reduce our vulnerability to them. Risk management, we believe, should be about lessening the impact of what we don't understand—not a futile attempt to develop sophisticated techniques and stories that perpetuate our illusions of being able to understand and predict the social and economic environment.' (See, Taleb, Nassim N., Daniel G., Goldstein and Mark W. Spitznagel. 'The Six Mistakes Executives Make in Risk Management'. *Harvard Business Review* October 2009.)

11. I have often argued with my students that when a day comes that we are not surprised at least once, we have not lived that day. As Alan Ball says in the film *American Beauty* (1999), 'It's a great thing when you realize you still

have the ability to surprise yourself. Makes you wonder what else you can do that you've forgotten about.'

12. Gardiner, Rita A. *To Do Or Not To Do? The Place of Ambiguity in the Work of Simone de Beauvoir*. Oxford University Press, 2012.

13. Kaufman, Scott Barry. 'Creativity and Schizophrenia Spectrum Disorders across the Arts and Sciences'. *The Creativity Post*. 19 November 2014. http://www.creativitypost.com/psychology/creativity_and_schizophrenia_spectrum_disorders_across_the_arts_and_science#sthash.xWVjRG1x.dpuf (accessed 19 October 2015). See also, *Frontier Psychology*. doi: 10.3389/fpsyg.2014.01145.

14. Frank, Robert H. 'Choosing the Right Pond: Human Behaviour and the Quest for Status'. *OUP Catalogue*. Oxford University Press, 1993.

15. Joshua Becker recalls Rabindranath Tagore's famous quote, 'We come nearest to the great when we are great in humility.' He observed, 'Humility is a funny thing. In fact, my grandfather used to tell us that he won a medal for his humility, but it was taken away when he began to wear it. Humility is the act of being modest, reverential, even politely submissive. It is the opposite of aggression, arrogance, pride, and vanity. And on the surface, it appears to empty its holder of all power.' (Find the full article at: http://www.becomingminimalist.com/the-hidden-power-of-humility/.) Milton Jorge Correia de Sousa also defended his doctoral thesis to argue that servant leadership is best exemplified when with greater power, a leaders also excels in humility. (Find the full article at http://discovery.rsm.nl/articles/detail/121-humble-leaders-most-effective-especially-when-in-power/.)

16. Kabir: *Bada hua toh kya hua,*
Jaise ped khajoor

Panthi ko chhaya nahin,
Phal laage atidoor.

17. Maltiben comes from a very poor family. She started out with just one cow and its calf, when she was married off to a physically challenged husband. Still, she developed an auto-watering system using a float valve for cows. Her husband gave her his full support and encouraged her in her entrepreneurial ventures. She educated her children, one of whom is now a police officer. She earns more than Rs 25,00,000 every year and has trained a large number of farmers from all over the country, sent by the dairy cooperative to learn from her. She has also served on the board of directors of SRISTI.

18. I have been teaching such open courses in the evening for the past few years which anyone can attend, no matter their age and qualifications. There are no fees for such courses. The content is often shared on open sources such as YouTube. You can watch five-part videos, from 2011 at https://www.youtube.com/watch?v=DYrllQzVKgQ.

19. Fleming, Lee. 'Breakthroughs and the "Long Tail" of Innovation'. *MIT Sloan Management Review,* 1 October 2007.

20. Robson, David. 'There Really Are 50 Eskimo Words for "Snow"'. *New Scientist,* 14 January 2013. https://www.washingtonpost.com/national/health-science/there-really-are-50-eskimo-words-for-snow/2013/01/14/e0e3f4e0-59a0-11e2-beee-6e38f5215402_story.html (accessed on . . .). Robson explains how in the 1880s, anthropologist Franz Boas studied different words the Eskimos used for 'snow', for example, *aqilokoq* for 'softly falling snow' and *piegnartoq* for 'the snow [that is] good for driving sleds', to mention just two. For the various Hawaiian words for ocean waves, see, Si, Aung.

The Traditional Ecological Knowledge of the Solega: A Linguistic Perspective. London: Springer, 2016. http://www.discovertsunamis.org/pdf/hawaiian_words_for_wave.pdf. For indigenous soil taxonomies, see, Krasilnikov, Pavel. *A Handbook of Soil Terminology, Correlation and Classification.* London: Earthscan Publications Ltd, 2009. Also see, Gosai, Kuldip et al. 'Indigenous Knowledge of Soil Fertility Management in the Humid Tropics of Arunachal Pradesh'. July 2011. *Indian Journal of Traditional Knowledge*, vol.10, No.3, july 2011, pp. 508–11.

21. National standards have to be changed so that no chaff cutter can be made without incorporating a breaking system like the one developed by Kazi. Incorporating such a feature must be imposed in the larger public interest as is done for seat belt or other such measures.

22. Laila Banu, S.M. Arthi, and Vinotha from Thiruvarur, Tamil Nadu, received IGNITE awards from Dr A.P.J. Abdul Kalam at an NIF function in 2011, for their suggestion that without wearing a helmet, a two-wheeler should not start. The NIF team got the innovation fabricated and it was appreciated at the exhibition at the Rashtrapati Bhavan the next year. This idea also indicates that when people do not feel the need for their own safety, some coercive tech solution may not be out of place.

23. For more information, visit www.nifindia.org/gtiaf.

CHAPTER SIX
FULCRUM OF FRUGALITY: A CIRCULAR ECONOMY

1. Securing the walls of the well with wooden frames and lining the walls with grass ensured the lateral recharge of clean water into technologies like Virda. During rain,

salts temporarily leach down from the top layers of the soil, thus letting clean water charge Virda, which floats on saline water. Virda, once sealed, can store water for months. After opening the well, it becomes saline in a month or two. See, Chokkakula, Srinivas and Sunil R. Patel. 'Virda: An Ingenious Method of Rain Water Harvesting'. *Honey Bee Newsletter*, Vol.5, No.3, 1994, p.7 also see Ferroukhi, Lyes and Srinivas Chokkakula. 'Indigenous Knowledge of Water Management'. Twenty-second WEDC Conference, 1996. http://wedc.lboro. ac.uk/resources/conference/22/Ferrouk.pdf. and the frugal innovation practice examples in the *Honey Bee Newsletter* from 1990 to 2015.

2. To learn more, see the final report for the GRIID project, at www.sristi.org/cms/griid/IDRC-Final-Report.pdf.

3. As quoted on the *e-Jainism* website, 'Aparigraha is the concept of non-possessiveness. The term usually means to limit possessions to what is necessary or important, which changes with the time period, though sadhus would not have any possessions.'

4. '59% Indian Women Are Anaemic: Study'. *Times of India*, 17 March 2015. http://timesofindia.indiatimes. com/india/59-Indian-women-are anaemic-Study/ articleshow/46589333.cms.

5. Geerligs, P.D., B.J. Brabin and A.A. Omari. 'Food Prepared in Iron Cooking Pots as an Intervention for Reducing Iron Deficiency Anaemia in Developing Countries: A Systematic Review'. US National Library of Medicine, Vol.16, No 4, August 2003, pp. 275–81.

6. See, Christopher V. Charles et al. 'Iron-deficiency Anaemia in Rural Cambodia: Community Trial of a Novel Iron Supplementation Technique'. *European Journal of Public Health*, Vol. 21, No.1, 27 January 2010. doi: http:// eurpub.oxfordjournals.org/content/21/1/43. It is claimed

that one cast-iron fish put in a cooking pot can provide for 90 per cent of the iron needs of a family for five years. For the full article, visit, http://www.luckyironfish.com/research.

7. Plessow, Rafael et al. 'Social Costs of Iron Deficiency Anaemia in 6–59-Month-Old Children in India'. *PlosOne*, 27 August 2015. doi: http://dx.doi.org/10.1371/journal.pone.0136581.

8. Gupta, Anil K. 'Land of Lepchas: Sikkim, 34th Shodhyatra'. *Anil K Gupta Blog*. 14 February 2015. http://anilg.sristi.org/?s=lepcha.

9. See my paper referring to this lecture, Gupta, Anil K. 'Dynamics of Internationally Aided Farming System Research Programmes: "A Gospel of a Dirty Hand"'. 1992. http://dlc.dlib.indiana.edu/dlc/bitstream/handle/10535/1812/Dynamics_of_Internationally_aided_farming_system_research_programmes_a_gospel_of_dirty_hand.pdf?sequence=1. Also see, Gupta, Anil K. 'Conserving, Augmenting and Sharing Water'. *Ideas 2012*. https://ideas.repec.org/p/iim/iimawp/11442.html. For news of this lecture regarding the army; see, 'Gospel of Dirt'. *Free Press Journal* 25 April 1952. http://www.freepressjournal.in/gospel-of-dirt/335970; and for the looming food crisis, see, 'The Threat of Famine'. *Time*, Vol. 86, No. 53, 3 December 1965, p. 52. http://connection.ebscohost.com/c/articles/54032361/threat-famine.

10. India ranks fifty-five among the worst eighty malnourished countries. See, 'Global Hunger Index 2015: Asia Fact Sheet'. International Food Policy Institute, 12 October 2015. https://www.ifpri.org/news-release/global-hunger-index-2015-asia-fact-sheet; and 'India's Global Hunger Index Rank Improves to 55 from 63'. *Economic Times*, 21 April 2015. http://articles.economictimes.

indiatimes.com/2015-04-21/news/61378666_1_hunger-index-fighting-hunger-india.

11. Rupert Riedl belonged to an artistic family in Vienna and was a strong advocate of citizen science, that is, science which relates to larger society. Influenced as he was by Konrad Lorenz's work, he wrote a famous book that has intrigued and influenced me a lot. See, Riedl, Rupert. *Biology of Knowledge: The Evolutionary Basis of Reason*. Chichester: John Wiley & Sons. See also, Wagner, Gunter P. and Manfred D. Laubichler. 'Rupert Riedl and the Re-Synthesis of Evolutionary and Developmental Biology: Body Plans and Evolvability'. 2004. *Journal of Experimental Zoology*, Vol. 302, Part B 2014, pp. 92–102. Here, the authors note, 'Throughout his life, Riedl was in awe of the intellectual atmosphere of Fin-de-Siècle Vienna, which emphasized the connections rather than the separation between the sciences, philosophy, and the arts, and constantly referred to it as his model for intellectual pursuits. Another strong influence of Fin-de-Siècle Vienna on Riedl's career was the cultural role that scientists could gain through the popularization of their work. From the early years of his career as a marine biologist, when he pioneered underwater film making, to his role as a citizen–scientist, who contributed to raising the awareness of environmental issues in Austria and beyond, Riedl has always paid attention to the public at large.'

12. Dick Baugh explains how a slight addition of carbon to iron during the period of heating gave the hardness and durability so necessary to shape swords and knives, both then and now. Find the full article at http://www.primitiveways.com/Steel%20heat%20treatment.html. Also see, Nicholas Bugliarello et al. 'Heat Treat Processes for Gears'. GearSolutions 20 October 2015. http://

www.gearsolutions.com/article/detail/6005/heat-treat-processes-for-gears.

13. Mikael Skou Andersen, in an introductory note on the environmental economics of the circular economy, in *Sustainability Science Journal*, Vol. 2, 2007, observes: 'Many adherents of the circular economy approach are strong proponents, on environmental and ethical premises, of material reuse and recycling. However, in a market economy (and in some planned economies as well), the prices of materials and natural resources will be too low and will mainly reflect the costs associated with mining and short-term values, but not with depletion nor the environmental costs. In such cases, only a limited range of circular options will make sense from the perspective of company managers.'

However, the current understanding is changing on the subject. See, Lieder, Michael and Amir Rashid. 'Towards Circular Economy Implementation: A Comprehensive Review in the Context of Manufacturing Industry'. *Journal of Cleaner Production*, 1 March 2016, Vol.115, pp. 36–51. China has enacted a new law on the subject, 'Circular Economy Promotion Law of the People's Republic of China', which took effect in January 2009 (as per the Standing Committee of the National People's Congress, China, 2008). The authors rightly argue that waste was not always treated in craft-oriented societies. Planned obsolescence without recycling and repurposing has created the problem. Also see, Jawahir, I.S. and Ryan Bradley. 'Technological Elements of Circular Economy and the Principles of 6R-Based Closed-loop Material Flow in Sustainable Manufacturing'. Thirteenth Global Conference on Sustainable Manufacturing—Decoupling Growth from Resource Use, 2016, Procedia CIRP, Vol.40, pp. 103–8. The authors note future goals very precisely, which entails 'envisioning a future where nothing is wasted; a future where every "waste" becomes an asset, and no value goes unrecovered; a future where all products at the end of their primary use are recovered and either reused, remanufactured, or recycled for multiple generations, has become more than a reality, but a necessity.' Grassroots innovators are a very crucial pivot of realizing this dream.

14. In the airplane industry, recent reviews are very instructive. See, LeBlanc, Rick. 'Airplane Recycling and Value Extraction: Industry Projects 12,000 Aircraft Need to Be Recycled in Next 20 Years'. *About Money*, 29 February 2016 http://recycling.about.com/od/ Recycling/a/Airplane-Recycling-An-Up-And-Coming-Industry.htm.

15. A simple definition of 'fatigue of metal-based parts' can be found http://www.epi-eng.com/mechanical_engineering_ basics/fatigue_in_metals.htm.

16. Gupta, Anil K. 'Frugal Innovation Is Not Just About Affordability'. *Anil K Gupta Blog*. 29 June 2014. http:// anilg.sristi.org/frugal-innovation-is-not-just-about-affordability/.

17. See, Gupta, Anil K. and Kirit Patel, 1994, *Beuniki Mo Loco* (crazy crazy fellow): Crazy Ideas and Innovations in Latin America'. *Honey Bee Newsletter*, New Series, Vol1. 1, No.1, pp. 7–10. The following are the numerous uses of old tyres that were found: In agriculture: (a) as drinking water troughs for animals and birds; (b) for fumigating fields to protect crops against pests, hailstorm, frost, etc.; (c) as wheels for animal-drawn carts; (d) as small boundaries/fences for vegetable gardens or nurseries; (e) as protection for saplings; (f) as a harness for animals; (g) as flooring in cattle sheds; (h) as protective coops for chickens against mongooses;

and (i) as motes or water lifting bags; in aquaculture: (a) as reefs for sheltering fish in the sea; and (b) as boats; in recreation: (a) as toys for children; (b) as swings hung from trees; (c) as a guard against stone battles; (d) as boxing bags for practising punches; in domestic life: (a) to make brooms (from long thread-like pieces of tyres); (b) to make shoe soles (I used to buy sandals and shoes made of tyre sole from Karol Bagh, New Delhi, till 1981 because these lasted longer); (c) to make mats (woven out of tyre threads, also pieces joined together as a mat, or wide pieces cut with designs to be used as doormats, or car mats as seen recently in Uganda); (d) as door hinges; (e) as fuel; (f) as waste bins; (g) to make hammers for soft pressures; (h) as chairs or seats; for aesthetics: (a) as flower pots; and other uses: (a) as buffers or shock absorbers in harbours or ports.

18. See, Choate, Mary. *Organic Lies: Misconceptions of the United States Organic Act in America and the World.* Arvada, CO: Coastalfields Press, 2007, pp. 63. Here, Choate observes that the d-Limonene derived from lemon juice can be used to control aphids. Moreover, the University of Georgia, USA, observes the following on its site: 'd-Limonene (commonly sold as Orange guard) is the major component of the oil extracted from citrus rind. It destroys the wax coating of the insect's respiratory system. When applied directly, the insect suffocates. Orange Guard is a water-based insecticide. Orange Guard is 100% biodegradable and water-soluble. The EPA calls d-Limonene a broad-based insecticide. It can be used for aphids, ants, mealybugs, gnats, ants, silverfish, roaches, fleas. Do not spray when plants are under stress. Avoid spraying in direct sunlight or the heat of the day. Avoid spraying flowers or flower parts.' (Find the full article at http://www.caes.uga.edu/extension/habersham/

anr/documents/Organic.pdf). For further reading, visit:
http://www.superfoodsrx.com/healthyliving/oranges-
and-cancer/ and http://www.anaturalhealingcenter.
com/documents/Thorne/articles/Limonene12-3.pdf.
Unfortunately, I could not find much Indian work on this
easy-to-use technology.

19. There are exceptions though. Once, the then chief
minister (and now the prime minister of India) of Gujarat
paid attention to our plea and distributed a pamphlet
containing low-cost, do-it-yourself (LC-DIY) practices
of pest control made by SRISTI to agricultural officers
in all talukas (or blocks) of the state within a few days.
We wish it had continued thereafter to remind farmers
of such alternatives developed by innovative farmers
themselves.

20. The visit materialized as a result of some senior
executives of a consultancy company working with the
Ministry of Railways and some executives from the
SNCF attending my talk in Paris on frugal innovations
at the grassroots level. That is how the idea for a visit
came up, and subsequently their interaction with two
grassroots innovators was also organized as a part of the
workshop.

21. Learn more about this project at http://nif.org.in/
innovation/modified_hydro_electricity_turbine/211.

22. Learn more about this project at http://nif.org.in/
innovation/tender_coconut_breaker_and_instant_
cooler/675.

23. For further reading on the innovation scholars-in-
residence at the Rashtrapati Bhavan in 2016, visit http://
pib.nic.in/newsite/PrintRelease.aspx?relid=136970;
http://pibphoto.nic.in/documents/rlink/2016/feb/
p201622901.pdf; http://www.thestatesman.com/news/

india/prez-selects-7-for-scholars-in-residence/126879. html; and http://presidentofindia.nic.in/innvoation-scholar16.htm.

24. Find details of the first batch of innovation scholars-in-residence at the Rashtrapati Bhavan in 2014 at http://presidentofindia.nic.in/innovation-scholars-scheme. htm; second batch 2015 at http://presidentofindia.nic. in/innovresi2016.htm, and third batch 2016 at http://presidentofindia.nic.in/innvoation-scholar16.htm.

25. Radjou, Navi, Jaideep Prabhu, and Simone Ahuja. *Think Frugal, Be Flexible, Generate Breakthrough Growth.* India: Wiley Jossey-Bass, 2012, pp. 288.

26. Few private sector companies follow sustainable methods of extraction of the herbs, so much so that in many cases, we have not yet even developed standards of sustainable extraction of natural substances.

27. For the key differences between nature-dependent, traditional societies vis-à-vis market-dependent, modern societies, see, Gupta, Anil K. 'Sustainable Institutions for Natural Resource Management: How Do We Participate in People's Plans?'. *People's Initiatives for Sustainable Development: Lessons of Experience.* Syed Abdus Samad, Tatsuya Watanabe and Seung-Jin Kim.), 1995 Chapter 15, pp.341–73.

28. I recall one such book, when a student suggested I read: Pateman, Trevor (ed.). *Counter Course: A Handbook for Course Criticism.* London: Penguin Books, 1972. This book which influenced me most regarding the triggering of questions in the classroom for which a teacher may have no answers. Likewise, there may be many books which very few people read, but they enrich the ecosystem by providing some sort of a trigger here and there.

29. Sen, Amartya. 'Ingredients of Famine Analysis: Availability and Entitlements'. *Quarterly Journal of Economics*, Vol. 96, No. 3, 1981, pp. 433–64.

30. To learn more about Micro Venture Innovation Fund, visit, nifindia.org/mvif.

31. Gupta, Anil K. 'From Sink to Source: The Honey Bee Network Documents Indigenous Knowledge and Innovations in India'. *MIT Press Journals*, Vol. 1, No. 3, 2006 pp. 49–66.

32. Gupta, Anil K. 'Innovation, Investment, Enterprise: Generating Sustainable Livelihood at Grassroots Through Honey Bee Philosophy'. In *Collaboration for Sustainability and Innovation: A Role For Sustainability Driven by the Global South?*, (eds James J.) Diego A., Vazquez-Brust, Cordeiro and Joseph Sarkis. London: Springer, 2013, pp. 217–32.

33. The multilingual innovations' database of the Honey Bee Network can be found at http://www.sristi.org/hbnew/honeybee_innovation.php?selectLanguage=hi&q= Honey bee multi language database on agricultural and other innovations by farmers.

34. The United States Patent and Trademark Office (USPTO) has recently started a discussion forum around patent applications and under certain conditions, such that any prior art revealed by anyone on the web can be taken into account while examining a particular application. But there is no doubt this will improve the quality of applications. This headway is particularly important for those developing countries, like India, which do not have enough examiners. But the substantive issue is how to enable communities and local innovators to read these patents that are put up for discussion in the USA and published in other countries? How 'public' is the public domain after all, and for whom? Will information in

English be accessible to the local communities that do not know the English language? How should a 'translation wiki', as was suggested by a student in Margaret Chong's class at Seattle Law School, be created for worldwide access by different language communities? One of my suggestions is that students worldwide can translate patents, say one page a week, for traditional knowledge or biodiversity projects in different languages and soon, we will have enough resources for tracking the unauthorized IPs. Another way to tackle this problem is that every patent applicant should declare that all the knowledge disclosed or used while making claims in their application have been obtained 'lawfully and rightfully'.

35. The NIF received inquiries from more than ninety countries (see, http://nif.org.in/aboutnif) due to its registering of grassroots innovations on different web portals on behalf of the innovators. D.N. Venkat, a grassroots inventor of the tree climber, exported the innovative device to twelve countries with the help of the NIF (see, http://nif.org.in/innovation/coconut_tree_climber/471), making the g2G model, or 'grassroots to Global', come true.

36. To learn more about the 'prior informed consent' (PIC) framework, visit, www.sristi.org/cms/files/pic_tech_inn_ideas.pdf;
www.sristi.org/cms/files/pic_traditional_knowledge.pdf; and
www.nif.org.in/sd.

37. Sinha, Riya. 'Rural India: The Silent Innovators'. National Innovation Foundation, July 2008. http://nif.org.in/dwn_files/Riya%20Sinha%20oiop.pdf.

38. To learn more about this project, visit: www.sristiinnovation.com/aaruni.html; and http://www.sristi.org/hbnew/hb_inno_detail.php?page=2152&search_case=Leaf%20curl%20in%20cotton&lang_name=en;

and http://www.thehindu.com/sci-tech/agriculture/a-tilting-cart-offers-relief-to-animals-and-workers-in-the-field/article407279.ece.

39. Second Policy Brief, IDRC, Canada supported projects under the Grassroots Innovations for Inclusive Development (GRIID) and SRISTI (Society for Research and Initiatives for Sustainable Technologies and Institutions). Also see, Gupta Anil K. et el. 'Values in Vogue: Institutional pathways for Sustaining Grassroots Innovations for Creating Public Goods'. *Ideas,* November 2010.

40. The idea of investing in venture funds which have never been known to invest in early state hard/manufacturing technologies still prevails. The hope is that, sooner than later, wiser sense will prevail and due course correction will be undertaken.

41. The Department of Science and Technology is investing in the vision and capability of the NIF much more now than ever before. The Department of Biotechnology has certainly turned over a new leaf in supporting young students recently.

42. BIRAC is an autonomous body under the Department of Biotechnology, Government of India. It provides risk fund support to young biotech innovators, start-ups and companies. In fact, in the entire innovation support systems of the Government of India, this is the only window of opportunity which supports very early-stage technological innovation ventures. Learn more about the BIRAC–SRISTI cooperation by visiting *birac.nic.in/desc_new.php?id=98;* http://www.sristi.org/cms/sristi-birac; and gyti.techpedia.in.

43. A TEPP programme was started in 1998 under the Department of Science and Technology and the Department of Scientific and Industrial Research, which

did fill this gap in the innovation ecosystem. But, for inexplicable reasons, it was wound up and replaced by PRISM, that has had limited effectiveness.

44. For more information on the Festival of Innovation, visit: http://presidentofindia.nic.in/foin2016.htm.

45. 'Suicides and Malnutrition among Weavers in Varanasi'. ActionAid, 2015. http://pvchr.asia/app/uploads/Suicide_&_Malnutrition_Report.pdf.

CHAPTER SEVEN

MOBILIZING SOCIAL AND ETHICAL CAPITAL
FOR SUPPORTING INNOVATIONS

1. Boehm, Christopher. *Hierarchy in the Forest: The Evolution of Egalitarian Behavior*. Boston: Harvard University Press, 1999. In a review of the book by John Henry Calvinist, Boehm observes: 'When lethal weapons were developed by humans, they could have . . . made possible not only killing at a distance, but also far more effective threat behavior; brandishing a projectile could turn into an instant lethal attack, with very little immediate risk to the attacker. This potent new extrasomatic means of fighting and threatening reduced the natural-selection pressures that for millions of years had been keeping in place apelike canines, innately disposed intimidation displays, and long, erectile body hair. To consider the immediate effect of weapons, one need only compare chimpanzee killings . . . [in which] it takes a group of several male chimpanzees ten to twenty minutes of ferocious gang attack to do in a stranger they catch while on patrol . . . My hypothesis is that weapons appeared early enough to have affected dentition, body size, hair loss on the body, and display loss, and they helped to ready humans for egalitarian society by making fights less predictable, and

by enabling groups collectively to intimidate or eliminate even a dominating serial killer' (pp. 175–81). The collective behaviour starts manifesting, leading to the emergence of social capital. He adds, 'Egalitarian bands amount to "intentional societies" . . . [as they] regularly create and maintain egalitarian blueprints for social behavior, "plans" that are implicit or (in part) explicit in the ethos, and well understood by the rank and file who implement them. The political notions and dynamics involved are not restricted to mobile foragers, for tribesmen all over the world are similarly egalitarian . . . Such people are guided by a love of personal freedom. For that reason, they manage to make egalitarianism happen, and do so in spite of human competitiveness' (pp.60–65). For the full article, visit http://www.thenewhumanities.net/books/Book%20Reviews60.html.

2. Tartar, the word indicating blacksmith communities in Japan, Turkey, South-East Asia and South Asia suggests a long tradition of smithy, besides of course central Indian tribal traditions of iron smelting. In another study of Japanese fold traditions, it is recorded that while the goddess of iron smelting was a woman, there was a taboo on women entering the blast furnace, so much so that even the man whose wife was menstruating could not enter the furnace. It was feared that the goddess will not like other women in her domain. (See, https://japanesemythology.wordpress.com/2014/07/06/the-goddess-of-iron-and-tatara-ironmaking/.) In Rajasthan, in the main gypsy or Lambadi nomadic community, the women help men in shaping iron tools, but that is an exception. (See, http://scribol.com/anthropology-and-history/forging-ahead-in-modern-times-the-ancient-lohar-blacksmiths-of-rajasthan/7 [accessed on . . .].) The skills that women were allowed to hone in ancient India were all ornamental or

culinary or artistic in nature, though in later times, hard work of a different kind was included in the list. The point here is that by denying them access to the skills to shape wood or iron, their creativity was curbed a great deal by cultural shackles.

3. Kitcher, Philip. *The Ethical Project*. Cambridge massachusetts: Harvard University Press, 2011. http://pages. uoregon.edu/koopman/courses_readings/phil620/kitcher_ ethical_project.pdf. Kitcher argues that both the evolution of codes and the ability of early human society to debate on the content of codes allow plasticity and exceptions within a range found congenial by the community. But ethical codes were not imposed externally, rather through an internal moral compass instead.

4. A database on indigenous common property resource conserving institutions can be found at www.sristi.org/cpri.

5. Hosetti, B.B. and M. Venkateshwarlu. *Trends in Wildlife Biodiversity Conservation and Management*. 2 vols. Delhi: Daya Publication House, 2001, p.184.

6. Bunzel, Ruth Leah. *The Pueblo Potter: A Study of Creative Imagination in Primitive Art*. New York: Dover Publication, 1929, p. 57. Bunzel observes that other tribes freely share their designs, except the Zunis who will never admit to copying their neighbours' design.

7. Gupta Anil K. et al. 'Grassroots Innovations for Inclusive Development: Need for a Paradigmatic Shift'. *Vikalpa*, Vol. 38, No .3 July–September 2013 pp. 103–22.

8. Conner, Clifford D. 'A People's History of Science: Miners, Midwives, and Low Mechanicks, Nation Books'. 2009. LouisProyect. http://louisproyect.org/2007/07/24/ slavery-technical-innovation-and-the-sugar-plantation/.

9. Satchell, Veront. Sugar, Slavery and Technological Change: Jamaica, 1760-1830. VDM Publishing, 2010, p. 284; and an excellent review of innovations by slaves:

Satchell, Veront. 'Technology and Culture'. April 2013, 54:2, pp. 382–88, in which Satchell goes back to an old debate about why slave communities did not develop. Accordingly he observes: 'Slavery, in this view, negates the use of advanced technology in several ways. First, it reduces the cost of labour, removing one of the chief incentives for technological innovation—the desire to lower labour costs. Second, slaveholders were backward conservatives, not rabid capitalists driven by the profit motive; profits, as a result, were expended on luxuries and consumer goods rather than on new and improved technologies. Quantitative rather than qualitative means were thus employed to increase production levels. Third, in an act of resistance, enslaved blacks would destroy new and expensive equipment. And lastly, enslaved blacks were unable to manipulate complex technologies. As a result of all these factors, slave-plantation economies remained static and economically backward. In recent years, a number of works have appeared that contradict this general thesis. These newer works argue that there is ample evidence to show that planters were neither backward nor conservative in their approach to their business. Rather, they actively sought to qualitatively improve their enterprises by not only utilizing, but also initiating and having manufactured for their specific use the most modern and advanced technologies available.'

Other sources cited by Satchell on the subject include: Seymour Drescher, *Econocide*; David Eltis, *Economic Growth and the Ending of the Transatlantic Slave Trade and The Rise of African Slavery in the Americas*; B.W. Higman, *Plantation Jamaica, 1750–1850* and *Slave Society and Economy in Jamaica*; Franklin W. Knight, *Slave Society in Cuba during the Nineteenth Century*; Russell R. Menard, *Sweet Negotiations*; Kenneth

Morgan, *Slavery, Atlantic Trade and the British Economy*; Eric Williams, *Capitalism and Slavery*; Manuel Moreno Fraginals, *The Sugarmill*; Eugene D. Genovese, *The Political Economy of Slavery*; Lowell Joseph Ragatz, *The Fall of the Planter Class in the British Caribbean, 1763–1833*; Jonathan Curry-Machado, *Cuban Sugar Industry*; Lyman L. Johnson, *Workshop of Revolution*; and Veront Satchell, *At Work in the Fields of Their Lords*.

10. See, http://teachinghistory.org/history-content/ask-a-historian/24411. Also see, Bloom, Paul. 'The Baby in the Well: The Case Against Empathy'. 20 May 2013. *The New Yorker*.

CHAPTER EIGHT
LESSONS FOR LEARNERS

1. Parthasarathy, Shobita. 'Fostering Grassroots Innovation: Lessons India Can Teach Michigan'. 10 May 2016. Michigan Radio. http://michiganradio.org/post/fostering-grassroots-innovation-lessons-india-can-teach-michigan#stream/0